BEHIND THE

GUN

Poncho's Last Walk

By

Bravo Charles

With Pictures By

Earl Almighty

Proceeds to benefit Infidel Inc. & other veteran nonprofit organizations.

Unedited Edition

ISBN 9781513654935

Printed by :

A Place To Copy
Raleigh, NC
919-876-2300

For

SPC (RET) Roland "Poncho" Carrizales

&

The 87th Infantry Regiment, 10TH MTN DIVISION (Light Infantry)

In memory of

COL James Sikes, SSG Bradley C. Beem, SPC Steven J. Mangold,
SPC Daniel T. Foley ,SPC Marc Nash, SPC Heath Choate,
SPC Michael Stebens, SPC Peter McCabe,
MAJ Larry Bauguess, JR.

Contributors

LTC (RET) Greg Alderete, LTC (RET) Scott Walker,
MAJ John Wasik, SFC (RET) Olin Rossman,
MSG (RET) Brian Szulwach, SGM (RET) Bill Poe,
MSG (RET) Thomas Corey, SFC (RET) Richard Hughes,
SPC Christopher Cooke, SFC (RET) T. Walker Peterson,
CPL Duane Nelson, Robert Loughhead, Kevin Labonte,
1LT Michael Mellano

"If there is a hell, it is here on earth, in the haunting uncelebrated darkness of every war ever fought. It seeps into the shallow graves of the innocent, shrouding the forgotten dead, silencing the hallowed cries of motherless children." – LTC Greg Alderete

Contents

Foreword

When the average person daydreams, he thinks of vacation get-a-ways, fishing and camping, family and happy hour. When a Veteran slips away we return with a hollow stare into sandstorms, mountain caves, freezing nights on countless patrols and best friends like brothers gained and lost during intense gunfights. We are Combat Veterans, friends forged under fire from "Behind the Gun". Steve Slane has completed a tremendous amount of heavy lifting to ensure our story is not only told boldly but told correctly. He takes us back to a long forgotten war zone into a faraway land that most folks never even knew existed Sure, Hollywood had exhilarated movie goers with the infamous 26 hour firefight in the streets of Mogadishu but what about the other months of tireless foot patrols, recons, ambushes, cordon and searches or the endless hours of port security overlooking the shark infested waters along endless miles of African East Coast's Indian Ocean beaches that dead end in Merca, what we recall as our home away from home.

Ft Drum New York, top of the world to most Americans, home of the 10th Mountain Division and top of the Mountain to those that served there. Thanks to the Base Realignment and Closure (BRAC) and plenty of political pull, Ft Drum became one of the most popular and most deployed bases for a Soldier to be stationed in the 1990s. Big Army had to justify why it had spent millions upon millions to rebuild the old Camp Drum and create a first-rate playground for, at that time, the cutting edge of military technology and training. In fact, the 10th Mountain Division had become the 18th Airborne CORPs "go to" unit and was tagged as such by maintaining a QRF status for most of the decade. And sough after it was, I remember vividly receiving my assignment orders as a new Lieutenant and rallying around the phone with fellow Artillery Officers to notice our branch and volunteer for combat duty once at Ft Drum (I laugh at the thought of that one now and again). As a young Field Artillery Officer attending the Officer Basic Course at that time I took note of comments by our instructor CORP at Ft Sill (home to the

Army's Field Artillery) that boasted of the 10th Mountain Division's readiness and the high probability of deployments, you see, that's what we all signed up for and after 10 years of a peacetime Army, we were ready to get into the game.

Soldiers from Ft Drum had been piece milled into the first Gulf War and assigned as *Augmentees to round out the already historic 101st and 82nd Infantry Divisions. I remember arriving to Ft Drum, my first unit of assignment and listening to the stories of those Soldiers that wore proudly the coveted right shoulder patch (indicating a combat rotation) and even some with Combat Infantry Badges, how exciting their stories were to a young Lieutenant who had only read about such adventure in history books and seen those actions in military training films. That's when I met Steve and the Soldiers from A Co 1/87 Infantry. We all shared the same desire, serve our country in combat. It may sound crazy but who wants to practice and never get in the game. As the Company Fire Support Officer for A Company 1/87 I had the opportunity to plan with the commander, support the company with the XO and 1SG and rotate among the platoons to provide supporting fires by way of forward observer teams and, best of all, to get to know personally the Soldiers of A Co.

Perfect practice makes perfect, that's what we did in A Co, all the way from 1SG Poe down. We trained hard locally in field conditions ranging from mosquito infested August 100 degree upstate New York summers to life threatening cold temperatures that could cause frostbite within minutes as the thermometer gages 30 below, either way it had to be down. We flew to JRTC(Ft Polk, Louisiana) and NTC (Ft Irwin, California) to hone our Infantry skills. We deployed south to Ft Bragg's shoot houses and urban training facilities, untold hours of training all that culminated in our preparation to take on Al-Shabaab or Al-Qaeda in the sweltering heat and Godless starvation of a seeming hopeless situation in Somalia. A mission, to restore Hope, we were prepared to take on whole heartedly because it was the right thing to do. I never heard anyone complain.

Through Behind the Gun, Steve has expertly and unselfishly managed to put together the stories of our lives as Soldiers in a manner that will lure your thoughts and senses to, at that time, the center of our universe, Somalia. Steve has provided an insight not only based from personal and collective experience but illustrates for you a roadmap of what led up to and the results of America's involvement in Somalia. Steve will leave you asking questions that go well on military operations and why we continually rush to the aid of our fellow human beings. God bless and protect the Warrior.

LTC (RET) Scott Walker

*An Individual **Augmentee** is a United States military member attached to a unit (battalion or company) as a temporary duty assignment (TAD/TDY) used to fill shortages or can be used when an individual with specialized knowledge or skill sets is required.

Introduction

Since its creation in 1943, and its reactivation in 1985, the 10th Mountain Division has been at the forefront of operations conducted by the United States. From the arduous terrain of the Eagle River valley in Colorado, to the snow infested woods of Jefferson County, New York, the division has trained thousands of Soldiers for specific operations in cold weather and mountainous terrain. Because of this specialized training, and the laser focus on fundamental infantry tactics and the esprit de corps that it builds, the 10th Mountain Division has earned a reputation as a go anywhere, perform anything organization capable of rapid deployment, swift adaptation, and mission accomplishment.

From its inception long before 1943, the 10th was designed to fill a specific niche in modern warfare. Knowing the Wehrmacht possessed three alpine divisions, and studying the effectiveness of highly mobile, lightly armed troops on skis from the Finnish and Greek armies, the Army authorized a unit capable of operating in harsh terrain. The 87th Mountain Infantry Battalion, activated on 8 December, 1941, formed the basis of the 10th Mountain Division. The battalion was manned with professional skiers, mountain climbers, and outdoorsman recruited specifically from colleges and the civilian sector. Experienced in operating in harsh conditions and high altitudes, these men would not only lay the foundation of the tough training the division would need to be successful in combat but would establish the 10th as one of the best trained divisions of World War II.

By 1944, the 10th Mountain Division would consist of three regiments, the 85th, 86th and 87th Infantry Regiments, which formed the combat units of the division that would defeat the Germans in the mountains of northern Italy during World War II. Of those Regiments, the 87th Infantry Regiment is the only operational Regiment today, with two battalions, the 1st BN and 2nd BN, stationed at Ft. Drum, NY as part of the modern 10th Mountain Division (Light Infantry) reactivated in February 1985. The Soldiers of this division are some of the best trained and most called upon men and women in times of emergencies since reactivation. Their training and ingenuity form the basis of modern tactics, techniques, and procedures that are used throughout the Army on the battlefield today.

Although it may not seem as though at first, this is not just a story of 1st Platoon, Alpha Company, 1st Battalion, 87th Infantry. It is not even a story of a light infantry company, detached from its parent unit and thrust into the harsh unknown with a completely different organization. It is the odyssey of two battalions, the 1st and 2nd Battalions of the 87th Infantry Regiment, and their intertwining throughout Operation Restore Hope, the US Army's deceptively benign name for a highly demanding, dangerous and lethal operation in Somalia in 1992 and 1993. The two battalions share the same lineage, the same history and experiences from past regimental members to gather strength and knowledge from and, ultimately, the same hardships and tragedies.

Undertaking the task of collecting, researching, compiling, and composing a collective of stories is never easy. Doing it over 25 years after the fact makes the task daunting. But the beauty of a project like this lies in the journey, both the author's and ours, from the time we answered the call to serve to the present day. It is a complex journey, one that has just as many victories and hardships back home as the actual time spent in combat. The story personifies the journey of the combat Soldier that many know from past wars and that present and future veterans learn all too often.

Our individual backgrounds are diverse, with each member having specific reasons for joining the military, and the Infantry for that matter. Whether the reason was destiny, academic, or curiosity, infantrymen across the organization have been thrust together throughout the years in a collective effort to accomplish missions. What set our organization apart from others is the type of training the Soldiers would undertake, starting at ft. Benning, GA. The author, along with most of the Soldiers in the Company, was part of a Cohort; recruits that are put together in Reception and complete Basic Training, Advanced Individual Training, and move to their first duty assignment as a group. The concept has been utilized on a small scale by Army combat arms units for years. The results of the cohort concept are phenomenal. In A/1/87 IN's modern history, cohorts have produced outstanding leaders. This group would be no different, with several of its members occupying distinguished leadership roles in and out of the military even today. But the real success is the teamwork and close friendships that develop out of the cohorts.

The term potential is often talked about and written in field manuals, and how the Army is designed to assess it versus experience. When working with cohorts, leaders have no choice, there is no real experience. This is where many members of the unit stood out. From the outset of the cohort's formation, many of the NCOs could tell who had what it took for increasing responsibility. The potential was evident in the train up leading to Operation Restore Hope at the National Training Center (NTC), Hurricane Andrew Relief, and Fort Bragg, NC, where our skills in infiltration, ambush, air-assault operations, and Military Operations in Urban Terrain (MOUT) were honed.

The key to relying on an inexperienced member of an organization is unyielding training and trust. Armed with a clear commander's intent, the author demonstrated that he, along with others in his cohort, could be trusted to do the right thing in the absence of supervision, which is the essence of the Army's Mission Command. This was probably the result of several years playing organized sports as a young man. He made sound decisions with little or no supervision, often anticipating the situation well in advance of others. Things like choosing and moving to over-watch positions, anticipating left and right limits, continuous improvement of machine gun positions, and preliminary pre-combat checks of himself and his Assistant Gunner aided the Squad and Platoon in deploying and being prepared for follow-on missions much quicker.

After the Army gave campaign credit to participants in Operation Restore Hope in 2014, the author realized it was time to tell the story. Reaching out to his Platoon and other members of 87th RGT who deployed to Somalia, he collected and compiled a wide array of viewpoints that captured the different aspects and phases of Somalia. The goal behind the book is to tell the story of the Platoon, the Company and the rest of the Battalion. It is important to the author that the memories are not only de-conflicted to tell the most accurate story (it has been over 25 years, memory becomes faded), but the story is from the viewpoint of the Soldier, the one on the ground who is getting it done. It is also important to note that the most important events documented in this book are not always the ones that involve body counts or the killing of the enemy in combat, but rather some incidents where decisions were made that ultimately saved innocent lives on both sides (The Gift).

One of the things that the reader will realize when reading the chapters is the raw manner in which the author conveys the story. This is Bravo Charles. With a matter-of-fact writing style and a sense of humor that borderlines on the macabre, he tells it perfectly. He captures the raw environment that is Somalia. If you are looking for a book that provides analysis on the strategic objectives or operational decisions of Operation Restore Hope, look elsewhere. If you want stories from American kids who found themselves in the Horn of Africa on an extended journey into the obscure, this is your book. This is told from the point of view of the Infantryman, a machine gunner, barely a year out of Basic Training, thrust into a situation that he just had to figure out as he went along.

Those of us that were fortunate enough to serve with the author understand his motivation to tell the story. Usually, when someone hears that you served in Somalia, the response is "Black Hawk Down, right?". Most are unaware of the fact that the majority of 10th Mountain's Battalions served in Somalia in the months leading up to, during and even after October 1993 in some fashion. This is his story, and we will forever be grateful for his willingness to take on the task.

I still serve today, as a staff Officer in an Armored Brigade Combat Team. In some respects, the experiences of my time in Somalia versus my time I have served with other units are similar. One cannot help forming strong bonds with those you serve with daily. The relationships I built and relied upon in Somalia were not unlike the relationships that held my Platoon together in Iraq over ten years later. Yet there are differences. It is likely because in 1992 no one from my Platoon had ever heard of Somalia. America was fresh off its victory in Desert Storm, and the events leading up to Operation Restore Hope indicated that it was to be a humanitarian mission. Indeed, the media started to lose interest rather quickly after the initial push into Somalia. Yet the grunts on the ground continued to go out every day on patrols, airfield seizures, cordon and searches, and security missions designed to stem the tide of militia activity aimed at controlling resources in the country.

The danger was underlying, rearing its ugly head in places like Afgooye, Kismayo, Merca, and Mogadishu. During that time, 1st Platoon kept up the discipline and the relentless op-tempo, all the while dealing with logistical issues and health issues like dinghy fever, malaria, and dysentery which did not spare one individual throughout the deployment. That discipline formed a bond between us, one that still exists today. It is that bond and experiences from

Somalia that I still draw on today in my current position in the military, and one that I will continue to draw on for the rest of my life.

MAJ John Wasik

"CAN'T SMOKE A ROCK"

"TO THE TOP!"

"CLIMB TO GLORY"

Tip of the Spear

While there were plenty of interesting experiences in the mission I'm about to detail, this book is about Somalia, though I will start by giving you a brief overview of my time in Haiti.

On the 19th of September 1994 we were on the USS Eisenhower as part of the 10th Mountain Division's 1st Brigade Combat team, about to make history as the largest Army-Navy combined air operation since the Doolittle Raids of WWII. Alongside us was the USS America which carried members of the 2nd Ranger Battalion as well as US Special Forces. I was the 1st Squad Leader for 1st Platoon of A CO 1-87 Infantry, and what had only hours before been an invasion had now turned into an occupation. However, the situation on the ground was still unknown and we were going in with the mindset that we were going into a hostile environment. For the second time in a year, I would be among the first Army troops into a hostile and foreign land. I would take the lessons learned in Somalia with me.

My first challenge was that I was leading a squad of soldiers who had only recently graduated from basic training. This was further complicated by one of my two subordinate team leaders telling the squad that he wouldn't kill anyone if it came down to it. He was a deeply religious person and was objecting on

14

those grounds. I reminded him that being a Godly person requires that he honor the oath he took. When he argued, I resorted to being a little less friendly, telling him that I would personally shoot him if we took fire and he refused to engage. It was apparently enough to change his mind.

I gave my squad their pre-invasion talk, telling them what to expect if things got hot. I told them the rules of engagement and simplified them in terms that were easy to understand; if you feel threatened, shoot to kill and let me deal with the consequences of your decision and I reminded them that they had been well-trained enough over the previous six months or so to know. If in doubt, "follow me", follow my lead and do what you're trained to do. I remembered how my NCO's in Somalia had done the same for me; simplifying otherwise confusing rules of engagement, which changed constantly. In fact, the rules of engagement probably changed 3 times prior to lifting off of the aircraft carrier that day.

"I just want to say thank you for volunteering to go on this mission with us. I for one feel much better about this since I'm going with you. You've been through this before and know what to expect." PVT Peter McCabe told me, referring to the fact that I had signed a waiver deferring my enlistment option to PCS (change duty station) and that I was one of a handful of combat veterans in the platoon.

"I wouldn't miss this for the world, Pete." I replied, adding "I wouldn't dream of letting you guys go without me. But thank you, that means the world to me." I said, and I meant it. I remember how sergeants like Wasik, Szulwach, Douglas, Laing and Ferriero had reassured me when I was in the same shoes as these privates in Somalia. Now it was my turn. Schmidt had been reassigned and tried to get my help to go in on the assault as a member of my squad. I tried, but I was denied. I had recently used my pull to send PFC Andrew Majuri to Ranger School over a sergeant who was trying to take the slot instead of going on this mission. That required a lot of higher ups to give Majuri waivers and sign offs.

And Majuri wouldn't disappoint, he ultimately passed Ranger School with flying colors.

Private Picianno's parents had shown up to see their son off before our departure from Ft. Drum when they told SGT. Rick Beem to make sure their son made it home. We all had a sense of immense responsibility for our soldiers. It was then I understood the NCO's that had led us in Somalia from a totally different perspective. Being completely responsible for someone's son in a hostile land is a heavy responsibility to shoulder. Imagine being the commander?

Then we went to the hangar area, just below the flight deck. I have no idea what that's called, I wasn't in the Navy. Once there, we received a pep talk from the commander and then started distributing ammo. Since I was once again in a shorthanded platoon, instead of an M16A2, I was carrying an M203 (M16A2 with a grenade launcher) and aside from a full vest of illumination and HE (high explosive rounds) 40mm grenades, I had four frag grenades and twice the normal combat load for 5.56mm ammunition. Now it was time to do what we'd spent all week rehearsing on the flight deck; load the black hawks and head into Port au Prince.

As I started toward the lift to the flight deck, someone handed me a gift; a 15lb, 3 & ½ foot AT-4 rocket.

"WTF is this for?" I asked.

"All the ammo has to go, so I'm distributing out the leftovers." The supply sergeant said.

"What am I going to do with a with this in a country that has exactly 1 armored vehicle?" I responded.

"Not my problem, sarge. Everything has to go." He said.

For some reason, we already had rucksacks that were so heavy I thought we'd be combat ineffective during the assault. The packing list for the mission was insane, none of it made sense. I believe Time magazine later published an article in October 1994 explaining the screw up, how that they had accidentally created a list with everything that was suggested during a meeting among the brass.

Rising up on the plane lift to the flight deck for "go time" was pretty cool, I must admit, and something not many in the Army ever get to experience. And I absolutely love air assault missions, and you'll probably be sick of hearing that by the time you're done reading this book. As chalk leader, I had my men lined up and prepped for loading the black hawk helicopters just as we had rehearsed all week. Enter Murphy. As I got to the door and people started getting on the birds as rehearsed, dropping their rucksacks at the door, I had to suddenly shift gears, yelling to everyone to take their rucksacks with them. The black hawks didn't have seats, something we had complained about them having all week and were told that's how we're going in despite our objections, with seats. Despite the initial confusion of this unexpected cluster fuck, we adjusted and got onboard.

We were the initial wave of the assault; our objective was to secure a port in the city. We'd be dropped in a field outside the city walls (yes, it was completely walled off) and maneuver to our objectives. I believe 2nd or 3rd platoon had a police station and I don't recall the third objective for sure, but I believe it was to secure a section of road between the other two objectives. As we soared across the Caribbean with our gunship escorts, the adrenaline began pumping like mad. I gave a look around the chopper and smiled at the privates to try and ease their apprehension. I remember being them once. If today was anything like Somalia, this would likely be the last time they felt *this* worried when they did something like this.

As we approached our objective, I could see smoke billowing out of a field near the objective. This really heightened the apprehension. I got the signal for the 2-minute warning; we were two minutes from the objective.

As the doors swung open, we were just a couple of feet off the ground, which wasn't level, when I jumped out. I landed in a hole and literally felt a "crack" in my ankle, followed by instant pain in my right ankle and knee. Other than that, the initial assault onto the landing zone (LZ) had gone perfectly. As soon as we were all out and in the prone, the black hawks quickly disappeared back to the ship. Time to move out.

Our LZ in Haiti

The load on our backs was ungodly heavy and my leg and ankle were killing me. When asked if I was good, I simply gave the thumbs up and began leading everyone off the LZ. We hadn't even gone 100 meters off the LZ when shit started getting bad. First, small arms fire rang out from somewhere in the general area, so everyone maneuvered and took cover. Then the combat medic got busy. I assume the sound of gunfire, the extreme heat, the overwhelming apprehension and these ridiculous loads we were carrying were just enough to send three of our guys into the "kickin' chicken"; they were literally having heat strokes. SGT Beem was helping out the medic by giving an IV to private Stroup as he lay there kickin' about.

As I looked over, I saw PVT Barton just off my flank about 5 meters. He had made a deal with me that if I couldn't turn him into a hardcore grunt by the time I left Ft. Drum, I'd send him to the motor pool as he had requested because he didn't think he was cut out for the infantry, though I disagreed with his assessment. I had seen something in the young 18-year-old Barton that he hadn't realized in himself, but it was a deal I am sure he initially regretted. Yet, here he was in all of his glory, carrying what would be tied as the heaviest load in the platoon as an assistant machine gunner, smiling back at me. Just like I had been part of an M-60 gunner in Somalia, now he was behind the gun.

"Still want go to the fucking motor pool, Barton?" I yelled back to him.

"Fuck no, sergeant!" he replied eagerly.

"That's what I thought!" I said smiling back at him.

Whatever and wherever the small arms fire was, it was sporadic and light and didn't seem to be directed at us at this point. Though it made me feel alive in a way I hadn't felt since leaving Somalia the year before. An adrenaline rush that can't be matched. Not being able to pinpoint a source, we decided it was safe to move because we really needed to clear away from the LZ more. Though now we had 3 casualties. As we tried to figure out what to do, a civilian truck happened by. So, having lots of guns and a big-ass rocket, we "borrowed" it and improvised a casualty evac that would allow us to clear the LZ and get to our objective. We also took the liberty of loading all of our rucksacks with the casualties onto the truck, after which they then were driven a short distance to set up a casualty collection point, as well as a cache for our rucksacks.

As we moved out, there was a nearby explosion, possibly two, followed by a few rounds of M16 fire. As I led the platoon toward our company rally point, we passed two sergeants from 2nd or 3rd platoon who's faces were cut up pretty good, both having taken shrapnel in the face. I asked if they were ok, one gave the thumbs up, the other looked bewildered. Their wounds didn't look very bad, mostly superficial, and no one could determine what had caused them; it was either grenades, or some improvised explosives. It appeared to me that these two technically qualified for the Purple Heart, though I know neither of them received it. "Operations other than war" strikes again.

We were down at least two sergeants; SSG Pavey, who had served in Somalia, had an injured back and SSG Williams was left behind in charge of the rear detachment. They had sent SSG Ferriero to 3rd platoon, SGT Wasik left the service, as did Douglas, Harris was gone, Laing had PCS'd and Szulwach was busy off being a Green Beret at Ft. Bragg.

When one of the other two squad leaders would later complain about my leading every mission one day while we were getting an impromptu Op order during a patrol, SFC Jones, who had gone to Somalia with me when I was a private, put it to them bluntly: I've been with SGT Slane when shit went down. I know what he'll do. You? I don't know you. I don't know what you'll do.

SGT Beem, CPL Grish and myself had proven ourselves to SFC Jones in Somalia and he let that be known. SFC wasn't the strongest tactician, though he was competent, but he was a great leader and knew who to lean on and when for carrying out the missions. His purpose in life was "the big picture", and he said it often. What SFC Jones was telling the other squad leader wasn't mean to be insulting. It just meant that now that we were in a real-world situation, he didn't have time to assess their reaction in combat situations because lives depended on it. This is when experience trumps all else and the combat veterans in the platoon had the most relevant experience. At the end of the day, we all want to go in one piece.

As we started to infiltrate into the port area, which was quite large, I spotted a small guard shack just ahead through my night vision (NODS), which I then pointed to using my infrared laser scope so everyone else with night vision could see my target. After briefly consulting with the platoon leader and platoon sergeant, I began maneuvering toward the guard shack with my squad. When we got there, the poor guy on guard practically shit his pants as I shoved the barrel of my rifle into the base of his skull, and reached down and grabbed an assault shot gun that was leaned up against the wall near his leg.

"Hey there, sweetheart! How are you?" I jokingly taunted my new friend. Yeah, I'm an asshole. Don't judge.

Next we made our way down to the main part of the port, where we then captured 3 additional armed men before settling in for the night, during which it rained. The next day, one of the other squads found some bunkers near a military outpost just up the hill from us which were mostly full of brand-new US made weapons, as well as some desert eagle .44's (really nice Israeli made handguns). An eventual subsequent raid of the military outpost went without resistance, though they had the firepower to have inflicted some harm on us.

Waking up in Haiti with my new toy, day 2.

The night we raided the outpost, a warm tropical rain had moved in, making the ground feel like putty while simultaneously producing a horrible, putrid

21

smell. We eventually made ourselves comfortable and settled in for the night, only to wake up the next morning and discover that some of us had been sleeping in a mass grave. One of the soldiers mounted a skull on a stick and jokingly introduced his new friend as "Bob", to which we laughed. We would later find the remains of several people, many quite small, in that area behind the outpost, and did so without much effort. As grunts often do, like those of us who had gone to Somalia, we joked away the horror of the reality. Although when Private Billy Ramos had sunk up to his waistline in the mass grave, and SGT Beem up to his knees, I really had nothing funny to add. It was what it was; horrifying.

One night soon after, while manning an OP (observation post) near the Haitian outpost, SGT Rick "Earl" Beem and several soldiers were struck by lightning during a sudden thunder storm. Earl was too salty to die by a mere lightning strike. So instead, SGT Beem soon got dengue fever for the second time in his life, making him the only human I know to have been struck by lightning twice, as well as the only one who caught two strains of dengue fever.

While our commander, CPT John R. Elwood, was on emergency leave, we had an impromptu QRF (quick reaction force) mission which involved gunfire, and I was reminded of my ankle as I lost my footing on the loose gravel at the port, and rolled it good. My foot was completely black when I finally ventured to take my boot off several hours later. Again, I finished my mission and was commended for taking quick action to disarm a Haitian while taking prisoners on the pier. However, the first sergeant who praised my actions that day shortly followed his praise by telling me "stick the muzzle of your weapon in your mouth, and blow your brains out", an order I ignored for obvious reasons. SSG Campos was standing with me looking every bit as confused as I was. It was one of several incidents with this first sergeant, and it was by no means the last.

During what was described as Haitian celebrations for democracy in late September, two grenades were thrown by assailants into a crowd of Haitians at the main port, killing several and wounding dozens more. A truly horrific scene, one repeated straight from Kismayo, Somalia. Our medics, like Doc Estes, did their best to save the wounded civilians.

Several times in the first 30 days, we received radio calls telling us to take cover due to sniper fire. As it turned out, they were usually cases of suicide, 4 if I remember correctly, with one or more of them rumored to have served with us in Somalia the previous year.

Third Platoon was seen on CNN firing a SAW (Squad Automatic Weapon) into a padlocked door after chasing a gunman. Why they assumed he was in a building with a door that was padlocked from the outside was an amusing observation on my part. Our battalion also initially secured the presidential palace and also escorted the newly deposed dictator, Cedras, out of the country. As exciting as all of the aforementioned sounds, it still wasn't actual combat. Dangerous? Somewhat, sure. Combat? No.

After several missions in Port Au Prince, we air assaulted into the mountainous region of Haiti near the border of the Dominican Republic and operated out of a Special Forces patrol base there. This time we took Chinook helicopters instead of black hawks. The surrounding area was pretty dense, lots of jungle in parts, with several sugar cane plantations being planted on the hillsides.

While out on our first patrol I helped SFC Jones and SSG Campos establish our location since the new handheld GPS devices we had were so new that they hadn't even decrypted them for use with the satellites, which made them inaccurate. Then, each squad presented a patrol route to the platoon leader and platoon sergeant to be approved so we could start patrolling.

My patrol route was about 10 miles round trip if I remember correctly, and took us up on a ridgeline full of jungle on an adjacent "mountain" (more like REALLY big hills). SSG Campos went with my patrol and we walked for hours before coming out of the bush into a clearing at a sugar cane field, surprising several locals.

"Hola! Yo soy el gallo grande!" I announced in Spanish (most were bilingual and I had 3 years of Spanish), meaning: "Hi! I am the big cock! (or rooster)".

"Ahhh, Hola!" an old man replied.

"Donde esta las senoritas?" I asked, meaning, "where are the women?"

After which I immediately began laughing, unable to keep a straight face after seeing his reaction. Imagine a huge guy with body armor and a grenade launcher asking you where your women are after you first make his acquaintance. It was pretty funny.

After settling things back down, we got some information about the area and then departed. Upon our departure, they offered us raw sugar cane to chew on while we walked, which we accepted for the walk back. By the way, if you chew on raw sugar cane long enough, your gums will bleed. But it gave us energy as we walked back to the ridge from which we had originated.

After a week in the mountains, we went back to the main base at Port Au Prince where we learned some bad weather was moving in. It had been fun patrolling in the high country, out in the bush again. Though the giant spiders there were just one thing among many that constantly tricked my mind about where I actually was, often finding myself confused and believing I was in Somalia, except here we had cots a lot of the time, as well as phone access. Life in general was much more comfortable than it had been in Somalia, though still tough and tense at times. However, overall, there was very little actual combat in Haiti.

I used to nonchalantly tell people how I once swam through a hurricane. While saying I swam might be a stretch, it isn't much of one. It's more like a subtle technicality depending on your preference or interpretation. But I'll let you decide.

As the 1st Battalion of the 87th Infantry was evacuated from their base in Port au Prince, Haiti with the rest of the members of the 10th Mountain Division's 1st Brigade during the onset of Hurricane Gordon in November, 1994, they forgot someone. Me. In fact, they forgot four of us to be accurate, and to be precise, not by accident. As A CO 1-87 was finishing loading the trucks just before sundown, our new first sergeant gave a command that I believe equated to little more than attempted murder.

"SGT Slane! I want you to stay here with some men and patrol the area!" he barked from the back of a five ton just as I had started to climb into the back of the last truck with the rest of my platoon.

"What? Are you serious? Are you going to give me a fucking boat?" I yelled back to him.

"Hahahahaha" he laughed as the trucks pulled away, leaving myself, Barton, Gross and Ratliffe standing in water up to our waists.

As the sun began to set, and the water kept rising, things really started looking bleak. We tried to find someplace, anyplace to take refuge as we stuck around the company connex as the storm turned into a full force hurricane with winds exceeding 100 MPH, a fury of lightening, and more rain than I've ever seen in my life. The situation was dire.

As the water rushed around us, we were in complete blackout until huge flashes of lightening would tear the dark from horizon to horizon as the wind and rain pounded us. The water had a strong current, it was rushing, like standing in a deep river or even in the ocean. We could see all manner of debris rushing past us as the sky would like up from the lightning, except that it wasn't just debris, there were bodies floating by. We spent the time mostly in shock. I desperately tried to come up with a plan. We had no radio, and no food, maybe a canteen of water between us, no dry anything; nothing. For the first time in my life I felt like I was a complete loss.

After several hours of trying to climb the connex or find any shelter at all (about 8), and when it seemed we were going to be in it all night, Ratcliff and Barton reported that they were getting hypothermia. They were both shivering and barely able to speak. Ratliff spoke as though he had been standing naked in subfreezing temperatures for hours on end, and Barton wasn't far behind him. This was dire. My worst fears of us drowning were now trumped by something I hadn't considered in a tropical climate. But it makes sense if you think about it. The water wasn't body temperature and the air temperature had fallen substantially when the hurricane made land. Over many hours, we were developing hypothermia. All of us. In the middle of what seemed like an ocean, with no land in sight, no way to get anywhere, no way to call anyone.......it was up to me. WTF. This is one of the biggest leadership challenges I ever faced, and it was life and death. Barton would later tell me over coffee twenty years later that though he was horrified and scared, my presence alone reassured him during this storm. Humbling to say the least. He obviously saw something different than I felt that night. Because to be honest, I really was at a loss.

After some group brainstorming, SPC Gross had reminded me of the extra tall tables that existed in the telephone tents that were closer to the entrance of the base than where we were. The tables were super tall, like up to my chest. We decided it was worth a try so I set out into the storm alone to find the tents, telling the other three to stay put and together. I have no idea how long it took me in retrospect, but I was away from the group for some time it seems, searching in the dark through submerged tents, trying to locate the phone tents. The phone tents had tables that were about up to my chest. After finally locating the tent, I could see that with the floor of the tent and the height of the tables, combined with being on slightly higher ground than where our company tents had been, this might just work. We started out in water at my waistline (I'm 6'4) and ended with the water at my armpits. For Barton, the water was over his shoulders in the deepest area back near the company AO where we spent most of the night to this point.

Gross and I drug our squad mates through the chest and shoulder high water and into the tent. This wasn't as easy as it sounds. We were in fully gear with full rucksacks, the water up over Barton's shoulders. It was like trying to keep someone from drowning with weights around their ankles as they were falling asleep from the hypothermia and barely able to walk.

After I was able to make the center pole fully erect again, and Gross and I worked the corners straight, I threw them each up on their own table, along with their gear and instructed them to get undressed and get into their sleeping bags which were dry inside waterproof bags in their rucks. I then ordered Gross to get on his own table and start getting dry, possibly even treat himself for hypothermia as I could tell he wasn't far behind the other two. And neither was I. Ratliff or Barton, I don't recall which one, stripped down into their underwear and tried to get into their sleeping bags. Realizing they were delirious, I kindly reminded them in a very SGT Slane way that they needed to strip EVERYTHING off.

Within a couple of hours, Barton and Ratliff would be acting normal again, as normal as possible given the circumstances, able to talk and even joke a little. As they drifted off to sleep, I sat in the dark, occasionally listening to Gross until he finally nodded off, but mostly I was thinking. I was infuriated with the first sergeant for doing this to us, beyond infuriated. I was furious that he took his apparent hate for me and subjected my soldiers to its consequences. As I sat there, I had realized that though we had been swimming in a hurricane all night with the dead, Barton was pretty together, as were the other two. But it was Barton that I was most interested in.

When I first met Barton, he had reminded me a lot of Spaceboy, my assistant gunner in Somalia, who our squad leader, SGT John Wasik would say, never fully transitioned into the Army. He had been stuck somewhere between hardcore, and confused, and nothing anyone tried would change that. Determined to not see Barton go down that same road, though I have no idea if he actually would have, I had spent that summer turning him into a soldier, and

27

in the process, he was broken, he was hurt and then he was......rebuilt anew.... he was hardcore. He was hard enough to air assault into this forsaken county, get past the horrors of the mass grave, and then swim with dead people all night, and not lose himself in any of it. While I'm sure the never-ending hours of this storm and its floating dead things technically damaged him, as it did me, he could walk away holding his head high. I had been extra hard on Barton trying to make amends maybe for what had happened with Spaceboy, I'm not exactly sure.

I'm not sure for how long I had before the sun would come up, but my mind went from analyzing the shock and horror of the night's events, to thinking of Spaceboy and then finally of where he had gotten lost. During the 12 to 14 hours we spent mostly submerged that night with only corpses to keep us company, I finally recognized something that I had seen in Spaceboy in Somalia in the instant I say his "light" went out in his eyes, like no one was home. I *felt* it in myself, only now recognizing it for the first time, though it had been there all along, just affecting me differently. It's ok if your glass cracks a little. It doesn't mean you're broken.

I was overwhelmed by a sense of doom that I can't explain, and I was thankful we were all alive. Though I wasn't sure how. For the last hours of the night, I couldn't find the love of God as the waves turned the minutes to hours, because my mind had gone searching somewhere else, somewhere else I had been and never really left, somewhere God wasn't readily found; Somalia. The climate here (minus the hurricane), the people, the chaotic nature of this place, all pointed to Somalia in my mind, where I had been reborn, behind the gun.

The Winter Soldiers

After graduating high school in Wilkes County, NC and starting college on a football scholarship at Elon College, I transferred to Appalachian State University in Boone, NC with the intention of playing football, after meeting with their coaching staff. That would not happen. I Instead enlisted in the US

Army as The Gulf War started up In the Middle East. After first enlisting for military intelligence with an airborne contract and going through the testing and background checks, I told my recruiter and the personnel at the MEPS (where you go to be shipped off to the Army) I wanted to be an Airborne Ranger......" whatever that is".

After waiting for several hours for a slot to become available, I was shown a video on the newly re-formed 10th Mountain Division (Light Infantry). It looked pretty similar to the Ranger video, but without the parachutes, and with snow. Lots of snow. When mocked by a SFC at the MEPS station for "giving up an easy job" to become infantry, I replied "I'm leaving college.... I don't want anything academic. I want to blow shit up." He shook his head and replied "I hope you like walking". I had no idea what he really meant. But it wouldn't take long to find out.

I won't spend a lot of time talking about basic training and infantry school, it isn't that interesting in the overall story here. About the most interesting thing about basic training aside from the lifelong friends I met, I was struck by a drill sergeant and promptly struck him back. He did a few calculations in his head, turned and walked away. Yeah, I could have been a bitch and squealed to someone, but the two of us handled it our way and it was never mentioned again. The Army still then allowed men to settle differences and establish dominance the old-fashioned way. Not officially, of course. But it happened a lot and no one complained.

Upon arrival at Ft. Benning, GA, I was placed with a COHORT in 1st Platoon, A CO 1-19th Infantry. A COHORT meant that most of us would go through basic training and to our unit (the 10th Mountain) as a group. Here I would meet the guys I would eventually spend the next three years and go on several deployments with.

Eric L Smith was assigned as my "Battle Buddy", the guy who would be my reciprocal shadow throughout basic and advanced training. We had a lot in

29

common having both been football players. I was from Wilkesboro, NC...he was from Wilkes Barre, PA. We were approximate the same height and weight, and were pretty much twins at 6'3"/6'4" and 230lbs. Though he had a much better tan.

Another of the more memorable guys in my platoon was a relatively quiet Texan named Roland Carrizales and his buddy Ramirez. Carrizales was an instantly likeable guy, though I had no idea at the time how important he would come to be in my life over the next 25+ years. Not that none of the others haven't been important, but his role would be much more pronounced.

Basic Training wasn't as rough as I had thought it would be, and was apparently much rougher than others had anticipated. A guy among the latter pissed his pants and quit on our first day "down range", really setting the tone for the next 4 months.

By 6 March, 1992, we graduated from basic and Infantry training and headed to Fort Drum, NY. I remember feeling like "wow....so now I'm an infantryman. That wasn't so bad." Yeah. No. The real training was just about to begin.

After reporting to Ft. Drum in several feet of snow and being escorted to A CO 1-87 IN (Infantry), I was taken to meet my squad leader, SGT Brian Szulwach (pronounced SCHUL-VACH). SGT Szulwach was as hard as they come. Ranger qualified and relatively new in the 10th having come from the 25th Infantry out of Hawaii, there was nothing ambiguous about him. You were either right or you were wrong, you were in or you were out. And it was up to you where you fell in that spectrum. In other words, take responsibility for yourself, you know your sh*t, do your job, and he'll take care of the rest.

I was first put into a room with Terrance Eaddy, who had a bit of a reputation of a guy you don't mess with. I wasn't so different. Also like me, Eaddy didn't have a problem with you unless you created one. After numerous warnings before going into the room, I walked in and was immediately offered a beer. No drama. Leading up to Somalia, he was one of my greatest mentors along with the other M60 gunner, Morris, who's place I would take.

Roderick Forde, George Perez (Chico), Tom Corey and Richard Hughes would be some of the Specialists or more senior privates in the platoon, with Corey and Hughes coming with the cohort just prior to ours. SGT Wasik was one of the team leaders in the platoon who would also make a big impact on me and eventually become my squad leader in Somalia. CPL McClelland, CPL Laing and CPL Schmidt were upcoming team leaders in the company and 1st Platoon. SGT Perez and SSG Pippen were the other two squad leaders in our platoon.

I then met the rest of 2nd squad of 1st Platoon. SGT Douglas SGT Ruddick were the team leaders, both were a couple of country boys, both were great soldiers and fit well with SGT Szulwach. The rest of the squad was from my cohort at Fort Benning: Spaceboy, Steve Mangold, Rick Beem, Tracy Briggs, Christopher Grish and myself. I think the rest of the platoon kind of made fun of this squad of "cherries" at first, but Szulwach would make sure that didn't last long.

Our A CO medics were Docs Busbin, Cooke, Davis and Estes. Being a line medic in light infantry unit was tough and took a special kind of character. These guys were great medics and soldiers who never complained and never let us down.

SFC Gary Mason was our platoon sergeant at the time. A Vietnam era vet who was close to retirement, he had a lot to offer us young soldiers. And man could he hump (walk with a rucksack).

2nd LT Bill Shomento was our platoon leader. He was a ranger qualified hard charger who I felt showed little regard for the men under his command (at times). I could easily say that of a lot of Jr. officers, it's not an uncommon trait when officers are young. But overall, I felt he was a great infantry officer and set a good standard for being hard and training hard. His favorite thing to do was

31

to take us on 5 mile "Indian runs" ....and they were grueling. Shomento leaned heavily on SGT Szulwach and our squad as the go to squad.

1LT Tom Ditamasso was our company XO. I believe he was from Rhode Island and was without a doubt one of the finest infantry officers I had the pleasure to serve with. By the time we would deploy to Somalia, LT Ditamasso had PCS'd (transferred duty station) to the 3rd Ranger Battalion where he would earn a silver star for gallantry in action during the Battle of Mogadishu, while fighting alongside the very battalion where he'd started his military career, 1-87th Infantry.

Our company commander was CPT Parks. CPT Parks was an outstanding infantry officer, and he loved to run. A lot. In the snow. Our first company run with him was approximately 20 miles in negative temperatures and 2 feet of snow. I did not know I could run that far. CPT Parks would also leave our company to become a member of the 75th Ranger Regiment before Somalia.

You cannot talk about an infantry company without talking about the man who really runs the show: The First Sergeant (1SG). And there has never been a finer 1SG than 1SG Bill Poe. The man stood about my height and had a piercing gaze that let you know you better square your shit away, because he would be watching. He was a Vietnam era vet who's combat experience was on the DMZ in Korea, something I was never aware of. Apparently, the communists in the north had several firefights and battles with American troops, knowing America was committed in Vietnam.

Prior to coming to A CO, 1SG Poe served in the 75th Ranger Regiment, in 2-75th RGR. He was then the NCOIC of the swamp phase in Florida for ranger school, and finally, as acting SGM of the entire Ranger Training Brigade (4th RTB). Just about everyone walking around 1-87 IN in those days who wore a Ranger tab, and there were a lot of them, knew him as the Ranger Instructor (RI) from Florida phase. For sure every single officer in the battalion under the rank of major that had a Ranger tab went through Ranger School under his piercing scowl. He was the epitome of everything Infantry, everything Ranger. Under his leadership, everyone carried the Ranger Handbook and every squad leader was personally accountable to him. The Ranger Handbook would be our bible and our training doctrine. Small unit tactics would be the core of our training (Ambushes, Raids, infiltrations, etc.).

Our Battalion command consisted of LTC Joseph Praesic (sp) and CMS Eddie Deyampert. CSM Deyampert, who is distinguished member of the "Old Guard", was a Vietnam Veteran who did 3 tours in Vietnam. When he walked, his boots made an unmistakable clicking sound, something he insisted in wearing long after departing the Old Guard.

Since we arrived in early March, I wasn't expecting the conditions we met during our first training exercise, which was a two-week event. After a SNAFU (f*ck up) getting my gear, I was transported to the field to join the company in the middle of the night. I am not sure if this was done on purpose or what, but I learned a lot about sleeping in the snow that night. Remember, at this point I had no training in it.... this would be my introduction. I was told it was -22 F that night. When I woke up at 0'Dark-thirty, my canteens were frozen, my boots were frozen, and I had a sheet of ice across my skull cap because my sleeping bag had a broken zipper.

SGT Szulwach seemed to expect to find me in this condition and gave me an impromptu lesson in cold weather survival, something that we would continue over the next two weeks. First and foremost, learned from that 1st night, sleep with your boots and canteens in the bottom of your sleeping bag, your body heat will keep them from freezing.

Another interesting aspect of field training with SGT Szulwach was that we would do PT (Physical Training) using things readily available in nature, such as logs, boulders and whatever else we could find. We never had an idle moment aside from laying in ambushes all night wearing our winter white camouflage in several feet of snow. Our "free" time was spent tying knots, reciting things from the Ranger Handbook such as the Principles of Patrolling, and learning everything he had to teach us.

After spending two weeks pulling an ahkio (sled) full of gear we never got to use (a tent and stove) through the snow while wearing snow shoes and dawning winter white camouflage, and doing some cross-country skiing, I got my first two official nicknames: Big Country (BC) and Mountain Man. SSG Pippen had named me Big Country after I chopped a tree down with a machete and built a fire to prevent hypothermia and frost bite our last night in the field. SFC Mason then called asked me "Kill anything today, Mountain Man?" as we did a 15-mile march back to the barracks…. but Big Country was the name that stuck.

We trained non-stop through the winter, which ended in June. (It actually snowed in July). We did trench live fire exercises, squad live fires, MOUT (Urban warfare) training using the WWII buildings on the old post, and weapons training and qualification on a wide array of weapons systems (M249, M16, M203,M60, AT-4's and LAWs). Sleeping in the snow became our "normal". I didn't know how to be cold anymore. We also took a company outing and did some downhill skiing at a nearby civilian ski lodge.

Competition was constant. There was always a drive to be the best soldier, the best fire team, the best squad, the best platoon, the best everything. We brought out the best in each other and built strong teams.

The next most memorable event from our first 9 months was our squad competitions. It was comprised of a week of events for time and qualifications (weapons). From what I remember we first did what we called the "Ranger Swim Test"….you get shoved off the high dive in full uniform and boots after being spun around blindfolded, jump in with full gear and rucksack for the gear ditch, and finally, swim the length of the pool in boots with your rifle (above our heads was the standard in my squad). We did 3 mile runs for time (18 minutes and 30 seconds for me), Bayonet course for time (basically an obstacle course where you stab everything and sprint for about 2-300 meters), 12-mile road march for time with full rucksack and weapon (1 hour and 53 minutes for our squad), weapons qualifications (Expert) and a few other things that escape me at the moment.

The most memorable event in the squad competition was the road march. We were told "Army Standard is 4 hours. Infantry standard is 3 hours. But our standard is Ranger Standard". Ranger Standard meant balls to the wall for 12 miles, leaving no one behind. And our time was amazing, 1 hour 53 minutes. The time the last soldier in the squad crossed the finished line. That soldier was "Spaceboy" .... being kicked, drug and carried by SGT Douglass. It was beautiful. One guy in the company finished in 1 hour and 43 minutes. Truly impressive.... except...." where is the rest of your squad, numb nut?" Szulwach asked him. Great question. And good point.

Next for A CO 1-87 IN came NTC (National Training Center) in Ft Irwin, CA...Death Valley to be specific. It is here where we'd learn desert warfare and survival. It was part of 1-87 Infantry's "train up" rotation. Panama for jungle training (JOTC), NTC for desert, Ft. Bragg, NC for MOUT (Urban warfare) and Ft. Polk, Louisiana for JRTC.... Swamps and whatever you want to call training in hell. 1-87 IN did jungle training Panama in 91, 95 and 96, JRTC in 94, and NTC in 91 and 92 and 93. As an opposition force (OPFOR) in NTC, A CO 1-87 IN set a record for tank kills. You might think Light Infantry doesn't fair well against tanks, but we did quite well. The opposing force was the "Big Red One", or 1st Infantry Division.

In NTC we would typically dig in during the day and walk all night ("patrolling"). During the rest of our 30 days in the desert, we would set up armor ambushes, live fire exercises, do recons and just bake our a$$es off in general. My favorite memory of this training was doing an Air Assault with TF-160, the Army Special Operations Aviators known as the "Night Stalkers". If you know anything about America's story in Somalia, you know that this unit of aviators had a big role to play there as well.

What was most memorable about that air assault was that we flew NAP of the Earth, which is a type of tactical flying at a low altitude using terrain features to hide your location. We flew fast, and so close to the mountains that it looked as though you could reach out the door and pick up rocks off the side of them. This was right as the sun was setting.

Then it was completely dark and we started false insertions, where the helicopters would land in various locations to confuse the enemy as to where you actually landed. During our last false insertion, LT Ditamasso exclaimed "Fuck this shit!" and jumped out and ran across the desert on his own. I wish I had followed him because what happened next was totally nuts. After we were finally inserted, it became immediately apparent that we had just been set down in the middle of an Armored company or battalion. Bradleys and tanks immediately opened fire in every direction. I died hiding behind a shrub from a .50 cal, firing on a Bradley with a 5.56 SAW. Basically, I was throwing rocks at a tank. And it was throwing car sized boulders back. Lucky this was all training and only blanks and lasers were used. I think maybe 4 soldiers survived the assault. LT Ditamasso was one of them. He and 1LT Scott Walker (our Fire Support Officer) ran around killing tanks during the chaos. And did quite well.

After NTC, SSG Daniel Ferrerio joined our platoon having come from Germany. As SGT Szulwach prepared for Special Forces Selection, SSG Ferrerio became our new squad leader. That also came with a new PSG, SFC Alton Jones. After first performing a military funeral for a WWII Navy veteran, we ended up in Homestead, FL immediately following Hurricane Andrew, along with the rest of the 18th Airborne Corps. They then restructured the platoon making SFC Jones the Platoon Leader and SSG Ferrerio the Platoon Sergeant. We would spend about 2 months in Florida for the hurricane relief effort.

Almost immediately after returning from Florida, we were sent to Ft. Bragg, NC for MOUT (urban warfare) training for approximately 3-4 weeks. Here I did something I am famously remembered for.... good or bad I am not sure, but the DoD captured the entire thing on video. During an assault, several members of

36

A CO "died" trying to get a grenade through a third story window. Our new 1SG, 1SG Rodriguez, called on me, the last guy standing to try. Except, I had forgot that I had injured my elbow the night before (My arm was black from my elbow to my wrist), and when I threw the grenade, I immediately knew I was in trouble. The grenade hit just below the window, fell back towards me, and I did what any rational person would do: I caught it. And I immediately threw it back through the window, where it exploded the instant it entered the room. It was then I heard a loud cheer like I was at a football game where I turned to see a bunch of brass and a guy holding a camera who said "Holy shit! I got that on film!" To which I gave a nervous smile and a thumb's up.

We got back to Fort Drum around December 1st, 1992 and I had probably slept in a bed a total of two weeks since March. I was then promoted to E4 and made the other M60 gunner in 1st platoon as Morris was preparing to ETS (Exit the Service). By December 4th, our lives would change forever.

Mission of Mercy

One cold December 4th evening in 1992, in upstate New York, some of us watched President George H.W. Bush address the nation and announce that the U.S. would intervene in the civil war of a small African country none of us had ever heard of before. A country where he said that people were starving to death in 'biblical proportions'. He told America that the 1st Marine Expeditionary force was already headed off the coast and that they would soon be joined inland by the Army's 10th Mountain Division. He assured America that these troops were 'America's finest' and that they would have the full support of the U.S. and the latitude to protect themselves while accomplishing this difficult mission. Not long after, on or around December 6th, our company, A Co. 1/87th Infantry, was put on alert and then on lockdown. All the phones were removed from the day room to maintain OpSec (operational security) and everyone was recalled to the base. We were now going to do what we'd all been trained to do.

Nearing the coast of Australia, the USS Juneau carried CPL Duane Nelson and the rest of G CO 2/9 of the 15th Marine Expeditionary Unit Special Operations Capable (MUESOC) and a team of Navy SEALs. After the president's announcement, they were notified that they too would be heading to Somalia. They began prepping to hit the beach and were told to expect heavy resistance.

On the morning of Dec 9th, 1992, CPL Nelson were the first ashore after the SEALs. Expecting a fight, they were instead greeted by a host of reporters shining lights all over the beach, taking away the element of surprise. The Marines immediately began pushing inland, securing airfields for the follow-on forces. Which would be us.

On Dec 12, 1992, approximately 18 hours after loading aboard a C-141 at Griffiss Air Force Base in NY and a brief stop in Egypt to pick up ammunition and supplies, we landed at Baledogle airfield outside Mogadishu, Somalia. We were the 92 men of A Co. 1-87 Infantry, counting our medics and Forward Observers (FO's). We had just flown nonstop to Africa, having done a midair refuel somewhere over the Atlantic because one of our NATO allies had apparently denied us permission to land (or so I was told). A midair refuel is quite an adventure, I must say. To be done correctly, the plane must speed up, slow down, go up and down, until it perfectly aligns with the refueling aircraft. I saw some hard, hard men lose their cookies that day, my friends. Even though I didn't puke myself, I suddenly felt that I understood the concept of "sympathetic puking".

The whole flight there, all I could do is wonder what we were going be doing, what it would be like, if we'd be fighting, if there were really that many people starving and what it would be like to see that. I'd grown up watching commercials about people starving in Africa and watching the reports of the biblical famine in Ethiopia. Those commercials and news reports were heart wrenching. Could I handle seeing it firsthand I wondered? All I knew is whatever I was going to be doing, I was ready to make a difference in whatever capacity my country saw fit.

Many of my African-American friends celebrated the fact that we were about to see the "motherland". While I couldn't identify with their sentiment, I genuinely smiled for them as they high fived each other in their excitement. There was even talk about Somalia being the site where the Garden of Eden had been. Either way, being both a spiritual person and a person who also believed in science, I viewed Africa as everyone's motherland since science tells us the human race began there. So, I also had some level of excitement about going there.

Initially, 1st platoon of A CO 1-87 infantry consisted of: SFC Alton Jones, SSG Daniel Ferriero, SGT Brian Szulwach, SGT John Wasik, SGT John Laing, (I promise the next name won't be John) SGT John Douglas, SGT Frank Harris, CPL Christian Schmidt, SPC Terrance Eaddy, SPC Roderick Forde, SPC George Perez, SPC Richard Beem, SPC Steve Slane (me), SPC Robert McEnaney, SPC Richard Hughes, PFC Thomas Corey, PFC Christopher Grish, PFC Steven Mangold & PFC David Spaceboy, here forth known as Spaceboy. Our attachments were PFC Roy Estes (medic), SPC Farley (FO) and 1LT Scott Walker (FSO).

After we landed, we still had no idea what our mission would be, if we would be handing out food or if we would be fighting the many warring factions in the Somali Civil War. We weren't even sure what type of environment we had just landed in. We exited the back of the aircraft expeditiously, many of us carrying extra weapons and gear along with our greatly over-loaded rucksacks and personally assigned weapons. Our bodies were instantly in shock in the 122-degree Somali sun. It had been -22 when we boarded the C-141 18 hours earlier. A total difference in temperature of 144 degrees, an unimaginable difference in temperature change in less than 24 hours. But apparently the airfield we were at was secure. The Marines that gotten to the airfield just a few hours earlier and were hauling ass. We were the first large US Army units to land in the country.

The only ones there sooner would have been pathfinders and Special Forces, likely coordinating with the Marines to secure the airfield and make way for follow on forces.

To make thing worse, I could barely feel my left foot due to the extremely tight ace wrap I had put on my leg to forgo medical treatment for what I would later learn was torn ligament(s) and cartilage. I had made the command decision that the treatment was unnecessary and got ready for business with the rest of my unit.

"Slane, are you sure you're OK?" SGT Wasik, my squad leader asked.

"Roger that, Sergeant! Good to go!" I replied.

"Ok...." He said.

Already I was carrying the heaviest weapon a light infantryman could carry, the M60 machine gun, I also had two M-16A2 rifles and a shit-ton (official Army term) of ammunition. My M60 machine gun had a name conspicuously across the feed tray. "Shannon", the high school and college girlfriend who had ripped my heart out over my joining the Army, saying I would never amount to anything after dropping out of college to serve. My M60 could break hearts and far worse to anyone who crossed us. It was total bitch, so the name fit. Terrance Eaddy's machine gun bore the name "Eaddy's Hoe", because he really had made that gun his bitch after toting it for the better part of three or more years. Without a doubt, one of the best M60 gunners in the entire Army.

Following close behind me was PFC David Spaceboy, my assistant gunner, who never came across as the brightest person I'd ever met, but he was a pretty good soldier in most respects and a good, decent human being. Maybe the best I've ever known in some respects as far as human beings go.

After clearing ourselves from the airfield, we proceeded to gather in a formation near the control tower. My squad leader. SGT John Wasik, performed the usual equipment and personnel checks and relayed instructions to us from the platoon sergeant, SSG Daniel Ferriero, about where we'd be moving to, and what we were to be doing. We then moved to an area in the Somali bush, away from the main airstrip, but still within the confines of this one-time Somali military airfield. It was already starting to get dark so we hurried to prepare to bed down in our new home.

Doc Estes accomplished pissing me off our very first day in Somalia. We hadn't been on the ground but for a few hours when he walked over and asked for a cigarette. This isn't generally a problem, as cigarettes are a commodity that we readily share with each other and I figured his must be buried somewhere in his rucksack. It was after he returned a few more times that I started to get agitated. While we generally share cigarettes, we expect that you at least showed up at the beginning of a deployment as reasonably prepared as possible.

"Doc, WTF? Did you bother bringing any cigarettes?" I asked.

"I brought a couple packs." He replied.

"A couple of packs? They told you that you're going to Africa and you thought a couple of packs would be good? Because you'd just run down to the fucking 7-11 and get some more once we got here? And where are your couple of packs now?" I asked him as I grew more agitated.

"I smoked them all at the airfield before we left, and then when we landed in Egypt." He said.

"Fuck-n-a, Doc!" I exclaimed in response.

I had brought eleven cartons of cigarettes and several rolls of Copenhagen snuff (chewing tobacco). Giving Estes the benefit of the doubt, I gave him one full carton of cigarettes and told him he had better pay me back. He didn't. However, a few months after leaving Somalia, I borrowed $20 from Doc Estes. I technically still owe him $20 I suppose. Consider us even.

As the sky grew dark, I saw what I thought was a giant rat scurry across the ground in front of PFC Christopher Grish's feet.

"WTF is that?" I asked as it stopped right in front of him.

"HOLY SHIT! IT'S A SPIDER!!" he said as he turned on his flashlight and instinctively stomped it into the red, Martian-like Baledogle clay.

Unlike many "normal" people, to this point I had no phobias in life. I wasn't afraid of heights, water, jumping, swimming, flying, nothing. Completely fearless, possibly to the point of stupidity. I certainly wasn't ever afraid of spiders. Until that moment. Now I was extremely glad that I had the largest weapon around. And a 9MM pistol with two extra M16's and 4 frag grenades to boot. Those spiders didn't stand a chance.

By now it was completely dark and we were supposed to be settled into our bags on our sleeping mats. However, hardly anyone had done so. My friends who had spent 18 hours celebrating going to the motherland were now singing a different tune. "Man, fuck the motherland" was now the general consensus.

Like myself, most people were sitting right on top of their rucksacks, as though they were some sort of spider-proof haven. Spiders can't climb a rucksack. Surely not. Especially not a spider who reminds me of a small dog. When I finally got so tired that I could no longer stay awake and after my guard watch had ended, I actually tried to fit my 6'4" frame completely on top of my rucksack. Which, isn't completely insane as I still had my unit's unique to the Army "Mountain Ruck", which was insanely large due to the extra gear one carries while training for Northern Warfare. And thank God for that training. After all, it was December! At any moment I might need to break out some "Mickey Mouse" boots, which are good to -60 F, and throw on some snow shoes, maybe even do a little cross country or downhill skiing, all while wearing my white winter camouflage. All things we were trained to do. But alas, it was 2 AM, I was on the equator in Africa, and it was probably still 100 fucking degrees F outside. Maybe 95. In any event, my skills in northern warfare that I had acquired over the last year were likely not going to serve me well here.

However, my training in the hottest place on earth, aka Death Valley, CA, was something that was relevant, as was our MOUT training at Ft. Bragg, NC. We were designated "Light Infantry", meaning we were trained for fighting in any environment, the more restrictive the environment, the better we were suited for it. We were experts in operating in small units of squad and platoon size. In our platoon, that actually meant 4-man teams at times as we only had 16 men. However, while I would argue that we were the best suited Army troops for fighting in the Alps, or the Antarctic.... maybe even the Apennines as our forbearers had done, I wasn't exactly sure why we were here, in what had to be the second hottest place on earth (I would argue the first). And seeing how we were already more than acclimated for winter weather having just spent the first part of December running in subzero temperatures, we were pretty much sucking buttermilk through our asses. And talk about pale? If I had removed my shirt during the daylight earlier that day, it's likely no other aircraft would have been able to land due to the glare of my snow-white skin. As I lay there like a giant bad ass Girl Scout crunched up as small as could be on my rucksack, all I could do is imagine what was crawling up to eat me. I slept about.... two minutes in total all night. Yay, me. Little did I know at the time, but after sleeping outside enough in Africa, none of this would ever bother me again.

Soon after the sun rose, SGT Szulwach came over and showed us his freshly caught Ranger breakfast. One of those huge-ass spiders he had caught with a pair of Leatherman pliers. A well-balanced meal for sure. There was probably enough to spider there to feed the entire platoon. How could people starve in a place like this. We could just send them all to Ranger School and they would never starve again. Szulwach had spent his first enlistment with the 25th Light Infantry Division, where I would eventually end my career. Stationed in Hawaii, he was a Ranger who had spent years acclimating to jungle environments, which Somalia was part jungle, part desert. I couldn't classify it as either. It was hot and dry but had an extremely dense, thick vegetation in many places. Desert in others. In the bush, the thorn bushes or trees that were more tree than bush, with thorns that could easily pierce the protective gear we wore. For us younger soldiers who hadn't even been out of basic training for a year, SGT Szulwach was our first squad leader. They gave him the task of turning us into soldiers as a group, and I think it was a pretty good idea. I'm sure it was a leadership challenge for him at times, but then again, because we didn't know anything when he got us, he didn't have to worry about breaking bad habits where tactics were concerned. We had none. But, by the time he was done with us, we were highly proficient soldiers. He taught us from the Ranger handbook and required that we each carry own a copy. We learned Ranger skills like knot tying and patrolling, ambushes and raids. All of which are Infantry skills, but Rangers are the gods of the infantry. And that's the way he trained us. He wasn't as well liked by all the lower enlisted as he was by me because he was considered a hard ass. But he was definitely respected by all. Besides, being in charge isn't a position of friendship; it's a position of responsibility and survival.

We then broke camp and moved to our assigned sector. Unlike any other infantry that would serve in Somalia except for the initial wave of Marines, we would have experiences like this that made us unique. We slept in the bush, a lot. Everyone that followed us to Somalia slept in buildings 99% of their time in country. I promise. For at least 1/3, maybe even 1/2 of my time in Somalia, I lived like the infantry I had grown up watching on TV and in movies. In the bush.

The area we move to was quite pleasant. It had ant or termite mounds that I had previously only seen while watching National Geographic specials on TV, or in their magazines. We set our gear down and began getting comfortable, building hooches (making a tent like structure out of a rain poncho, supported in the middle by a stick no longer than an M16 and tied at the corners with bungie cords) to sleep or get shade under, and making a perimeter. Suddenly, SGT Wasik screamed.

"HOLY CRAP!" Wasik yelled as his gear went skyward in all directions and he ran from beneath it.

"What's up, Sarge?" SSG Ferriero asked him.

"My gear is full of fricken termites or ants or something! They even have eggs already!" he replied.

No way, this I had to see. As we gathered around his rucksack, he pried it open with a couple of sticks. Sure as shit, there were THOUSANDS of ants of termite looking things, moving around all over inside his rucksack, many carrying what appeared to be eggs! He had probably left his gear there for all of about 30-45 minutes, max. And it had been colonized. We were all really loving our new home now!

45

After settling in, we were told to gear up for combat patrols outside the wire. We were wasting no time at all. We came to do a job, and a job we were going to do. And this type of mission would help acclimate us, as well as better familiarize us with our surroundings. What would we see outside the wire? Would we see starving Somalis? Would we see the guerrilla fighters that we'd all seen on TV? We had no idea what to expect. Being one of two M60 gunners, I would likely go on multiple patrols, being loaned out to squad or team size elements as required. We didn't have a full platoon, just 16 men to start out, with a full-strength platoon being 35. Chico settled in quickly, pulled his boonie hat over his face, and started a siesta in his claimed spot. Being from Arizona, somewhere I had once lived, the heat wasn't anything to complain about.

SGT Wasik led my first patrol, which included myself, Spaceboy, Mangold, Grish and Forde. It was probably only 10 or maybe 11 AM when we left the wire through the main gate at the Baledogle airfield, and it felt like it was 120 degrees F already. It was hot and dusty and you could hear every single one of us breathing like we were gasping for air within 30 minutes of our patrol. And my knee was absolutely killing me. Though I dare not complain and get sent to see a medic and end up with a profile. No way I was going to allow that to happen. Where my platoon went, I was going, come hell or high water. And it felt like hell for sure.

Steve Mangold & John Douglas during a foot patrol

About an hour or so into our patrol, we found what appeared to be a mine, most likely an anti-vehicle mine rather than an anti-personnel mine, by the looks of it. For some comic relief, I announced that I would handle it, and started to do mostly as I was trained by removing my pistol belt and LBE, but holding up my bayonet, which is a big no-no when dealing with mines, especially anti-tank mines. And I knew this, I just wanted to be funny. As I got down on my stomach and pretended to low crawl toward the mine, SGT Wasik got a little excited.

"Slane! Stop fucking around, man!" he yelled out.

"I know, I know! Sorry, Sergeant!" I said as I backed off and jumped to my feet.

"We're going to have to mark this somehow and have the engineers come take care of it." SGT Wasik dictated to the group.

We weren't actually prepared for this scenario. This made things much more real to me. We were in a very dangerous place. We had nothing to officially mark a mine with so that someone wouldn't come along and get killed. We looked around and improvised as best we could by using things made of wood rather than metal, and SGT Wasik marked the mine on the map. Whatever came of it, I do not know, but I assume the engineers came and took care of it.

Soon we found ourselves near some buildings that appeared to be shot and blown up, with some very large, burned out, anti-something type gun. Some fighting had definitely occurred hear at some point in recent history, though not for some time by now. Spaceboy posed near the hardware and I snapped a picture of him. He may have taken one of me also, I don't recall, but if he did, he neglected to give me a copy. We soon returned to our patrol base and another patrol left out. This would be how we operated for the first few days in country as we acclimated to Africa.

On that 2nd day, we had started to see locals. They seemed generally friendly and glad to see us. The truth of that I cannot say. As we headed off away from a group of locals after a brief stop during a patrol on our 3rd day, a man with some camels emerged from the bush and began crossing the road. He was carrying an AK-47. However, as soon as he saw us as we readied our weapons, he dropped the weapon and proceeded to walk away briskly with his hands in the air. We didn't know who he was, but what was apparent is that he wasn't carrying this weapon because he was a guerrilla fighter involved in the civil war. He was just a nomad who was armed for his own protection. SGT Douglas and a few others literally chased him down to give him his weapon back. At this point we had no interpreter, so, all we could all do is make stupid gestures and talk like we were talking to deaf people.

On or about our third or fourth day, maybe sooner, we began manning the front gate to the airfield. All the things we had trained for were now being done for real. We had sector cards on the wall where my M60 was mounted, and at each position around this one time Cuban and Russian airfield. Suddenly and without a warning, a fury of activity in front of us a couple of Humvees came racing down the road with a red jeep which had some sort of weapon mounted on it. Seeing the Humvees, I relaxed my aim a bit, but not so much that I couldn't still fire if needed. As the jeep got to the gate, I could see that it was one of our soldiers behind the wheel.

Vehicle with a 105mm recoilless rifle seized in Baledogle around 16 Dec. 1992.

We gathered around and marveled at our prize, everyone asking what the weapon was that was mounted in the back. I didn't really ask the specifics of "how" we had acquired the jeep, though if you zoom in on the picture and look at the back of the seat, there appears to be an answer in the form of one well-placed bullet hole. Anyway, some of the older soldiers knew what type of weapon was mounted in the jeep and told us that it was a 105mm recoilless rifle and the ammunition in the back of the jeep was flechette rounds. I asked what a flechette round was and the answer was more than troubling.

"Basically, thousands of tiny arrows with razor blades flying at you...." Someone explained.

That sounds fun. We continued to operate from our patrol base for about a week it seems, rotating between pulling guard at the gate and running foot patrols in the surrounding area. On what may have been our last or next to last day at our patrol base, a group of reporters showed up. This is not something I expected. During the Gulf War, the US had allowed unprecedented access to its troops by the press. Even escorts for the press. However, there was none of this going on here in Somalia. While the press may have received the occasional escort or help from the military, they certainly weren't embedded with us nor receiving any sort of regular protection. With them was an Irish aid worker, maybe showing them around, acting as a guide. In three weeks, she would be dead, killed in an ambush in Afgooye, a place we would soon follow.

As I sat trying to look inconspicuous under my hooch, a reporter and cameraman stopped by and started asking me questions and taking pictures of me. I honestly remember little of what they asked except how I felt about being away from home on the holidays. I said something about I had planned to see my youngest brother Noah at Christmas who was six at the time but had to tell him that wasn't going to happen. They soon left me alone and moved along to question others, including Paul Dehart, whom I had gone to basic training with at Ft. Benning, GA. He was attached to 1st platoon and was part of our company's Anti-Tank or AT and mortar section.

Nearly a year later, I found out that those reporters had put a picture of me on the front page of their Newspaper, USA Today, and had written about a two-paragraph narrative on me in the inside article. When I saw the picture, I realized that I really didn't look that inconspicuous sitting under my hooch, with a small American Flag waving in the wind.

"Christmas in Somalia" – USA Today, December 23, 1992 edition.

No, I don't really remember saying that or much else, I was nervous, but I probably did. After about a week in country, we moved over to some run-down buildings that looked like old military barracks. It would be a Christmas to remember, for sure. We also started performing our first air assaults to surrounding villages and convoy security missions to and from Mogadishu.

Looking for the Ish

"The old 1st of the 87th infantry traded their skis for helicopters and went tear-assing around 'The MOG', looking for the shit......" – Paraphrased from the film "Apocalypse Now"

After about the first week in country, we moved toward the other side of the airfield into some old Somali-Russian or Cuban barracks. The buildings were full of bat shit, dead animals and other *creature* comforts of home. We spent our spare time cleaning them as best we could. Any shelter from the hot Somali sun was better than none. Szulwach even crafted a Ranger broom to assist our bat-shit cleaning efforts. I wondered what was next? Maybe some Ranger cookies made from bat droppings? Yum....

Ranger broom!

Within our first five days or so being in country, aside from foot and a few mounted patrols (on vehicles), we also started performing missions that would become routine during our time in Somalia, and something we always did a lot of in general in the 10th Mountain, Air Assaults. Air Assault missions are my absolute favorite type of mission. I'm sure you'll get sick of hearing that, but I can't help it. Now that I'm an old man, I miss getting into a ROARING Black Hawk helicopter in my "battle rattle" (combat gear), with lots of my best friends and butt loads of guns and explosives, and flying around hostile countries, "looking for the shit". Eventually in Somalia, we would find tons of Ish. Almost too much Ish to handle.

Our first Air Assault mission was to a small village somewhere west of Mogadishu and Baledogle. I couldn't tell you the name, because I never heard it. Since I wasn't going with my own platoon the other platoon apparently didn't think I needed to know. This mission was done in broad daylight and even consisted of performing false insertions, something we had done when we flew with the famed Task Force 160 during our time in Death Valley. A false insertion is exactly what it sounds like. The pilot pretends to land and let the troops off in several different locations, so anyone watching has no idea which site the troops got off at. It could be all of the sites for all they know. However, we weren't flying with Task Force 160, or even our own 10th Mountain Aviation unit, which was also good.

For this mission we were flying with some unit out of Germany and the first thing our pilot yelled to us was something like "Got a map?" as he pointed to void with wires hanging out in the helicopter dashboard where his GPS equipment was supposed to be. And just as we were on our final approach, he screamed back to the chalk leader "I think this is it! If it's not, just fire up a flare and I'll circle back and pick you up!"

"Oh boy…." I thought to myself as we began to close in on our landing zone (LZ). "I'm about to get dropped off 'somewhere' in the middle of butt-fuck Somalia, who knows where. But if I'm lost, shoot a fucking flare and the fucking guy who left me here lost, will somehow find me again, and then miraculously find the fucking base we just left and have no idea how to find again?"

My view from a black hawk helicopter over Baledogle.

I'm guessing he was just fucking with us. Well, mission accomplished. It actually worried me a little.

As soon as the wheels touched the ground, we were out the door about 10 meters and hit the dirt in the prone position (on your stomach facing out with your weapon at the ready), and as soon as the last man hit the dirt, the helicopter lifted back off and smothered us in a fury of dust. As soon as it was gone, we were able to lift up our goggles and start our mission.

Once everyone was at the rally point, we spread out and began walking through the town. Within about 3 minutes, a single shot echoed out and we all kissed the dirt. I've been here just a few days and someone already hates me. It felt a little like going to a new high school, except everybody had guns and various scary exploding things. I remember looking around and seeing what I think was a general at the rear of our formation, just taking a knee. I guess he didn't want to get his uniform dirty. And besides, who wants to shoot the enemy's general?

After scanning the surrounding area and unable to locate the source of the shot, we picked up and started moving again. Spaceboy and I headed over to link up with elements of another platoon.

I had been "loaned" to my old platoon sergeant, SFC Gary Mason and SFC Mason wasn't very happy about it. He had basically demanded that he get the other, more experienced M60 gunner, Terrance Eaddy, a demand my current platoon sergeant and platoon leader ignored. I didn't take offense to his demand. Eaddy had been an M60 gunner for probably the better part of 3 years by then. I hadn't even been out of basic training for a year at this point, and had been made a gunner just days before coming to Somalia after putting in my time as an assistant gunner to SPC Morris who had ETS'd (got out of the Army). To compound matters exponentially with SFC Mason's disappointment, my assistant gunner had shown looking like a bandito out of an old western. He had the two belts of M60 ammo he carried (I carried 8 to 10) crossed over his chest.

"WTF is up with that shit?" Mason asked Spaceboy.

"What do you mean, sergeant?" Spaceboy innocently asked.

"You look like a goddamn bandito. Poncho Fucking Villa. Why the hell are you carrying your ammo like that?" Mason asked.

"I dunno, sergeant..." Spaceboy replied.

I had tried to remedy the situation prior to leaving. He had slipped through the pre-mission inspection because he had the ammo in bandoliers like he was supposed to. Sometime between the inspection and boarding the birds he had gone "full bandito" on us. By the time I noticed, we were boarding the Black Hawks.

"Badges? We don't need no stinking badges!" I said, quoting a line from an old western (The Treasure of the Sierra Madre), hoping it would lighten up the situation.

"Get that fucking monkey dick out of your mouth when you're talking to me!" Mason said, referring to my cigarette, a phrase I had grown quite accustomed to over the previous year when he was my platoon sergeant.

"I think cigars are monkey dicks, sergeant. This would be more like a cat dick or something." I replied.

"Move the fuck out." He ordered.

Sheesh, this is fun. I had always imagined I would experience combat with someone funnier, I guess. Nothing worse than killing and dying with people who were grumpy. I had always imagined a more festive demise. Mason was grumpy and ready for retirement. It probably didn't help that he was overweight by Army standard, probably by far the heaviest person I'd ever see in uniform, especially in an infantry unit. Add in the fact that we just air assaulted into the interior of Somalia at the hottest part of the day, and you have a pretty grumpy sergeant on your hands. Mason was tough and carried the weight pretty well as he was well over 6 foot. As a private, I had trouble keeping up with him on our first road marches. He couldn't run very well, but he could "hump" (march in full gear). He was a Vietnam Era veteran and had finally made it to war, though far past his prime and just as he was exiting the military.

Once we got to our position and set up, a vehicle went speeding across the field away from the town. I immediately swung the M-60 around and started tracking him, waiting for the command to fire. If I had to guess, whoever had shot at us was in that vehicle. They were speeding away starting at about 350 meters out in front of me. I could have turned their vehicle into a burning hunk of Swiss cheese from this distance. However, we didn't see any weapons and a call came over the radio to hold our fire. The rules of engagement (ROE) trump whatever we *know*. Just enough more excitement to keep the adrenaline up.

After an hour or so, I started seeing something strange in the distance heading right toward us. At first, it looked like a couple of camels. But as they came into full view, it appeared to be camels as far as the eye could see. It was a caravan of nomads. I felt like we were having a true National Geographic moment now for sure. It was really quite amazing to see as they passed by, the camels laden with their tents and packs of belongings. There must have been 50 camels or so in the caravan, maybe more, some carrying people and some of the people walking. Some of them were armed, but it was pretty well understood that these weren't the type of people we had to worry about. They weren't from Somalia and they had no part in the civil war here. They basically moved through routes that had probably been established for hundreds, if not thousands of years, from one place to the next. Many of them spoke several Languages, including English, which makes sense if you think about the nature of their travels. It probably took a good half hour or so for the caravan to get past us and then we got word it was time to move out. Whoever we had gone to intercept was gone, likely in the vehicle that sped off earlier. We had found a small cache of weapons in the town, but nothing like the larger caches we'd find later during our tour.

We would perform another air assault or two before Christmas to get a feel for the land and establish a presence. People needed to know we were there so the "bad guys" would leave the population alone, I guess.

A day or so later, we did a sweep of "Wally World" (I believe it was) after reports of armed bandits or fighters (I'll say it 1,000 times, there's no difference). Leading up to this point, I don't remember much of what happened, so it must have been unremarkable, but now as we walked across a huge field, spread out, and took up positions. Just as it was getting dark, I heard some shots ring out to my right flank.

"What are they shooting at?" Spaceboy asked innocently.

"Well, if I had to guess, they're probably shooting at 'bad guys'. What the fuck do you think they're shooting at? Keep your eyes open..." I replied.

After a few minutes, a report made its way to us that one of the other platoons had engaged at least one armed Somali. But now I got to eat the words I had just said to Spaceboy because after a while, the loud annoying animal noises we had started hearing were said to be that of a camel. What the fuck they had actually shot while engaging these guys, or guy, was a fucking camel. As far as I remember, the Somali they had shot at got away.

"Slane, you guys good?" SGT Wasik asked.

"Roger that, sergeant." I replied.

"We're going to hold these positions for a while, so stay alert." He told us as he went off the check on the others.

"Roger" I said again.

For about an hour, I was pretty jacked, waiting for the "ish" to find me as I lay there periodically traversing the terrain. Then I realized that the Ish wasn't coming. 100 meters away and now nothing. And as luck would have it, we spent the whole night in those positions, on the edge of a field, listening to that fucking camel whale away all night, hoping to find "the shit".

"Why don't they send someone over and just shoot the fucking thing in the head?" I whispered out into the dark to no reply.

"Fucking ridiculous." I added.

So, there we were, my bandito buddy (he tried wearing the 60 rounds like that for like a week), sitting alone in the dark with nothing to do but listen to a camel die, or engage in some Spaceboy psycho-babble. Suddenly I loved the dying camel. Don't get me wrong, I love Spaceboy like a brother, but shit. And then he uttered the famous, drive Slane homicidal phrase that I would hear every time we ended up alone in Somalia, or so it seemed.

"Slane"….he said.

"What…?" I replied.

"Why are we here?" he asked.

"What?" I said back confused.

"What are we doing here?" he specified.

"Listening to a camel die." I instinctively said, knowing he wanted a deeper answer.

After hours upon hours, the night suddenly got quiet. Except, now I could see the sun coming up over the horizon. Yep. We laid there all fucking night, listening to camel in his never-ending death throes. I came to the conclusion that camels are fucking drama queens. What other explanation is there?

As we picked up and headed through an area with some houses and I opened a gate to walk through when I was mutually surprised by quite a site for my 22-year-old eyes. He had to be the oldest living Somali on the planet. Old by any standard. And he was buck naked with nothing but a bit of a robe or something folded and over his shoulder. He looked like he had just seen his death, and I thought maybe I might be looking at mine. WTF?

"Uh….subax wanaagsan (Soo-bah wanox-sun. It means good morning.)" I said, holding my hand up in their Islamic tradition.

"yuuuuuhhhh……su…..bax wa….naag….san" the old man was finally able to utter as he had one hand raised back to me, and was shaking like a dog shitting razor blades.

"Yeah….buh buh, now…" I said, trying to avert my eyes and move along.

It wasn't quite fully light out yet as we traversed the streets and alleyways of the town. Spaceboy and I could see SGT Wasik and the rest of the squad one alleyway over as they suddenly had some excitement. SGT Wasik whipped around and faced the opposite direction and postured himself behind his M16A2 and maneuvered toward a suspicious individual, while shouting commands to him and to the rest of the squad. He thought the guy was shadowing him and had been about to do something, though it turned out that it may have been nothing.

About 10 minutes later, an individual happened out into the alleyway quite abruptly, and I thought in a threatening way and possibly armed.

"FUCKING DROP IT!" I shouted from behind the gun, as I hit the dirt and took a prone position, my adrenaline pumping like mad.

As I lay there contemplating the fate of this guy, SGT Wasik and the others quickly came over and detained the individual, and subsequently let him go. Again, it had been nothing. A short while later, we took several rounds of small arms fire as we neared the end of the village, but could never locate the source.

Back at the airfield, it was time for some hygiene and breakfast, followed by weapons maintenance, some sleep and maybe some guard duty. I believe we were rationed to just 2 or 4 quarts of water per man, per day, and 2 MRE's (Meals ready to eat.... basically, barf in a bag), and half a canteen cup of water per day for hygiene. At some point, though I don't remember exactly when, it was rumored that we would be cut back to just one MRE per day. Personally, I would have preferred that we be forbidden to eat ANY MRE's at all, and maybe have some real food instead. In an ironic twist, I would eventually lose 35 lbs. in Somalia. With my broad frame and being 6'4", I looked as though I were starving. But were there only about a week or so in at this point. Going home is a long way off. Eventually, I sprawled out on my sleeping mat in the shaded platoon room, where it was only a brisk 170 degrees and zonked.

Hellfire Christmas

SGM Larry "Super Jew" Freedman, a Delta Force soldier, would become the first fatality in Somalia while conducting CIA paramilitary operations. His vehicle struck a mine or improvised explosive, wounding 3 and killing 1. Their mission was so secretive that after the wounded and dead were flown to a US Naval vessel, they had no idea who they were treating, or what to do with Freedman's remains.

Though we still were basically sleeping exposed to all the fun creepy crawlies that wanted to curl up in our bags with us. As we started to make the barracks once again resemble a military post, Navy Seabees began building up a base right next door. They had machinery and lumber to aid them, things we lacked. SFC Mason procured a "shitter" for us after talking with one of their NCO's. However, the shitter cost me a pair of jungle boots (You all owe me $60.00 plus interest).

The rooms in our "barracks" were small and only one was occupied per platoon. This meant that most of us would still be sleeping outside. Early one morning, Spaceboy showed us the guest he found under his sleeping pad. A millipede that was about 18 inches long. He tried to step on it and crush it but to no avail. He finally jumped up and down on it 3 or 4 times until we heard a "crunch".

Our Barracks at Baledogle

We were limited to one half of a canteen cup of water a day for hygiene, which was challenging to say the least. With that water, we had to shave, brush our teeth and give ourselves the old infantryman's "whore bath", which was basically washing our balls and underarms. If you did any of that in the wrong order, you might imagine your disappointment. Most of our uniforms were now permanently caked with the red Baledogle clay, and I hesitate to describe what we smelled like. We also started to learn that underwear was our enemy. After patrolling around in this climate with no clean underwear and no showers, my balls started going to war with the insides of my thighs. Doc Cooke from 2nd platoon had his platoon use foot powder on their man junk and suggested the same to us, so we did as he directed. And it worked, but, no more wearing underwear.

After a few days of patrols around Wanlaweyn (Wally-world) and Baledogle, it was time to go to Mogadishu, something we would do quite regularly as convoy escorts. As we started out in our Humvees and got outside the wire, we began driving east toward Mogadishu. Before too long, we started seeing new sights as we got into territory we'd not seen to this point. Just a few miles outside of Mogadishu, we stopped as an OH-58 Kiowa (scout helicopter) sped over the top of us, followed two minutes later by 3 Cobra attack helicopters. They were flying pretty low and fast as though they were after something. Sixty to ninety seconds later, the ground suddenly and violently shook as we heard a large explosion.

"BOOOOOOOM!!!!!!"

"What the fuck was that?" someone asked.

"I think those Cobras just took something out!" SGT Douglas replied.

After a few minutes on the radio, it was confirmed that the Cobras had flown just ahead of us and taken out a vehicle with a .50 cal mounted on top. The black smoke now visible, we prepared ourselves for any possible counter attack from survivors. However, there were none.

The blown-up vehicle was barely recognizable as it lay smoldering in the bush off the main road. No one even had any idea how many people had just been blown to meet Allah. Though we were about a kilometer away when the Cobra unleashed one of its Hellfire missiles on the unsuspecting militants, the ground shook where we were as though we were in an earthquake (closet thing I can relate). Had the Cobras not taking out that vehicle, we probably would have had a really, really bad day. My M60 was the biggest weapon we had, and though we had two of them, taking on any size force with a .50 cal would have been challenging, depending on who fired first.

As we entered Mogadishu, I was initially surprised at how many people there were. My adrenaline still pumping, I was on full alert as a vehicle drove by that wasn't much different than what the Cobras had just taken out a half hour before. Except manning the .50 cal was a Pakistani in a bright blue helmet, which was an excellent sniper target I thought to myself. Maybe it was a clue as to why so many of them were being killed which President Bush had used as a catalyst for sending us here. I was glad that we were NOT under UN control, and never would be. We had our own rules of engagement and a command structure that didn't include anyone in the UN.

Pakistani Soldiers wearing the UN Blue helmet and beret in Mogadishu, December 1992.

We conducted a small patrol, though because I didn't spend most of my time in Mogadishu, I can't really tell you what area it was. As we exited our vehicles and prepared to set out on foot, there was what I believe to be an Italian soldier standing there. He was extremely neat and clean, looking (and probably smelling) nothing like us as we walked past him covered in grimy, red clay-covered uniforms. As he stood there in his neat uniform and shiny boots, he seemed to raise his nose at us, for which I winked at him.

"Stay alert, cupcake!" I said as I walked by him, not knowing or caring if he could understand me.

"Man, he sure is pretty!" someone else uttered.

All I remember about the location of the patrol that was distinguishable from the rest of my surroundings is where it ended. It was a very large and elaborate white building that I believe had two floors and some type of gardens in the back. It was in fairly good shape and it seemed extremely out of place given everything I had driven and then walked past to get there. It seemed like a presidential palace someone had said, or maybe an embassy of some kind, though there were no guards around it.

Eventually we found the headquarters for US forces, which included a PX of sorts. I grabbed a few Marine t-shirts (they didn't have any Army t-shirts) to wear under my BDU tops, and looked for whatever "Poggie bait" I could find. They had none. When we told one of the Marines where we were stationed upon his asking, we were advised to get back there before dark since we didn't have a base in the area, which sounded reasonable to us.

We pulled back into Baledogle airbase just after dusk and spent the evening "smoking and joking", something that we wouldn't get much time to do for our entire time in country. Then we hit the rack and prepared for our turn pulling guard.

The next morning, we got up around 5 AM and pulled "stand to", a military tradition where everyone gets behind their weapons in a position and prepares to be attacked. My position was near the main road coming from the airfield and I was thoroughly bored with the idea until a lonesome Marine happened down the road.

"Halt! Who goes there?!!" I challenged to the unsuspecting Marine.

"Lance Corporal Keen!" he replied.

I then gave him the challenge phrase (no, I don't remember it) to which he only stuttered in response. So, I proceeded to the next step in the process.

"Advance to be recognized!" I ordered, kind of giggling to myself, knowing that the Marines and Army were likely not communicating about challenge and passwords.

"Halt!" I ordered again as he got within 10 meters of the bush I was hiding in.

"WTF are you doing running through my perimeter at O'dark thirty, dude?" I asked him.

"I have a blah blah blah blah blah." He responded as the words started to meld together as I became disinterested in the details of his mission.

"Yeah, yeah, yeah. Alright, maybe you should check with someone next time you decide to go prancing around the countryside all alone and find out some passwords! Go ahead, get the fuck out of here!" I said as he then returned to his double-time pace down the road. "And Merry fucking Christmas!" I added since it was Christmas eve.

The Somali Air Force at Baledogle

After a delicious Christmas breakfast of MRE's (I had the ham slice), we began writing our own "12 days of Christmas" song while we gathered in a circle as a platoon and played hackie sack. It was around this time that we got our first VIP visitor, General Gordon Sullivan, a four-star general who was the Army Chief of Staff, a member of the Joint Chiefs of Staff, and the future acting Secretary of the Army (appointed in August 1993).

General Sullivan gave us a good speech in telling us that we were there to make a difference for millions of starving Somalis. He informed us that we were now receiving hostile fire and imminent danger pay and that we had earned the former wartime shoulder sleeve insignia (though that was not officially announced for several months), which meant that we were now veterans of a "war", and would wear our 10th Mountain Division patches on our right shoulders for the rest of our military careers. General Sullivan was a good leader. I don't say this because I was ever *personally* led by him per se, other than being a member of the Army which he commanded, but I say this because of the way he presented himself and the importance of our mission. I found him to be inspiring. After a short talk and some one on one talks with members of our unit during which he handed out a few Army Chief of Staff challenge coins, he moved on to the next unit elsewhere late in the afternoon just before dusk. Now it was time for our Christmas eve festivities; guard duty at the main entrance to the airfield.

Christmas Eve 1992 with 1st Platoon, A Co. 1-87. "The Rock"

After spending a couple of hours working out the lines to our 12 days of Christmas in Somalia, things quieted down a bit and people began rotating between sleep and duty. Estes provided some serious comic relief while sound asleep inside the small building just to the side of the main gate.

Next to the room containing my machine gun was another small room but with no windows facing the road. This room was our command post, so to speak. In it you would find the platoon sergeant or platoon leader, the RTO and radio, and the medic, Estes. Or Testes as we often affectionately referred to him. The room was extremely cramped to say the least, and whoever was in it took turns manning the radio at all times. It didn't matter where the person was, the hand mic could reach to any point in the room.

On this particular night, I was manning the SAW, so I was outside the building. It was quiet and probably about 90 degrees still at near midnight, when I heard the most blood curdling sound you can possibly imagine. I am not even sure I can adequately describe it in writing to even come close to doing it justice, but here goes.......

"SSSNNNNNAAA YEEE AAA EEEEE AAAAAAAAA KKKKKKKKEEEEEEEE!" in the highest pitched, 'I'm being eaten alive', nearly-crying voice of Doc Estes.

Needless to say, there were suddenly a dozen grunts surrounding the small building, weapons ready and pointed, ready to kill this monster and likely anyone it was on. Just to be safe. The only window to this particular room was in the back, and several of us approached it in a rapid manner, with weapons locked and loaded, prepared to light this fucker up.

My heart was racing like mad. Somalia was full of snakes and not just any snakes, some of the deadliest snakes in the world to include Black Mambas, Cobras, Spitting Cobras and Asps. Everything in Africa could eat and kill you it seemed. I'd already seen spiders as big as rats and watched giant ants kill a bat. I saw a grown man try and kill a millipede or centipede (I didn't count the legs, etc....) by squishing it with his entire body weight, to no avail. Scorpions were often seen, too. And now our medic was being eaten alive by a huge fucking snake, at least by the sounds that he was making in his final death throes.

This would be the one time that it was ok to turn on a flashlight without a red lens to dull the light. And as we did and pointed our weapons around the room, the only thing visible was the look of pure delight on Steve Mangold's face, contrasted by the total terror on the face of Doc Estes.

"Dude, hahahaha, it was the cord to the fucking radio mic!" Mangold tried to explain as he laughed.

Apparently, Mangold, or someone else had reached over and grabbed the hand mic of the radio to perform the hourly radio check and in doing so, had pulled the cord across Doc's throat and body, giving the sensation of a snake slithering across him. Nothing but laughter could now be heard erupting in the quiet darkness of the Baledogle airfield and it continued for some time. This is something our beloved Doc would be known for from now on. Something that when we were all bored and depressed, deprived of sleep and in need of a good laugh, we could just throw it out there.

"Fuck you guys!" he would reply in his dry, monotone voice. "You guys are assholes."

"Merry Christmas! Now get back to sleep so Santa comes!" someone replied.

He was right, we were assholes. Probably something we have in common with everyone else in our MOS or similar MOS's. We usually came off as cocky assholes. To each other this wasn't a problem. But we generally get a bad rap for not "playing well with others". And it makes sense if you think about the job infantry has to do, which by the end of this book, you'll have a much better appreciation for. But if you were about to get your ass kicked by some bully at school on the playground, who would you want on your side? The captain of the chess team and his debate team buddies? OR.... the captain of the football team, along with the meanest, nastiest players on that team, all of whom believe they are indestructible and can't be beaten. There is something inherently dangerous about people who seem to fear nothing and believe that they can do anything. And by the end of our time in Somalia, Doc would be just like the rest of us.

Christmas morning was full of cheer! By lunch, it was over 120 degrees outside. And by the end of the day, we were told the heat index had been a brisk 153 degrees. Beem and Wasik sat on the railing outside of our platoon CP as we all discussed Christmas, or anything trivial to keep off the topic. SGT Wasik was making his rounds to each member of the squad and seemed to be handing something out, when he finally came to me with two closed fists.

"Pick one." He said.

"What?" I asked.

"Pick a hand." He responded as I complied.

"Merry Christmas, Slane" he said as he opened his hand, revealing a small cookie.

"Seriously?" I laughed.

"Yeah, or you can have a butterscotch candy...." He replied.

"Nah, you can give mine to someone else, it's ok." I said.

"Are you sure?" he asked.

Our Christmas tree…

I don't know why, but the reality of it being Christmas had hit me at that point and I suddenly felt depressed. SGT Wasik was a genuine guy who had made a genuine attempt at bringing even just a little bit of Christmas spirit to us and I kind of mocked it. And I felt guilty for doing so, later apologizing for being a bitch about it. As the sun began to set, we got together as a group with a small thorn bush a few of the guys had decorated and we sang our 12 days of Christmas in Somalia.

Rick "Earl" Beem (left) and SGT John Wasik, on Christmas Day, 1992.

"On the first day of Christmas the Army gave to me, a bird in a fucking thorn tree!

On the second day of Christmas the Army gave to me, two duffle bags, and a bird in a fucking thorn tree!

On the third day of Christmas the Army gave to me three MRE's, two duffle bags, and a bird in a fucking thorn tree!

On the fourth day of Christmas the Army gave to me, four frag grenades, three MRE's, two duffle bags, and a bird in a fucking thorn tree!

On the fifth day of Christmas the Army gave to me FIVE! PAIRS! OF! SOCKS! Four frag grenades, three MRE's, two duffle bags, and a bird in a fucking thorn tree!"

You get the picture. After the sun had set, we listened to our Navy and Marine neighbors enjoy the feast they had next door. We had learned that they had a nice ham dinner with all of the fixings. Poor bastards. They could have had a spaghetti and meatball MRE. It came with real candy. Rather than sit around feeling sorry for them, I spent Christmas night on duty on a small hill in an OP on the edge of the airfield. Even got to have a bit of Christmas excitement as a technical vehicle came dangerously close to trying to enter the airfield through the bush. Shots rang out as E-87 (I believe) approached and the vehicle fled. I'm not sure who shot at who, but the situation cleared up quickly.

Peace on earth, and goodwill toward men. I'm manning an M60 in the Somali bush, ready to spread goodwill to whoever stops by, and watching people shoot it out just a short distance away. But, oh what a beautiful, beautiful sky.

SPC Terrance Eaddy, M60 gunner, 1st platoon on Christmas 1992.

Beledweyne

Just after Christmas in 1992, on 28 December, we were given our first major mission, an air assault to the border town of Beledweyne, Somalia, which was just along the Ethiopian border in the disputed Ogden region of Somalia, in The Shebelle Valley. The city also had a major water supply running right through it, The Shebelle River. The Ogden region had been in dispute with Ethiopia and had seen its fair share of war throughout the years. It would be the furthest westward mission that we had in Somalia and a mission that would be our first joint mission with another country.

The city was also the birthplace of General Mohamed Farrah Hassan Aidid, leader of the United Somali Congress (USC) and later led the Somali National Alliance (SNA), the man who had driven out President Mohamed Siad Barre's forces from Mogadishu, and a man who was largely responsible for both the Civil War in Somalia, and the mass starvation of the Somali people. Aidid was someone who was always on the US radar, and his followers were always mentioned during mention briefs in areas we believed me might encounter hostilities. He was responsible for much of the violence in Somalia, and would later become the target of a bounty issued by the United Nations (UN) and enforced by the US. He is also the man responsible for the incident later known as "Black Hawk Down", which would take place in about nine months.

Beledweyne had a fairly good airfield that could be used to fly in follow on forces and supplies to the region. We were to secure the airfield (a mission typically called an airfield seizure) and then be relieved in place by the Canadian Commandos as they were called, the US equivalent of Airborne Infantry. Airfield seizures were missions typically done by the Ranger Battalions at that time (Operation Just Cause, Operation Urgent Fury), so it was a mission of great importance to us, as we felt it really established us as a unit. This mission would also be the fourth or fifth of many Air Mobile or Air Assault missions that we would perform all over Somalia during the next several months.

71

It would be a pretty long flight compared to any other air assault missions we would do. The city was about 150 miles northwest of Baledogle, and 200 miles northwest of Mogadishu. To make the long flight to Beledweyne, our Blackhawks were fitted with external fuel pods as the Blackhawks would not be refueling there since no friendly forces had been there and established a presence yet. Hence, the purpose of our mission. Little or no resistance was expected, but what we would actually find there was unknown.

We were very well versed in getting on and off Blackhawks for Air Assault missions, but we had never flown with these extra fuel pods before. It was one thing the crew chiefs had to point out to us when exiting the aircraft. So, we took a couple of practice runs to make sure we didn't run into or get our gear caught on the pods as we exited the helicopter. Then, it was show time.

Flying over Baledogle to Beledweyne

We took off from Baledogle sometime in the late morning or early afternoon and began our long trek to Beledweyne, which was almost a two-hour flight as I recall. I remember being thankful for being so high up in the air and feeling much cooler than I would be on the ground. People tried to talk, but Blackhawks are really too noisy to be able to make much out for a conversation for extended periods. After about an hour in the air, somewhere near the

Ethiopian border, we took fire from the ground. I was told that it was the Ethiopians and the return fire we saw going back at them, was our Special Forces taking care of business, though I have no idea personally. Soon we were updated by the chalk leader that is was nearly show time.

Air Assault into Beledweyne

As the helicopters swooped down into the fields around the airfield outside of Beledweyne, we could see Somalis scattering to get out of the way. As soon as we touched down, the doors flew open and we exited the Blackhawks expeditiously, and took cover behind our rucksacks until the helicopters lifted back off and left. Immediately we linked up at our rally point, did a quick head count, and moved out to our assigned sectors as rehearsed. No shots were fired, but our adrenaline was still rushing. Once in position, we began the buildup our positions as best we could, dug fighting positions, and settled in for the night. We could see lots of civilians off in the distance and closer to the city, but at this point they kept their distance. Spaceboy and I dug in as best we could and used our rucksacks for additional cover in front of our position. Behind our position,

73

we used our e-tools (shovels) and tent stakes and put up a poncho for shelter (often called a hooch) and got ready to settle in for the night. We were occupying a large field around the airfield with little or no cover, only a few bushes. The stench was terrible. We would later learn that we were in a field they used to discard animal remains.

"Digging in" is something that the infantry does a lot in training, something for some reason I didn't think we'd do often in the real world unless we were fighting tanks. But, apparently there's actually a reason they have us dig so many in training. And we made sector diagrams, too, just like we did in training. To accompany the diagrams, we had sector stakes to control the direction of our fire to the right and left while firing at night, since you can't see left and right visual markings in the dark. During our training at NTC in Death Valley, we did a lot of digging in. Luckily this ground wasn't as hard as it was in some of the places I had tried to dig in while in Death Valley. I once spent hours digging in there, only getting about a foot into the rocky ground and covering my hands in blisters. But at least here the ground wasn't so tough.

One of us had to be up at all times and Sgt. Wasik made regular rounds to check up on us and make sure we were ok. I really hated sleeping in the Somali bush, or anywhere outside in Somalia due to the insanely large spiders, millipedes, ants, scorpions and a half dozen or so of the deadliest snakes on the planet. It never failed that I would see one or all of the above mentioned while in the bush and it really wasn't that uncommon to see any of them in buildings. So, inside or outside, it really didn't matter. Everything in this country wanted me dead, it seemed. Needless to say, it was a long, mostly sleepless night that was mostly quiet. The only exception was some sporadic gunfire that was clearly not any of our weapons, followed by return fire by a SAW (Squad Automatic Weapon) probably 500 meters or more from where I was. While it put us in a heightened state of alert, we were apparently in no immediate danger. SGT Wasik reported seeing a UN vehicle heading into the city and taking fire as it went as he watch through his night vision goggles. I did the same through my

PVS 4-night vision scope mounted on the M60. I spent the entire night mostly alert and behind the gun. Someone had commented that the gunfire had only been "happy fire", whatever the hell that is, but they were sadly misinformed.

As the sun began to breach the horizon, I remember how absolutely beautiful the scene was. It seemed like it was right out of a documentary about Africa and I was the host of Mutual of Omaha's Wild Kingdom. Which would make Spaceboy that poor son of a bitch assistant Jim(?) who always had to do the dumb shit, like wrestle the crocodile or ride a lion, while the host of the show narrates his ridiculous deeds to the rest of the world. I wondered if maybe Spaceboy would mind wrestling a Black Mamba or something to amuse me while I ate breakfast and made my coffee. No dice.

I proceeded to heat up a canteen cup full of coffee while Spaceboy stood watch. As I took a few minutes to enjoy some hot joe, I sat in wonder of the situation I was in. I remember seeing some large birds off in the distance, probably vultures or some other pretty bird, gathered in a large group. I started hearing the city in front of me coming to life as the sun rose higher in the morning sky.

By 8 AM, the locals began to emerge from the city, making their way toward us a little at a time. By 9 AM, they began filing past our positions like we were on exhibit in a zoo. Some could speak English, most could not. They would try and ask for food or try and sell us things, even offer us wives.

Locals walking near Beledweyne.

Around noon an older man, probably in his late forties or early fifties, clearly considered an elder in this culture, came by with 7 or 8 of his daughters and began bartering with me. At first, I had no idea what exactly he was trying to "sell". The oldest daughter might have been in her mid-twenties, the youngest probably about 12 or 14. Confused as to what exactly he was after, I called for Mohammed, our interpreter.

"He is trying to see if you are interested in taking some or all of his daughters as wives." Mohammed explained.

"What? That one couldn't be but like 14 or so...? They marry them that young here?" I asked.

"Yes." He responded.

"Well, how many of them is he trying to marry off?" I asked.

"All of them. As many as you can afford." He said.

"Afford? I have to pay him to marry any of them?" I asked.

"Yes. It's a custom here. You pay the family to marry their daughters." He explained.

As we talked, each of the girls smiled as though presenting themselves for judging in a beauty contest. And to be honest, they were surprisingly beautiful. Not exactly what I expected in the middle of a third world country. For years I would tell people that Somali women are actually some of the most beautiful women I've ever seen. And I had been away from the civilized world for a few weeks by now and wouldn't have minded having a girlfriend, I guess. But I've said that about a lot of women at a lot of different points in my life. Basically, I figured out I just really like women. However, I wasn't interested in marrying one or any of these women and I certainly wasn't going to pay to do so.

"Tell him thank you very much. His daughters are very beautiful, but I can't marry them." I told the interpreter to tell him.

I think the guy may have asked the interpreter if I was gay or something. Then the man smiled at what I had said, and then motioned at Spaceboy as to possibly inquire if he was interested. Spaceboy just had a goofy smile and said nothing intelligible. Which wasn't unusual. After they left, he started up with his philosophical statements and questions about their culture and what had just transpired. He also noted that they were quite beautiful.

After the parading of potential brides was done, children began coming closer and closer and getting curious. One asked me what my name was in pretty good English. I have no idea where my response came from, but it is something I used for the rest of my time in Somalia.

"Mohammed Ali Babba!" I replied.

"Mohammed Ali Babba?!?!?!" he asked excitedly.

"Mohammed Ali Babba!" I repeated.

"You muslim?" he asked, his eyes as big as baseballs at this point.

"Yes, I am muslim!" is the 2nd white lie I replied with.

The children began talking amongst themselves in Somali. I had no idea what exactly they were saying, but hearing the occasional "Mohammed Ali Babba" thrown into their conversation, I knew it was about me. They seemed genuinely pleased that I had a name that they were comfortable with, and even more pleased that I was apparently Muslim. I began to play a game that I used the interpreter to explain, as well as at least one kid in the crowd that seemed to understand and speak English pretty well. I called it "Mohammed says", obviously a spinoff Muslim version of Simon Says.

"Mohammed says......touch your head with your right hand." I said as I demonstrated.

"Pick up your left leg!" I followed up with and then quickly pointing to those who failed because Mohammed hadn't said.

After several rounds of Mohammed says, it was time to sing some songs. My favorite of which was "Old Mohamed had a farm". Spaceboy seemed pretty amused with the whole thing, but eventually, the leadership in the platoon was not. And they were right.

"Slane, we gotta get these people out of here. It's not safe to have all of these kids gathered around your position." Sgt. Wasik said.

Spc. Slane playng "Mohammed says" with the children of Beledweyne.

"I know, I know. You're right." I acknowledged before telling them that play time was over and they had to leave.

By now the Canadian planes began landing, carrying troops and supplies. Some of us got lucky and were able to trade or MRE's for the Canadian equivalent which were MUCH better. And I was just about to be one of those lucky bastards when the Canadian Commando I was bartering with was quickly informed by one of his comrades in passing that our meals were shit, and not to bother. Fucker. The deal was off and I was stuck with shit. Again.

The second night was slightly busier than the first while the Canadians settled in. No planes landed after the sun went down because there was no way to light the runway, but their camp was bustling with activity as they settled in and erected tents. Tents? And they're infantry? We never got tents. Not in a field environment. They weren't infantry. Not in my book. Infantry would be sleeping out here in the dirt with the rest of us. I was pretty convinced that these were actually POG's (personnel other than grunts) as we affectionately referred to non-infantry in the Army. Perhaps Canadian infantry was just soft? No, in reality they were the pride of the Canadian military, a famous airborne commando outfit and even though they slept in tents, we were proud to have led the way to Beledweyne for them.

A few more sporadic rounds of automatic gunfire shattered the night, but again, nothing in my immediate AO. Just enough to remind me that I was in a country where no one was safe. Not ever. And enough to keep me awake most of the night again.

The third day was rather awkward. This was to be the day we flew back to Baledogle after being relieved in place. By early morning, we were all over the tarmac with our gear, no longer manning the positions we had held for the previous two days. We spent the time trying to find some Canadian soldier who had no idea how bad our MRE's were so we could trade. No dice. We waited and we waited, then we waited some more. Wondering why were still in Beledweyne.

By early afternoon, an American General who had landed earlier was preparing to leave. He asked how we were getting back to Baledogle. SFC Jones and SSG Ferriero told him they didn't know, and then went off and talked to him and his staff for a few minutes. After a while, they returned and told us that the general was sharing his plane with us and would give us a lift back to Baledogle. As it turns out, SFC Jones personally knew the General, and it was our very own MG Arnold, 10th Mountain Division Commander. I guess that's good news. Laying around a tarmac with no shade when it's 125 degrees wasn't as exciting as you'd think. So, we were pretty glad to be going back to our base.

While in midflight to Baledogle, we had noticed that no one seemed pleased with our dirty appearance and certainly not with our smell. We had been in Somalia for over two weeks already and still hadn't had a single shower. But, fuck you very much. We're doing our job and smelling pretty for generals wasn't actually part of our job description. The general sat with a captain who seemed to be his man-bitch. He would hand him things to read, give him a pen, I was pretty sure he was even straightening his hair, maybe even doing his nails. Mid-flight I watched in horror as the captain proceeded to feed the general. He pulled out an MRE and neatly trimmed off the top of the pouch and proceeded to remove the contents in a highly organized, military manner. First, he opened the box to the main meal and removed the sealed contents. I believe it was the Ham Slice MRE. He quickly snipped the top of the package open, and very nearly moved a very precise amount of ham out of the package for the general to bite. I wanted to roll out of my seat laughing as this replayed itself with each part of the MRE, down to the cookie. How far removed from the reality of the military does one have to be to have a man-bitch daintily feed him an MRE, like he's the Princess of Whales or something. This situation escaped none of us dirty, stinky grunts who were ruining his fine meal and man-bitch time in the back of a C-130. It was like being a third wheel on a date. One of the most awkward things I've ever witnessed.

CPL Schmidt took the time to ask General Arnold when we'd be going home. The general's response pleased no one.

"You should be glad you're in Africa. The weather back at Fort Drum is terrible." The General responded.

His words were a chilling reminder that some officers are completely out of touch with their troops. General Arnold sat in his headquarters in Mogadishu in an Air-Conditioned building, with hot chow, showers and all of the comforts of life, including a man-bitch who fed him his MRE's. However, General Arnold was a capable and effective leader by all other accounts, though being in touch with the reality of your troops should factor into that equation as well. We had just missed Christmas with our families and have been flying and patrolling all over the shit hole, taking fire from an unknown enemy, sleeping in the dirt whenever we were actually able to get sleep, eating next to nothing and every other unpleasant thing I've previously described. Being thankful I was in Somalia was not at the top of my list. Don't get me wrong, I was proud to do my job for my country, as was every man with me. We just didn't appreciate the disconnect.

After the plane landed and we unloaded, we were walking by another Air Force plane that had pallets of water in the back. We hadn't had water in a while and had sat on that damn tarmac in Beledweyne for hours, so we asked the flight tech to toss us some water. The plane began taxying down the tarmac as he threw water to us, but he didn't let up. He made sure all of us pathetic dirty bastards that were chasing his plane down the tarmac got some nice fresh bottled water.

After getting some fresh water, we gathered ourselves together and started walking back to our former Russian (we were told) Barracks and settled in for the night. Guard rosters were made and equipment was accounted for. Time to get some sleep. Mohammed Ali Babba would soon be recognized all over Somalia, but for now, he was tired.

The end result for this air assault mission was a success. The Hawadle militia withdrew from Beledweyne upon our arrival, rather than risking a fight, and the Canadians were able to begin securing the city.

Several months after we left Beledweyne, a 16-year-old Somali prisoner, Shidane Arone, was beaten to death by two Canadian Commandos. Mefloquine, the anti-malarial drug they took, and we also took, was suspected as causing psychosis and leading to the killing, though this was never proven. The following are known side effects of Mefloquine:

"Serious side effects include potentially long-term mental health problems such as depression and anxiety and neurological side effects such as poor balance, seizures, and ringing in the ears. It is therefore not recommended in people with a history of mental health problems or epilepsy." ~ The American Society of Health-System Pharmacists.

The only side effects I might add would be "May cause spontaneous insulting of Michael Jackson, resulting in riots and potentially holding one's self at gunpoint." I'm sure you'll understand this much better, later on in this book.

The Shidane Arone incident had so outraged the public in Canada and all over the world, that this famed Airborne Commando unit was recalled to Canada where they were subsequently disbanded completely.

Into the Unknown

In January of 1993, two Marines would be killed, and several wounded in several attacks around Mogadishu.

After our return from Beledweyne, our platoon was stationed outside the Brigade CP (Command post) as a QRF (Quick reaction force). Basically, if anything happened, we'd be the first to respond in force. By this time, we'd been in Somalia over two weeks. Though we had yet to come under direct fire, our purpose there and how everything would play out was still a great big mystery, though one thing was clear: Somalia was a dangerous place. While there had been shots around us, we still were pretty green.

Wanlaweyn (Wally World) was a pretty interesting place where locals had maintained a roadblock from which to extort money from anyone who drove down the main road. Something we had dismantled promptly upon our arrival. It was difficult to figure out the difference between the "bandits" in Somalia and the clans. All bandits had clans, and the clans were also blamed for the crisis that had required our presence here, so, the lines are blurred for me. Food was stolen from relief agencies for profit, to feed fighters in the clans, and to subdue rival clans through forced starvation.

The call came that there was a large disturbance in Wally World, and A Co. was to move out expeditiously. Apparently "bandits" had been trying to loot a large warehouse in town that contained large quantities of food. After securing the warehouse, the officer on the scene had decided to give the food to the people since we weren't going to stay to protect it. It didn't take long for the situation to go from bad to worse from there.

People began getting wildly out of control and what followed was a full out riot. Suddenly, an order came out that probably hadn't been echoed since the Civil War (half kidding).

"FIX BAYONETS!" echoed out gallantly as though we were preparing to charge at The Battle of Gettysburg.

What a strange order to give while trying to control a crowd of unarmed people in what was dubbed a "humanitarian mission". What purpose did the bayonets serve? I mean, I know what they're for......were we expected to start gutting people? I hardly thought this was a lawful or wise order to give, but carrying the M60, it also wasn't an order I'd have to follow. Bayonets could only be fixed to the M16's and M203's. The situation was eventually calmed and the food handed out without any bloodshed.

A Somali approached us carrying an MRE box and seemed interested in trying to sell us the box.

"Yeah, that's what the fuck I want. More MRE's" I said.

He shook the box and I heard a loud thumping around, mixed with a strange animal noise. It sounded like a cat getting its balls ripped off, that's the best I can describe it.

"WTF is that?" we asked.

"DIK DIK!" he replied.

"DIK what?" I said.

"DIK DIK!" he said, opening the box just enough for us to see the head of a small deer like animal poking out. He then removed the animal and held its legs in each hand as it continued its weird screams and thrashed about.

"No wonder these people are starving! Look at the size of their deer!" I said. "It's like the size of a cat!"

What we were seeing was in fact a tiny antelope called a Dik-Dik, something we would grow to see quit often during missions into the interior. For many years after leaving Somalia I would often jokingly reminisce about the numerous dik-diks running through the bush. And how it reminded me of my first wife, to whom I was married for all of about 3 minutes after Somalia, and who had never stopped dating after our wedding. <Sigh>, memories. I digress.

Near New Year's we got an unexpected visitor. President George H.W. Bush had flown to Somalia to see firsthand the last operation he would carry out, as he only had a few weeks left in office. Though the RTO's were told to maintain radio silence where the president's arrival was concerned, our company, Jovino, RTO famously replied "Roger, I copy Air Force One" over the radio. Well, so much for keeping it a surprise. Since our radio equipment wasn't encrypted, it wouldn't take much for anyone to have heard the announcement of Air Force One in the area, though it was in the form of helicopters, not the actual plane. Anyway, now Bush was in the bush, staying in Baledogle, and he brought his own diks; The Secret Service.

As night fell, I was given a shift guarding the entrance to the Brigade CP. Inside was the leader of the free world, whom I had yet to see. Suddenly two secret service agents emerged behind me carrying towels, heading off to do some hygiene.

"You guys know the password to get back in here, right?" I asked them.

"Yeah, yeah, yeah, we got it." One of the two hastily replied, seeming annoyed that a lowly Specialist in the Army would bother them with such trivial shit.

"Okie dokie. It's getting dark, just making sure you know the drill to get back in." I said smiling to myself, wondering if they really knew "the drill".

I don't know for SURE that they were secret service, but that's what I was told. Either way, they were part of the presidential detail. We're just going to go with them being secret service. It's much more fun that way. You'll see.

After about an hour or so, it was dark out. I hear them before I could see them as they blabbed in the dark, stumbling closer to me. And then I could make them out.

"HALT!" I yelled out, raising the M16A2 I was using to pull guard.

They didn't stop.

"HALT! WHO GOES THERE!" I shouted again. And again, they didn't stop.

"SCHICK SCHICK!" rang out as I charged my weapon and repeated "I SAID FUCKING HALT!"

"WHOA WHOA WHOA, Hold on! He's going to shoot!" one said to the other, holding his arm out in dramatic fashion and stopping his comrade.

I gave them the challenge phrase.

"Huh?" one replied.

I repeated it again and got no reply.

"Now is when you'd give me the password" I said, knowing who exactly it was, but with plausible deniability of actually knowing.

"Um." I said then hesitated, then blurted something out.

"Nope." I responded to his incorrect guess.

He then followed with something else.

"Nope, wrong again! Advance to be recognized. Slowly." I ordered them as they took a few steps slowly toward me.

"Halt! Far enough. Now put your hands on your heads and walk backwards towards me, one at a time" I ordered.

As the first idiot stumbled backwards in the dark, I forcefully steadied him, checked for weapons, and then turned him around so we were face to face.

"Oh, hi! I remember you! Remember that password thing we talked about when you left? Yeah. I sort of wasn't fucking kidding." I said before letting him by and then telling his buddy to follow. Neither of them looked happy, which made me extremely happy. We're in the most dangerous country on Earth and I'm guarding the entrance to where the leader of the free world is probably sitting down to a nice dinner of MRE bbq pork, and you thought you could fuck around on my watch? I had no aspirations to being THAT guy, the one on CNN who was on guard the night the President of the United States was killed because I shirked my duty.

"You fellas have a great night!" I said smiling as they walked back into the compound.

While our platoon was on QRF, one of our squads spent a couple of days in the bush securing a downed helicopter. I believe they spent two days guarding the site until the helicopter could be retrieved. Other missions included guarding VIP's to and from Mogadishu including Robert Oakley, the former ambassador to Somalia who was key in negotiations with the local clans and warlords.

On one particular security mission to Mogadishu, several in the platoon spent the night in the back of a fastback Humvee pulling security in the Bakaara Market. My squad leader, SGT Wasik, literally had to smack my assistant gunner (AG) Spaceboy because he kept falling asleep, apparently opting for sleep over staying alive. SGT Wasik regretted doing it, but shit, this is a combat environment and in the most dangerous city in the world. In the most infamous market in that city. Death is a constant here, and if you ever spent the night in Mogadishu, the constant sound of gunfire all around you and the thud of the Pakistani .50 caliber machine gun reminded you at all times that you were no longer in Kansas. And if you brought Toto, better forget his ass, Dorothy, because these mean, skinny motherfuckers will kill and maybe even eat him. I digress.

On January 6th, 1993 we were told that we had a mission to guard a food convoy further inland towards Baidoa to a city called Burhakaba. Finally, now this sounds like making a difference in a country we were told had 300,000 people more about to die of starvation! We were also told to put on clean uniforms because the President wanted to attend our mission brief and pre-mission inspection. I didn't really think that meant I would actually see him, let alone meet him. After getting our gear on, we went to an abandoned building in the airport and waited around. As I stood there, I noticed the biggest fucking monitor lizard I have ever seen in my life sitting in a tree, looking like a hungry dinosaur about to prance on one of us. I mean, this thing was at least 3 to 4 feet head to tail. It was a Rock Monitor (*Varanus albigularis*) and it was menacing. I quickly got out of the proximity of the tree he was in when a caravan of vehicles pulled up.

SSG Ferriero called everyone over to where he was standing as the President and his security detail began emerging from the vehicles. Several Secret Service and some Special Forces-type guys fanned out and started combing the area, looking in bushes, behind rocks and all over in general. Extremely thorough. Except, as impressive as it was to watch, I don't think even one of them ever saw the biggest threat to national security looming just over their heads; my friend, Mr. Rock Monitor. I couldn't help but wonder what would happen to our president the minute this thing jumped on his head. I couldn't stop whispering and quietly laughing, which drew the stern eye of more than one of the president's security detail. It was like a schoolmarm giving a troubled student a serious case of the stink eye. I smiled back as though to say "HI! I remember you!?!?! Remember the password?"

The president and some other important looking people listened as the commander explained the details of the mission, often referring everyone to the map. As my secret service buddy walked by, I couldn't help but make noises in an attempt to draw their attention. Specifically, I was making my best attempts at a muffled machine gun sound, as though it had a silencer. Stupid, I know. But I wasn't alone, and we were highly amused with ourselves as the schoolmarms constantly whipped their heads back our direction, trying to see who the joker was. Our only instructions were to keep our weapons pointed down at all times around the president, which was a lot less lenient of a restriction than most people had around him. I even heard other soldiers, sailors, marines or airmen weren't even allowed to have a weapon within 500 meters of him. Well, I spent the night guarding the compound he slept in, so I guess I clearly got a pass there. And now, we were about to embark on a military mission in the most dangerous country in the world, so, another pass. I like the fact that I got to shake the hand of a sitting US President while carrying an M60 machine gun and a 9MM pistol, as well as having shittons of ammo.

There were only a few of us from the company that were picked to meet with the president, so I probably should have been more reverent about the whole thing maybe. I dunno. George Bush was 22 once, and had been in the military. I'm sure it wasn't his first time around a wise ass. Nonetheless, I was a wise ass willingly in his service and a true patriot. And, he was one of my heroes. George Bush senior is one of the few presidents in the modern era who actually served in combat, having been the youngest pilot to get shot down during WWII. And now, I was getting to make history with him. I started to wonder if I'd be nervous when he came by, which, made me nervous. Until, I remembered myself that is. I'm Steve Fucking Slane. He'll be glad he got to shake my hand someday.

One thing that instantly stuck me was his height. I had always heard that most presidents are tall, and he was nearly as tall as me. He reminded me of my own grandfather in many ways and demanded a similar respect just by his presence.

Left to right: Unkown, Rod Forde, Terrance Eaddy, SGT Schafer (in back), Daniel Ferriero, George Bush, Steve Slane, John Wasik and Tom Corey.

As the President came up to us, he took a minute to talk to each of us and then shook our hands. He seemed very genuine, though he lied when he told me I'd be back home by the end of the month. And then we took a picture that hangs on my wall to this day. A picture that would reunite several of us two decades later when the Army Times used it in an article about Somalia being given wartime campaign credit.

Now that all the hand shaking and dick grabbing was over, it was time for business. We mounted up and headed out. The drive to Buurhakaba was uneventful but memorable because it's the only place I saw something even resembling a mountain in the form of a very large hill that seemed to surround the city. We weren't there very long it seems. I believe a few trucks of food stayed here as we continued to Baidoa, where over 1,000 people a day had died during the worst of the famine. I wasn't sure what to expect. So far, I have been in Somalia over two weeks and I haven't seen a single starving person.

Baidoa would be the exception, though I chose to try to limit my own exposure to that exception. Once there, we dismounted our vehicles and headed out on a short patrol. We ended up in a sort of fenced in area that had troughs or tables around its perimeter. In the middle of the area stood two young, potbellied children, malnourished and visibly victims of the famine we had all heard so much about. I wanted to go over and offer them some food, but I probably didn't have anything they could eat, and we weren't allowed to feed them anyway. It was a heart breaking scene to say the least and I tried to venture no further around the area, though I had to. I didn't want to see anything else.

I spent the ride back to Baledogle hoping and wishing that the convoy of food we had protected for them would be enough for everyone there. This would be my only mission where I directly did anything I would remotely consider humane, and the only place in all of Somalia that I went where I ever saw a person who was outright starving.

When we returned to Baledogle, we made another trip to Mogadishu. It was uneventful but eye opening as usual. The fighting clans having mostly abided by their cease-fire, there didn't seem to be much going on at the moment. We now turned our attention to the south as we prepared for a large Air Assault mission about halfway between Kismayo and Mogadishu to a place called Merca. Our immediate attention would be to stop the roving band of thieves that had so exacerbated the famine in this country. From Merca, we would eventually conduct numerous more Air Assault missions where we'd cordon and search villages and cities and eventually lay in ambush like hunters on a Safari, and even venture into the middle of the civil war.

A Tough Goat to Swallow

Aside from guarding numerous military convoys between Mogadishu and Baledogle, constant guard duty, quick reaction force duty, our initial air assaults to a few small villages and then into Beledweyne, December in Somalia for us consisted of never ending foot patrols. One of the more interesting aspects of Somalia was that there was an international presence, though we were by far the largest. Canadians, French, Italians, Belgians, Pakistanis and a group that was most memorable to me for reasons that will become apparent, the Moroccans. Out of most of the aforementioned nations, which is not meant to be all inclusive, the Moroccans were in the contingent of predominately Islamic nations that had sent troops to Somalia.

The first thing that was most apparent about the Moroccans was that their military equipment was greatly antiquated. It seemed to me that their jeeps were similar to those the US military might have used as far back as the Korean war or even WWII. Their personal equipment was pretty much the same. Older style helmets contrasted with our Kevlar, no body armor (that I recall), and older style weapons and LBE's (Load Bearing Equipment – eg, vest with pistol belt, holsters, ammo pouches and canteens). One other notable trait of the Moroccan army worthy of mention is that they always started their days by baking bread. And the bread was very good, though I don't think there was anything particularly special about it other than not being an MRE. We would try and procure Moroccan bread whenever we could, especially since we were rationed at two MRE's per day.

What the logistical issue was with food and water was, I cannot tell you. But one reason you're reading this books is because at this point in my career, I was a lowly M60 machine gunner rather than an officer or a senior non-commissioned officer. And because of that fact alone, while reading my book you are more likely to hear what the privates and specialists endured and bitched

92

about when it comes to bad command decisions or logistical issues such as food and water. Many books I've read by officers, especially field grade or above, are nothing more than a glossed over version of the events that support "the establishment's" storyline, along with a lot of mutual dick sucking with every other officer of any significance that served with them. In those accounts, everybody who is anybody did a good job, no matter how bad they might have fucked the pooch on things like, I dunno......getting food for the "everybody who is basically nobody to them"; the rest of the fucking Army.

You see, the enlisted ranks are earned by being a fucking hard ass and by being good at their job. While plenty of that is true with the commissioned officer's, there's another aspect of being an officer and that's what's called "the good ole boys club". If you cause waves in the good ole boys club, your career advancement will suddenly grind to a halt. This is why some of the best officers I served under never made it to be generals or full colonels.

Historically, commissioned officers represented the upper class in society, the privileged in what can best be described as a far outdated caste system. Though those days of kings and peasants might be forgotten by the public at large, the ideals are still very much alive among those who run our government and military. Though I am making a generalization here, I admit. I was also different than a lot of the guys I knew being that I was born into a wealthy family and a family that was at least at one time better connected than most of these elitists now in charge of me. But like my grandfather had done in WWII by enlisting instead of getting a commission, I dropped out of college and enlisted, much to his dismay.

In the enlisted ranks, the only officers you need to worry about keeping happy are your platoon leader and your company commander. And to keep them happy, you don't have to be a spit shined golden boy. You keep them happy by following orders and accomplishing their missions.

So, in reading my book, you're going to get it like I saw it and you're going to get my opinions and my honest perspective about everyone, including the dickheads who screwed us over on food, or coordinated air lifts out of Beledweyne for everyone yet somehow "forgot" my entire company, leaving us stranded there longer than the rest of the battalion. They were sorry bastards no matter what they say about each other in their own books. As far as I am concerned, the only officers worth a shit in Somalia at that time were my own company officers, the battalion commander LTC Jim Sikes, and the brigade commander COL Kip Ward. Sorry, but I don't know any of the officers in the other companies, no offense, but those aren't really the officers I'm referring to. But then again, I'm not part of the good ole boys club so who cares. I know, I know, that's tough to swallow. Of course being a lowly specialist, I lacked perspective to adequately assess most of the rest.

Sorry! Now that you understand the WHY behind us being so damn hungry, let me tell you about the amazing food the Moroccans cooked for us this fine day.

I headed out this day on loan to another squad and I believe SGT Laing led the patrol along with CPL Schmidt. Quite a distance down the main road stood a dilapidated building very near the airfield where the Moroccans had set up camp. As we started walking past them when they motioned us over and we obliged. And man am I glad we did.

Once we got over, they invited us into what appeared to be a bombed out building in the middle of which was a huge wok type pot over an open fire and it was full of food. It smelled absolutely amazing. Immediately they started gesturing for us to take our gear off by even offering to take my weapon while another removed my Kevlar. Everyone followed suit and started removing their gear and placing their weapons up against the wall. I placed my flak vest down on the ground for a place to sit after one of the Moroccan's motioned for me to sit by patting the ground next to him.

After each of us were seated, the man who seemed to be in charge told one of his soldiers something, at which time we were all presented with a small loaf of bread. I still wasn't quite sure what was going on, or what was cooking over the fire, but I was pretty sure we were about to get fed. The officer in charge broke off a piece of bread while holding the loaf out in front of him for all of us to see, then held the piece of bread out that he had broken off and made a scooping motion, which he then followed with scooping his bread into the large bowl of what looked like a stew, and took a bite.

"Spaceboy, wrong hand, dude." I told Spaceboy. "You stick your left hand in there and we're all going to end up leaving here hungry." I added.

In their culture, it is proper to shake hands and share a meal with the right hand. The left hand is considered unclean and is used to perform hygiene and clean filth. As you read this book, you might think me somewhat of an ignorant person, I don't know. While I admittedly am not "PC", I genuinely respect all cultures, and in fact, all human beings by default. Likewise, if you give me a reason to not respect you, like shooting at me, I reserve the right to gleefully send you to whatever god you serve, without hesitation.

My first bite was hesitant as I had no idea what the fuck I was eating. Could have been camel dick stew for all I knew at that point. As the started to consume that first bite, I was pleasantly surprised.

"Man, this shit is good!" Schmidt said.

"Hell yeah!" Laing added."

And it was. It was absolutely amazing. It was some sort of lentil bean stew with lots of meat in it. While the meat was a little tough, it was very tasty. Though we couldn't talk to them, nor them to us, we seemed to have quite a bit of dinner conversation. Someone almost accidentally reached for the bowl with the wrong hand (probably Spaceboy) and to my surprise, they merely politely corrected him, reminding him to use his right hand, which he did.

"Damn, dude, this is delicious!" Mangold said as he devoured another bite.

For an hour of our lives in Somalia, we had a temporary sense of normalcy. Disregarding the fact that we were sitting in a bombed out structure with people we couldn't speak to, because it just didn't matter. They were good people, and Mangold, Beem, Spaceboy, Schmidt and Laing were family to me. We ate and laughed while gesturing to our gracious hosts for some time, when SGT Laing announced that we needed to get back.

"Gritty bread, mine had rocks in it. And I loved it." ~ SGT Rick "Earl" Beem, January 2016.

Which was fine, I had eaten more than I should have, so I eventually got up as everyone else finished their meal. As I started putting my gear back on, the officer in charge walked up and point at me, and gestured, smacking his bicep as he flexed it, then pointed back to the food, and made an eating gesture as though he were saying "Hey, you're a really big guy! Are you sure you're full? There's plenty left so help yourself!" I patted my stomach and gestured back that I was full and tried to thank him as best I could for the meal. Soon, we all had our gear on and waved a hearty goodbye to our new friends, and started to return to Baledogle.

"That was some good fucking food." Laing recalled.

"Dude, it was goat! I saw the carcass laying off a way from the building." Schmidt said.

"Man, I don't give a fuck what it was, it was delicious." I said, to which everyone concurred.

"You know what's funny? I was talking to the Marines that are sleeping on cots in the hanger and they said every time they leave the hanger; the Moroccans steal their cots!" Schmidt said.

"Hahahaha, fucking POG's (People other than grunts. Making them bitches in our world), who gives a shit? I'd kill to sleep on a cot." I said.

"No shit!" Mangold added.

Eventually we made our way back to the platoon CP where the next squad was gearing up to head out. After telling them what we had experienced, everyone was a little jealous and hoped that they might be as lucky.

One of the last things that happened in Baledogle that I recall was E-87 having a firefight out near Wally World where six Somalis were killed, and several more wounded. One account of the incident can be read in LTC Greg Alderete's publication "Land of Unkown: Memoirs from the Basement of Hell", a good collection of various experiences in Somalia, including his own. The collection is aimed at educating the people of our country about the fact that Somalia was in fact a war, and for the personal sacrifices of everyone who served there, and our fallen brothers and sisters, a war we don't want forgotten, though it mostly is.

It was eventually discovered that at least half of the dead were innocent bystanders who were already falling prey to a roving gang of bandits or "technicals" as we called them. Most of the wounded technicals had escaped the scene, leaving behind blood trails, but were never found. While we went to Baledogle on occasion, we would never be here again as a unit after January 9th. By that date, we had taken hostile fire between 2 and 4 times already, depending on who you were, and what missions you performed. For myself, it seems like I had been under fire 4 times by then.

Corporal Punishment

Around January 8th or 9th, we started securing the port city of Merca, south of Mogadishu. After Air Assaulting to the city and conducting the initial sweep of the city, we started a rotation where we would do two days of port security, two days of check point security, and then two or three days of running other missions, such as Air Assaults to conduct cordon and searches, patrols, ambushes, and reconnaissance. I don't recall taking any fire during our first sweep of Merca. I took the opportunity to introduce myself as "Mohammed Ali Babba" to the local children after running into many who used to point at us and run their fingers across their throats and say "You! Christian!" They made it abundantly clear they wanted us dead. They were raised to hate Christians. The viewed us as enemies. Enter my alter ego, a Muslim American Soldier named Mohammed Ali Babba. Not only did it seem to put them at ease, they seemed very excited to have a Muslim among the ranks of the occupying soldiers.

Merca would be a place that I would be very familiar in on and off over the next three months. Here, as well as in Afgooye, Beledweyne and Barawe and several small villages around Somalia, it would be common for children to run up to me, patting the spot on their arms where my tattoo would be while excitedly shouting "Mohammed Ali Babba! Mohammed Ali Babba!". I have nothing against Muslims or any other religion. Being from part Armenian descent and having a great grandmother that escaped the Armenian Genocide in Turkey and Armenia around the turn of the century, I was raised respecting everyone else on earth by default. Even though Muslims had slaughtered my people, to include my great grandmother's mother, I had no interest in repaying the violence on anyone as retribution.

The port of Merca had initially been secured by a group of Islamic Fundamentalists when we arrived in Merca. They actually had done a good job protecting the flow of food and were heavily armed. This group, which we called "Ali Tihad", was always suspect to us and eventually we would have problems with them. But initially, they seemed ok. I suppose. Don't get me wrong, they didn't rush up and hug us or anything. But they also didn't start shooting at us right away, either. And they were actually doing a righteous thing by protecting the shipments of food that came to Merca.

We were technically supposed to have a day of downtime, but that usually consisted of more missions or additional guard duty. Aside from our interpreter,

Mohammed (such a unique name, isn't it?), we had other Somalis who assisted us from time to time. Sometimes they would accompany us on missions, some even armed. Others helped in the daily task of keeping people in order. Corporal Punishment was one such Somali. While he would occasionally accompany us on missions, his primary use was that of "enforcer" of the masses. I don't know his real name, and he couldn't tell you if he wanted to. He had no tongue. Someone decided Corporal Punishment didn't need a tongue and removed it for him, presumably by force. I'm not sure who gave him his rank and name, that distinction is blurred. Possibly Mangold, Harris, Perez, Szulwach, Laing or Douglas. Maybe Schmidt. I can't remember now, but I can tell you the name fit. In the famous words of SFC Jones, "If the shoe fits...."

Corporal Punishment was all of about 5'2", 110 lbs., had a cheesy 70's style porn mustache, and a genuine smile that you wouldn't soon forget. Especially when he was done kicking ass with his trademark instrument of pain; a hardwood cane. We usually only saw him at the port in Merca, and only saw him in action when crowds would begin to gather at the entrances to the port and then got unruly. He wielded his cane with such precision and fury, I would have thought twice about crossing him. If a fight broke out in a crowd anywhere near us, or people got out of hand, it would literally take two seconds and heads would start rolling. I still see him in my waking dreams, airborne, swinging his cane, and it impacting upside the head of a would-be Somali rebel rouser. I hear the hardwood "crack", like a Louisville Slugger, and I see the eyes of his target rolling back in their heads as they fall to the ground unconscious. I'm sure I don't need to try and explain the irony of his name. Corporal Punishment.

Keeping the port secure was constant work. When we first came to Merca and secured the main roads, the port and a base of operations, we were the first at the port. There were sixteen of us pulling two hours on, and two hours off of guard duty. We tried several variations in attempts to get more sleep. Sixteen men guarding what would require at least twice that many to adequately secure. We tried several alternative guard rotations, one of the worst being six hours, hoping that it would provide some well needed sleep to all of us at some point. It is nearly impossible to function with two hours of sleep. A REM cycle of sleep is about ninety minutes and it takes most people an hour or more to fall asleep and even begin a REM cycle. With the two-hour rotation, you were basically being woken up while you either just started a REM cycle, or were right in the middle of it. The effects of this were devastating after many days. You felt ten times more tired than you were before you laid down. You could barely hold a thought. You felt completely insane at times. And at your absolute worst, you bitched and acted like a 13-year-old girl on her menstrual cycle. Everyone did it at least once. We were all guilty of being a whiny bitch at one time or another. It's ok. You learn to accept it.

On my first or second night at the port, I was pulling an either four or six-hour guard shift. I don't remember which. And it really doesn't matter. I was already extremely sleep deprived before we started this shit. It wasn't uncommon to go two or more days on 2 to 4 hours of sleep. Many times when you were given the opportunity, it was either too hot or your mind wouldn't slow down enough to let you sleep. And on this particular night, my brain REALLY, REALLY wanted to sleep.

Because there weren't technically enough of us to protect the area we were given by the book, I was manning a machine gun by myself. Something we almost never did. We almost always had another person with us. It's a golden rule in the Army. You always have a buddy. When I started my shift, I was very alert. I was someplace new and knew that there were people here who wanted us dead. At first, that was enough to keep me going. However, after three or four hours of staring into the dark from across sandbags, I started having a very hard time staying awake. At first, I didn't realize it was happening. I kept jerking awake like I had done driving a car at night on not enough sleep. Almost as soon as I would jerk awake and convince myself I was good to go, my eyes would start closing again, and the cycle would repeat itself every 30 to 90 seconds. Two minutes at best. I couldn't try smoking to stay awake or a sniper might make a nice hole in my head. I couldn't go make some coffee, the light from a fire end the same way. I couldn't leave my post either. I was trapped alone with no way to keep this going all night. I still had two or three hours to go.

Finally, after my head bounced off my machine gun when I had basically passed out, I was scared enough to continue staying awake. I realized that in this state someone could walk right up to me and slit my throat and then proceed to kill the rest of my platoon. The thought of that was all it took. I was wide the fuck awake and stayed that way until my shift ended early the next morning.

The next day half of us were sleeping in a small building that we used as our CP when an officer did something that really pissed us off. As several of us were lying awake, he came in the room as though he was sneaking and unseen, grabbed a couple of the M16's laying in the middle of the room, and quietly crept back out as though he was a cat burglar who had just pulled of a heist completely unseen. He then came back in the room and yelled at everyone to wake up and commenced to chewing our asses for not having anyone awake and watching the weapons.

"Sir......I was laying right here, watching you take our weapons." Mclehaney said.

"Me, too..." I added.

"Then why didn't you stop me?" the officer asked.

"Um, because you're an officer? And I figured you had some reason for taking them? And they're basically yours?" SPC Perez argued.

"That's fucked up, sir!" Perez told him, continuing the debate.

At first, the officer rejected our arguments and threatened us with various forms of punishment. Needless to say, we were not enjoying being fucked with like a bunch of privates in Basic Training. He talked to our platoon sergeant and platoon leader, demanding better security. SSG Ferriero and SFC Jones both argued angrily with the officer until the situation finally yielded to calmer heads. I'm pretty sure the officer was just really fucking tired too. However, now that we'd been sitting here arguing about how we watched him steal our weapons and whether or not our security was sufficient, my break was over. No sleep for me. Thanks, dick. I appreciate that. Glad we had this exercise in utter fucking uselessness. What's another day without sleep to me? I'm not even sure I remember what sleep actually is at this point.

I got up to take a piss. And lucky me that they built us some "facilities" to utilize. As I walked over and pulled my junk out, I marveled at the workmanship I was witnessing. The American ingenuity. Series of water bottles with the bottoms cut out, taped end to end to form long tubes buried down into the sand. As I finished and put my dick away, I was sure to wave to dozens of Somali's standing in plain view of our makeshift latrine. Yes, some genius decided the location of our urinals was to be in plain sight of the rear entrance to the port. While the urinals faced a wall, a wall facing the ocean, anyone on either side of the urinals got to see non-stop cock and ball action all day long. But thank God no one at sea could watch us urinate. Because that's just creepy. A crowd of women and children watching grown men urinate is fine. Acceptable in almost any culture around the world, especially those that were strictly conservative in their already strict beliefs. So it's all good. But God, pirates and sailors watching me piss from out at sea? I think not. Sounds pretty dubious at best to me.

"Hi! How the fuck are ya? Hot out today, ain't it?" I said as I buttoned my pants and walked about wishing I could piss in private, believing I had done my part to keep diplomatic relations with the locals at their best.

Ferriero (back left), Wasik, Corporal Punishment (center), Schmidt and Slane at the Merca port

Our augmented security seemed to fluctuate with shipments at the port. When large shipments of rice and oil were unloaded, trucks would load up and move the shipments in guarded convoys, throughout the rest of the country. And when large shipments did come, there were plenty of extra security concerns due to crowds and the additional workers that would be inside our perimeter during the day. At the end of the day, the workers would file out into the street and the crowds would eventually dissipate. One of the first few ass beatings Corporal Punishment issued was when a man who had stolen literally a pocket full of rice started getting attacked by the crowd at the gate. Corporal Punishment ended up beating both the man, and many in the crowd. Apparently he was territorial about his beatings.

Aside from Corporal Punishment and our additional local port security, there was the cookie girl. She was probably about ten to twelve years old and would bring trays of the absolute worst cookies I have ever tasted, and sell them to the laborers who unloaded the ships. After just a couple of rotations pulling security at the port, she was one of our favorite locals. You'd think that given this girl had at least 16 big brothers who carried even bigger guns, no one would mess with her. But that wasn't the case.

After a bit of commotion near the Cookie Girl one day, we went to investigate what was wrong. Our interpreter had told us that one of the workers took one of her cookies and had refused to pay. The Cookie Girl had stood her ground until we got involved. Once she understood what was going on, it's almost as if she just put her hand on her hip and looked at the people her dispute was with and said "What now, mother fuckers?" And she was right. What now indeed. The worker paid for his cookie and we let him go. And that was that. Except Corporal Punishment gave the guy a good whack on the way out the gate for good measure. Then smiled at us, shook our hands and made the rounds getting praise for his ass kicking prowess. And the Cookie Girl paraded proudly near us every time she saw us after that, knowing that we had her back. And word travelled fast. I don't recall another cookie thief for the rest of our time in Merca. Though I still can't figure out why on earth anyone would steal a cookie that tasted like that.........

Over the next few months, which are covered in later chapters, we would have lots of interesting adventures at the Port. We regularly took small arms fire and took plenty of prisoners who would take their chances trying to breach our perimeter at night. After the port was built up with sandbags and more permanent positions from which to pull guard, we settled into a rotation that allowed us to get sleep once in a while, while still maintaining security. And we never ate those fucking cookies.

Merca

The security model for operations in the Merca area was pretty simple, even to someone who wasn't privy to the "why" or the "what" like myself. First, the initial sweep of Merca to establish a presence followed by routine security patrols through the town to maintain that presence. Second, secure access to Merca to restrict the movement of weapons to and from the city, and to deter potentially undesirable types from entering the city. This was done by setting up checkpoints along the main routes to Merca. People could voluntarily register certain types of weapons but they would be left at the checkpoint upon entering the city. Thirdly, simultaneously secure the port of Merca which is where the relief shipments entered this part of the country. Rounding out the summary of security would be a QRF force at the Merca base, and constant convoy security for the shipments coming into the port as the supplies went out to the surrounding areas. I believe elements like the 10th Mountain Division MP's were largely responsible for the convoy security. The MP's were one group of 10th Mountain Division troops that saw almost as much of the country as the infantry did, and likely as much combat.

As I understand the situation from the ground, with the city largely secured, the command made contact with the local authorities to establish a power sharing framework among rival groups. Yep, nation building 101. Likely something you never knew about the mission in Somalia, and also something we had said we weren't going to do here. Also something we started immediately upon our arrival in the country. The power sharing was between at least 3 or 4 main groups; elements of Aidid's SNA, elders from two or more clans, and an Islamic fundamentalist group we called "Ali" or "Ali Tihad" because the full name is difficult to pronounce, and we don't speak that Paris talk. We're just grunts, gunslingers. As you may have already anticipated, Ali will be a group you'll hear more about later on in the book.

Checkpoint security is dangerous business and I'm surprised it went as well as it did, but that's a testament to the leadership at each platoon level in my opinion. Running a successful checkpoint requires lots of teamwork, and lots of people looking out for each other at all times. One wrong move by anyone on duty at the checkpoint, and soldiers would be hurt or killed, as would civilians. We confiscated lots of guns at the checkpoint. If the gun was registered, the individual could pick it up when he left Merca. But the idea was to keep guns from flowing into Merca, and I think it was a pretty solid idea.

As the M-60 gunner, my position was on the roof, overlooking the road and the stop point on the way into Merca. On the road was a sandbagged position in which two or three soldiers would be stationed at any given time. Then, there was the sergeant of the guard. He was responsible for making sure everyone was doing their job and that everyone had everything they needed. He was also responsible for resolving any "unknowns" at the checkpoint, which would happen from time to time.

"I'd like to register my RPG!" one Somali walked up and announced one day in broken English.

"Oh? And where is your RPG?" someone responded as the sergeant of the guard walked down to see what was going on.

"At home!" he responded.

"Do you have any ammunition for your RPG?" the sergeant of the guard asked.

"7!" the man cheerfully answered.

"Well, go home and get it and bring all the ammunition with you so we can register it." The sergeant of the guard said (I don't recall which one).

Well, the man complied. Except, when he got back to "register" his RPG, he was a little more than disappointed when we kept it. Not exactly a weapon we considered required for standard home safety.

During an incident with another platoon, a solider accidently discharged his weapon, hitting the man in the head. Every effort was made to save his life and he was medevac'd to Mogadishu (in record time I was told) where he died. Everyone at the scene, even the Somalis, said that it had been an accident, albeit a tragic one. Such is life behind the gun. Pay attention.

Another memorable incident involved our 2nd platoon medic, Christopher Cooke, who chased a vehicle down with nothing but a 9mm, broke the window out, and pulled the driver of the vehicle through the window onto the ground and held him at gunpoint, while the rest of his platoon followed. When they arrived,

Cooke explained that he had seen a gun as the man had tried to get away, hence chasing him down.

Our first few times at the checkpoint were tiresome to say the least. Just 16 men to rotate basically half of us on, half of us off, in such a way that we might be able to get some sleep. Four hours was pretty standard by my recollection, something we settled on at the port as well. However, with four hours "off", you were lucky to get 2 of that actually sleeping. When you weren't on duty, you had to eat, do maintenance and maybe some hygiene. And during the day, it was impossible to sleep when it was so hot.

SGT Wasik, SGT Szulwach and SSG Ferriero posing with weapons seized at the checkpoint.

One of our initial rotations between the checkpoint and the port at Merca was made memorable in my mind by an incident involving Doc Estes and SSG Ferriero.

"Sergeant Ferriero, I can't pull guard duty or radio watch." He explained to SSG Ferreiro.

"What the fuck are you talking about now, Estes?" Ferriero inquired.

"I'm a medic and by Army regulation, I cannot be made to perform infantry duties, including pulling guard and radio watch." He explained. "I can only be responsible for medical equipment."

Wrong move, Doc........on many points. Especially for giving us the answer we so desperately needed.

"Medical equipment, huh? I tell you what, Estes." Ferriero began.

"Yes, sergeant?" Estes asked.

"I'm going to tape a g0ddamn band aid to the middle of the floor, right here. And I want to sit here all fucking night and guard that band aid. Oh, and if someone calls on the fucking radio? Answer the mother fucker since you're just sitting here with nothing to do. We good now?" Ferriero asked.

"Yes, sergeant." Estes grudgingly replied.

We were tired. We were really, REALLY tired. We were sixteen men in a platoon that by Army standards should have contained around 35 swinging dicks. And since we were a platoon sized element, we were given full platoon sized or even company sized missions. And I say company sized because by my estimation, and the estimation of almost anyone with us, most of the areas we secured would require a full company to properly secure. This checkpoint, however, was probably fine for a full-strength platoon. However, with sixteen men, we had to decide how to best split our time. Did we want shorter guard duty so we didn't fall asleep? Or did we want longer guard duty so that any sleep we did get when we weren't on guard would be worth getting since a full rem cycle of sleep is about 90 minutes, and it would probably take you at least 30 to 60 minutes to get there. We were exhausted beyond description so Doc not "wanting" to be awake most of the night was totally valid. However, believing he could fuck the rest of us over by not doing something as simple as radio watch was completely out of the question. Eventually we settled into 4 hour rotations so some sleep became possible.

My view at the checkpoint as a vehicle is waved through.
Copyright 1993 Steve Slane.

Checking the vehicles like the one depicted in the first picture was especially nerve racking for everyone involved. For me, I had to keep the M-60 trained on the crowd of people while my comrades did the dirty work of searching. The plan was that if anything happened, they would jump off to the side and I would open up, along with another person in the guard position down on the road. Though I clearly had the best vantage point.

SPC Steve Slane posing with seized weapons at the checkpoint.

One thing I did enjoy about the checkpoint was that the building was better shaded than most of the places I spent my time in Somalia and it had a great view of the Indian ocean. The building looked like it had once been pretty nice but had been shot to hell during the civil war, but inside it had several rooms

109

which eventually had cots placed in them so we could feel a little normal during our downtime. I would often spend my time listening to Enya at night because it calmed me down and helped me sleep. That is opposed to groups like Metallica and Alice in Chains that I would listen to before Air Assault missions, especially if it involved a raid or an ambush or other faster paced and more dangerous missions. At night, if I was somewhere where I could possible get rest, it was Enya.

Another interesting feature of the checkpoint was its mortar position situated in the rear. It was something that we would eventually utilize quite a bit by my recollection when we'd take fire at the port. SSG Ferriero, SFC Jones or one of the other NCO's would make a call over the radio for support from the mortar section, and within seconds the beach and port would be lit up by parachute flares, known as white phosphorous M83 illuminating rounds. These rounds would turn day into night and help us defend the beach and locate whoever had attacked us. I recall at least 3 such incidents at the beach, so I am sure it happened more often than I recall.

While we had plenty of stressful events at the Merca checkpoint, and the nature of the duty there was particularly dangerous, I don't recall ever taking fire there. In fact, we even found ways to amuse ourselves given the amount of weapons and ammunition that had been confiscated there.

Most grunts are just giant kids in many ways, kids with pyromaniac type tendencies. We like to shoot and blow shit up, and we fear very little, which can be to our detriment at times. However, give grunts a bunch of weapons of every type in the modern era, from WWI to present day, and you'll see the kid inside each of them come out.

Det-cord was a particularly fun thing to have and believe it or not, we had a quite a bit of it confiscated. At this point in my career, I had very little explosives training so it was something the older guys had to help us younger guys out with. Later in my career I would learn all about C-4 and how to make demo-knots using det-cord when blasting caps weren't available, shape charges, improvised claymores and even employ bangalore torpedoes to breach obstacles. Det-cord was distinguishable from another similarly looking cord called time-fuse by its lack of tick marks. Confuse the two and you're dead. Det-cord burns at some unbelievable rate at around 4 miles per second. If you confused it for time fuse, you can see your potential dilemma.

Well, this was my introduction to det cord and the introduction was a fun one. Application? Improvised bottle rockets. Yep, we would cut a length of det cord and hold it in our hands and light it. Instantly it would zip through our fingers and out into the air, where it would disappear.

C-4 was something we also had quite a bit of, albeit mostly in several claymore mines we'd confiscated. And, like the det cord, we found a good use for it, though not for pure amusement. Supplies in Somalia were extremely lacking to say the least. So, things like the fuel tabs we used to make hot coffee were in short supply. A couple of the NCO's had a good solution, one that they readily taught us younger guys. Cooking with C-4.

Sounds insane, right? Cooking your meal or coffee with C-4? If you were one of us, you would have just jumped on aboard and had some hot coffee or cocoa, maybe heated yourself an MRE concoction or any number of things. Imagine being able to make Ranger pudding and have it hot? Yum.

We'd eventually get hot chow while on checkpoint duty, not all the time as I recall, but occasionally. On one such occasion I was cooking a cup of coffee with CPL Schmidt when the one of the supply guys or possible a cook came over and got excited that we were cooking up some coffee.

"Where'd you guys get the fuel tabs?!?!?!" he asked excitedly.

"Fuel tabs? What the fuck are you talking about?" Schmidt replied.

"Right there, what you're cooking that coffee with!" the POG exclaimed.

"Oh, this? This isn't a fuel tab." Schmidt informed him.

"It's not? Then what is it?" our POG friend inquired.

"It's C-4" I replied nonchalantly.

"Yeah, right…" the POG replied.

"No shit. Look." Schmidt said, pulling out the broken open claymore mine that had been laying behind him with a big chunk of its C-4 conspicuously missing.

"Holy shit!" the POG yelled, and jumped back quite a way as though he was about ready to retreat.

"Dude. WTF are you afraid of? It's C-4. It requires two things to explode; heat and pressure. You can light, or you can stomp on it without a problem. But if you stomp on it while it's lit, watch out…...so, unless you're going to jump up and down on our fire, chill the fuck out." Schmidt explained to the bewildered POG.

Mr. POG never did seem fully accepting of our explanation and to my recollection, stayed away from us. His loss. We had hot coffee, mocha to be exact. Just mix up some coffee and cocoa powder, add three or four creamer packets all in a canteen cup of water, cook over C-4, and VOILA, another infantry trait is realized; I'm a fuckin' Barista.

The Baptism

"I indeed baptize you with *water*; but one mightier than I cometh, the latchet of whose shoes I am not worthy to unloose: he shall baptize you with the Holy Ghost and with *fire*." Luke 3:16.

Being a Southern Baptist Sunday School teacher and superintendent at a small mountain church in the foothills of North Carolina prior to joining the Army, I had already experienced two of the three baptisms mentioned above. I was first "born again" and made a public profession of faith at the altar, and was later baptized in a ceremony meant to symbolize my spiritual rebirth. We had already experienced some light fire on various missions with some frequency. However, I had no idea what it was to be "baptized by fire" until one night in January of 1993, at the age of twenty-two in a suburb of Mogadishu I'd never heard of, Afgooye, in a country I'd never heard of until I was sent there to fight people I never knew hated me. And many of them, if not most of them, hated me. They hated all of us. If for nothing else, for being "Christians". They automatically assumed that every American was Christian, and they clearly hated Christians. Small children would walk up to us and say "You! Christian!" and run their fingers across their throats to express their love for us.

This would be TF 2-87th's second large scale operation in Afgooye in the month of January of 1993. After the killing of an Irish Aid worker during an ambush carried out by Somali guerrillas, we tightened the noose around the city during two air assault operations involving door to door house calls; technically a cordon and search. During a command mission to gather intel in Afgooye, the BN TAC took fire, prompting larger scale operations.

Though not present when the TAC took fire, I have the combat action log for that day and I heard plenty about it while we were in country. According to the log, after the BN TAC took fire, they fired and maneuvered on two Somali fighters in the Afgooye market. Now, when I say "they" and referring to the BN TAC, we're talking about the guys in charge. The log specifically states that the BN commander, LT COL Sikes, personally did this. In fact, it says that when the assailants proceeded to take females as hostages in the market, the BN commander himself was the one that called their bluff, firing at them, causing them to drop their weapons and flee. I'm not sure that was a move out any hostage rescue manual as standard operating procedure (SOP), but hell, it worked and it was gutsy.

I read one newspaper clipping that mentioned similar missions that we're about to talk about in Afgooye, but the facts listed in the article do not align with

113

any operation in Afgooye that I am familiar with, the date of the article being the only familiar factor, aside from numerous black hawks air assaulting into the city. Other than that, the article is completely contrary to the official combat action log and the firsthand accounts of approximately 300 grunts on the ground, including myself. Though the reason for the inaccurate article may be that the person writing the article left before things got interesting. I don't know, don't care. Here's the "skinny".

Psy-ops (psychological operations teams) prepped our arrival by dropping leaflets around the city, warning any violent factions of our impending arrival. Why, I have no idea. It seems to me the point of an operation like this would be to neutralize the enemy rather than merely make them change locale. But, what did I know? I was just an M-60 gunner in a light infantry battalion. I do what I'm told and only give my opinion when asked. That is, until now.

The mission began as all did. We would first be given an op order and go over its details to make sure everyone knew what they were doing and what the mission was. After everyone was satisfied that the plan was understood, we would begin prepping our equipment. This usually involved filling our canteens, packing our rucksacks, performing individual equipment checks and then inspections at the squad and platoon level. Sgt. Wasik was technically my squad leader, but as an M60 gunner, I was always usually under direct control of the SSG. Ferriero, the platoon sergeant, or SFC Jones, our acting platoon leader.

Spaceboy, my AG (assistant gunner), was always a challenge. He had decided that his "share" of the 1,200 rounds of ammo for the M60 was 200. The ammo weighed approximately 8 lbs. per 100 rounds, so, in addition to Spaceboy's AG gear of about 30 lbs., he would carry 16 lbs. of ammo. This was of course in addition to all of the standard gear and packing list that everyone else carried. Water weighs just over 8 lbs. per gallon, and we all carried at least 4 quarts (approximately one gallon) of water. Spaceboy also carried the M203, already making his load heavier than a standard rifleman without the addition of the M60 gear and ammunition. Our rucksacks would weigh at least 60 lbs. on

114

most missions, depending on the packing list. All of this meant that Spaceboy's 5'4" and 145 lb. frame was carrying 75 percent of his body weight in gear and ammo. The other AG who would later become the other M60 gunner, Tom Corey, had a much heavier, stronger build than Spaceboy and carried at least half of the ammo for his gunner, making his load even heavier. Corey was a natural leader and an infinitely better soldier than Spaceboy, and since Eaddy was the senior M60 gunner in the platoon, I had no say in who my AG was. (Corey would later go on to serve in the 3rd Ranger Battalion and ultimately serve as a Green Beret for the rest of his career. He still maintains that Somalia is the toughest deployment he's ever done, and that A CO 1-87 was the best trained infantry unit he served in.)

My load was even heavier than Spaceboy's, but I was also about a foot taller and weighed 235 lbs. before deploying to Somalia, nearly 100 lbs. more than Spaceboy weighed. While I was significantly leaner after just a couple of months in Somalia. Having been an athlete my entire life, setting the power clean record in high school and playing college football, I was much stronger and much better suited to carry such a heavy load than Spaceboy was. Spaceboy and I normally had 1,200 rounds of 7.62mm ammunition between us for the M60. Subtracting his 200 rounds, or 16 lbs., that left an additional 80 lbs. in ammunition for me to carry. Though the Army manual stated that a properly fitted M60 crew also had an ammunition bearer, our sixteen-man platoon was ill-equipped to provide anyone for this role. Add in the gun itself, approximately 23 lbs., a PVS night vision scope weighing approximately 5 lbs. including its mount, and six quarts of water, I already had 120 lbs. of gear without even putting my Kevlar, pistol belt with 9mm, or rucksack on. On many missions, each of us would also carry a 60mm mortar round for our mortar platoon. Luckily, that wasn't the case this time around. All suited up and ready for business with a 60 lb. rucksack (if I was lucky), I was 6'4" and well over 400 lbs. of nicotine, caffeine and pure hate. Since I was someone who could squat a Volkswagen and bench press 400lbs., carrying this much weight was a walk in the park. For like the first 10 minutes or so. Unfortunately, I never had a 10 minute "walk" in the Army, not even to take a dump.

After hours of mission prep, Sgt. Wasik inspected the squad and went over final questions about our mission before making our way to the tarmac at the Bale Dogle air base, which was our current home. It was just before dusk in the early evening or late afternoon. Our Blackhawks in a single formation on the tarmac, we loaded up and were ready to go.

Air assault missions were admittedly my favorite type of missions. The sounds and feeling of flying in a Blackhawk at up to 200 knots is a complete rush. The heavy thud of the engine and the dull chop of the rotors, the violent shake of the helicopter......it was like the best amusement park ride times 1,000. Because we didn't fly a straight line to Afgooye from Baledogle air field, the flight seemed like it was about twenty to thirty minutes.

As we neared the objective, SSG. Ferriero, the chalk leader, yelled and signaled that we were two minutes out. As the pilots began their approach, I could feel my adrenaline building and my heart pounding with excitement. As we got into position and jumped out of the sides of the Blackhawk, I was suspended in mid-air for a millisecond and pulled backwards, the safety seat straps had somehow gotten caught on my machine gun. I broke free and took position behind my rucksack for cover, until the LZ was clear and we were ready to begin moving in to the city. As Specialist Cooke from 2nd platoon jumped out of his helicopter, he stepped on someone; Corporal Peterson, one of the scout platoon's snipers who was laying in the field in a ghillie suit, so well camouflaged that Cooke had literally stepped on his leg.

"Hey, watch it, dude!" Peterson said to Cooke.

"WTF? How long have you been laying there?" Cooke asked.

"Three days" Peterson replied.

Peterson, Smith, Whitling, Choate, Nash, Warren, Garcia-Bochas, Ursulo and the rest of the scouts had gone in days ahead of us and were laying unnoticed in and around our LZ. Jason Adams and our company scouts had done the same.

Within the hour, it was growing dark and we were staged just outside the city, ready to sweep our assigned sectors. A few minutes after we crossed our line of departure and had started down the dark alleyways and streets in our assigned sectors, a call came over the radio for everyone to return to the line of departure, that we were going to "start over". Everyone was pretty confused by the command until we go back up to the road and saw a General and his staff officers and a reporter and cameraman. Apparently the General wasn't ready for his big photo of our mission and now that his hair was done and his stars sparkly, he wanted a re-do. Ok, whatever. I wondered what the Somalis thought of that scene. Soldiers quietly creeping into and across streets and alleyways, getting to a certain point, and then going in reverse. Only to re-appear ten minutes later. Did they understand the concept of a time-out? Or a do-over? Can you do that in a combat environment? I have no idea, but it felt ridiculous.

Things were pretty quiet at first and going smoothly. Anyone who's ever served in the military, especially in a combat environment, knows that this is exactly when everything goes to complete shit. And in exponential bounds. Why should this night be any different?

By pure chance, I had discovered that the safety mechanism on my M60, a type of trigger lock, was completely unmovable and jammed. Meaning, I could not take my gun of off "safe" and turn it to "insanely dangerous", the only other setting this gun has. I informed SSG. Ferriero and Sgt. Wasik and asked if we could take a minute to try and fix this. Spc. Forde came to my assistance and tried to help me, but it was dark and we couldn't see shit. We both tried to force the trigger lock back into place to no avail. The only thing I could figure out is that I'd need to take the trigger mechanism completely off. This is when Spc. Hughes walked up to provide the ultimate aid, a flashlight. Believing this would be safe due to the red lens we all had in our flashlights, I gave the go ahead to proceed. If you've ever experienced something that seemed to happen in complete slow motion, the next ten minutes, and especially the first three seconds, were exactly that. Though in reality, it all happened pretty quickly.

The first thought that crossed my mind, and may have exited my mouth, was "What the fuck......?" as Hughes turned the flashlight on with Forde, Hughes and myself all standing up, hovered around the M60. Apparently Hughes had neglected a bit of soldiering 101, he had forgotten the nifty red lens cover for his flashlight. Forde took the flashlight and turned it on. The three of us were completely illuminated as we stood under and directly in front of a tree. I remember the look on Forde's face, the nervous smile with his gold teeth shining brightly in the luminescent glow of Hughes' fucking floodlight. Somehow the lens cover had been removed, a mystery we've never figured out.

"You stupid mother fucker!" Forde said. This was the first full second.

"CRACK! CRACK! CRACK! CRACK!" as several rounds ripped into the tree trunk we were standing in front of. Immediately we did what we were trained to do, we kissed the fucking dirt. As we did, the flashlight somehow had gone airborne, illuminated the area before landing on the ground directly between, but out of reach of all three of us. That was the second full second.

Bewildered that none of us had been hit, we were wildly trying to stomp and kick the flashlight while lying on our bellies as the world around us simultaneously erupted in fire. Three seconds and the flashlight was out. I proceeded to remove the trigger mechanism from the gun and frantically tried to remove the tiny spring that was between me and my removing the trigger lock. Sgt. Wasik began maneuvering the squad, bring everyone online in the direction the initial fire had come from. People returned fire from various positions, half the platoon being isolated about 30 meters away. I fired back with the only thing I could; my 9mm. But I only had one magazine of ammo.

"Let's flank these mother fuckers!" SSG Ferriero yelled as fire began to be returned from two additional directions. Except the fire was being returned at us, not just the Somalis that had originally fired on us.

"You might want to wait until I get the 60 back together!" I yelled back as I felt the tiny spring from the trigger lock hit the palm of my hand.

"You have a 9mm, don't you??" SSG. Ferriero replied.

"I'm not flanking shit with a 9mm! And I only have 3 fucking rounds! That's enough for me, you and Spaceboy to kill ourselves if we get overrun!" I screamed back as someone opened up in our direction with a SAW and I finished putting the trigger mechanism back together.

We were now caught in a good old crossfire, from three different directions. The rounds were so close; we were getting dirt flung into our faces. One direction was our Somali welcoming party; the other two directions were "friendly fire". There is a saying in the military: there is no such thing a friendly fire. There is just fire. For a split second, the thought of dying, or maybe just the *feeling*, crossed my mind. And some might think I am crazy for admitting this, but it was then that I truly believe I heard the voice of God, right in my ear, as plain as day. I actually looked to see if someone was over my shoulder talking into my ear.

"You're not going to die here." I heard as I literally felt any fleeting fear leave my body in an instant. Though our situation wasn't improving.

From the water tower overlooking the town, SGT Pavey, a company scout, was in an over watch and could see everything perfectly. LTC Sykes ordered him to engage at the center of fire, meaning, at first platoon. No one was actually sure who was who, but thankfully, SGT Pavey knew that we were friendlies.

To make matters exponentially worse, a Cobra attack helicopter swooped by and turned back toward our direction. As it began its approach, a long stream of tracer rounds ripped just a few meters in front of it (probably appeared closer than it was as I could barely make out the helicopter). When it became apparent that this helicopter was on a target run, I rolled over on my back and grabbed the IR light from my helmet band on my Kevlar, and held it toward the sky, literally praying that what I had heard about these lights wasn't true. Only visible to someone wearing night vision, which this Cobra crew certainly would be, I had heard that it can sometimes be mistaken as a muzzle flash, of which there certainly were plenty of them by this point. I had no idea if it was true, but I had little choice other than to try and make sure they could see it and hope to God that I wasn't about to get vaporized by one or more of its legendarily lethal weapons systems. It's chain gun, its 2 inch rockets, and its hellfire missiles. I had always heard the chain gun could put a bulled on every square inch of a football field. I wasn't sure if that is accurate or not, but I certainly didn't have enough real estate to hide on that came anywhere near as close to being the size of a football field. And it would have to be logical for the Cobra crew to look down and see where all the fire was concentrated, us, and assume that's where they need to dump their payload.

"I remember that night. I remember taking cover and the tracers were flying everywhere. I looked over at that reporter and laughed. He looked like a giant fucking sea turtle, trying to bury himself in that red clay, like it was sand on a beach. It was fucking hilarious." ~ Interview with Spc. Christopher Cooke, A co. 1/87 Infantry medic, 2nd platoon, December 2015.

By this time, none of us that were pinned down were returning fire. It was obvious that we would only make the situation exponentially worse. Not to mention, at this point, I had no idea who was who. At what seemed the last possible second, the Cobra abruptly pulled out of its attack angle and flew off into a safe direction.

"Cease fire, goddamn it!" I could hear SFC Jones yelling into the radio from about 30 meters away where he was with the rest of the platoon, a command SSG. Ferriero had also echoed several times.

120

Within a few more seconds, all was calm, the firing stopped completely. We began to get up once we were sure it was all clear. Sgt. Wasik and SSG. Ferriero checking with each person to see if we were alright. I got up and dusted myself off, confused as to how I wasn't shot. I was the biggest fucking target in the platoon. How did they miss me with those first three shots? Spaceboy looked thoroughly confused. Like he had just landed on another planet. Glazed over look on his face. We walked over toward the rest of the platoon.

"Dude, those fucking rounds were hitting so close I was getting dirt in my mouth!" Corey said.

After SFC Jones got the scoop on what had started the entire incident, he asked how I got my M60 fixed.

"I took the trigger lock off." I said.

"How did you know that would work? I've been in the Army for 17 years and I didn't know that would work. I wouldn't think that would fire like that." SFC Jones said.

"I didn't know. I've been in the Army for 1 year and it just seemed logical. And firing won't be a problem. It's not firing that will be a problem. Just pray I don't trip or anything." I said.

"That's pretty impressive, Slane." SFC Jones said.

After we had gathered our wits, we headed over to a road on which the company commander and RTO were on. I saw the look on the RTO's face as we approached, his eyes conveyed guilt and shock.

"I am so fucking sorry! We called that Cobra in on you guys!" he said excitedly.

"It's all good, fucker." I said.

Now that I had my baptism by fire, I was ready for a baptism by water. I was really fucking thirsty. Something about nearly dying can make you thirsty. I mean, like, REALLY FUCKING THIRSTY. I felt like I had cottonmouth, my mouth was like sandpaper. I reached down and pulled out one of my canteens, removed the cap, and eagerly took a huge drink.

"PFFFFFFFFFFTTTTTTTTTTT!!!" as I instinctively spit the water out.

"It's fucking saltwater!" I said.

I checked another canteen, same result. I tried my two quart canteens. No dice. All saltwater. I was drinking the fucking Indian Ocean. I asked for someone else's canteen, no dice. Every single one of us was walking around carrying 6 to 8 quarts of salt water. Within about 30 minutes I was so desperate, I tried adding Kool Aid I had stockpiled from MRE's. Same result, tasted like sweet saltwater. Later, being driven mad by thirst, I added an iodine tablet, then two, hoping it would fix the problem, logically knowing it wouldn't. Then I added more Kool Aid. Barf.

We later learned that the water purification system that pulled water from the Indian Ocean had reversed its filters, which gave us pure ocean water to quench our thirst. Oh, how I loved the Army in that moment.

Things got a little heated just a short time later as E87 took fire near the bridge. A Co 1-87 then move into a blocking position as E87 tried to flush the fighters out, but to no avail. Night-Sun (our eyes in the sky) reported seeing two fleeing Somalis dropping their weapons and heading into a building. We pursued but were unable to locate them, though their weapons were retrieved.

We continued our mission, kicking in doors and searching houses, confiscating any weapons we found. We got several crates of ammunition, some grenades and a few assault rifles. Turning over anyone found with the weapons to be detained and questioned. Nothing too exciting. But the longer the night went on and the thirstier I got, the more my head began to hurt in a way I can't describe. I had no sweat left. Not a drop of moisture in my mouth, or anywhere else on or in my body. We repeatedly requested water and were repeatedly told it was on the way. It never came.

Eventually we made our way to what seemed like the center of the village and into a large, two story villa. There were several Somalis inside and we just came in and made ourselves comfortable. I went out onto the back balcony, claiming it along with a few others as my bed for the night. I lit a cigarette since I was in much danger of being shot by a sniper based on how the house was position, nor did I really care if I was. I sat down and took the M60 apart and put it back together in working order, complete with the trigger lock. I smoked my cigarette and re-thought the events of the night, wishing I had something to drink. Anything.

1st platoon plus attachments, Afgooye, 1993. Only building with windows in the entire country.

We were told that the building we were occupying was actually one of the Presidential Palace, a summer palace. It was here that Earl (Aka, Rick Beem) would later tell me that he went to the rooftop and had a talk with God. He looked up into the unadulterated Somali night sky and saw the big dipper as he

123

prayed. And God answered. In much the same way he had spoken to me and Earl felt an inexplicable peace flow over him. And from that day forward, like me, he never again was afraid of dying.

Maybe the combination of nearly dying, coupled with severe dehydration, that contributed to the whole scene. He isn't exactly sure. But, try telling someone who's had an experience like this that it isn't real.

"EVERY time I see the big dipper now I am reminded of that place. But it will never be as bright and in my face as that night. I guess being in a country with 4 working lightbulbs will do that……" Rick "Earl" Beem, December 2015.

Just before the sun rose, we got up and got ready to move. The commander had instructed everyone to meet at a rally point just outside town and that they were bringing us water. Now that's the best fucking news I've heard all day.

After we arrived at the rally point, we did the rucksack flop and began waiting with the rest of the company. As the Somali sun rose over the horizon and the heat began climbing, the minutes seemed like hours. The hours seemed like days. When I finally heard the helicopter in the distance, I felt like I was dead. I looked around and everyone else looked like they were dead, too. About 120 infantrymen sprawled out around a burned out building and the field surrounding it, so dehydrated we could barely comprehend that our wait for water was over.

Within a few more minutes, a large transport helicopter appeared with the largest fucking water blivet I've ever seen. All I remember of the time that followed its arrival was drinking so much water that I got sick. Finally, following my baptism by fire, I had the baptism by water I had awaited all night.

I would later find out the that could only be described as the group premature ejaculation of fire was started by two of the most senior NCO's in the company, all that remained of the Vietnam Era veterans that still in the Army. I loved those mother fuckers. They shot at absolutely everything and everyone. And on more than one occasion, they reminded me of that fact.

The next day we again patrolled Afgooye and again took sniper fire, albeit very brief. As the shot or two rang out, a sergeant in 3rd platoon was conspicuously taking cover and facing the wrong way. He was facing directly at me and the rest of 1st platoon.

"Pssst! Turn Around! He's behind you!" I informed him with a smile on my face.

How he didn't notice that he was out of place by facing the opposite direction of everyone else, I had no idea. It made me laugh. People do strange things. The rest of our 2nd day in Afgoyee was pretty eventless. We only confiscated a small number of weapons this time.

"This is exactly how I remember the salt-water mission. I remember that night perfectly." SSG Ferriero, December 2015.

A Chemlight for Marvin

I don't know, but, somebody told me this…. I'll just tell it from the 1st person like I was there. But, I wasn't. Just sayin'…….

Interrogation in a combat zone can be a challenge to say the least. For starters, you usually don't speak the Lainguage of the person you're interrogating and it's likely that they don't speak yours, so an interpreter is normally required. Secondly, there must be some compelling reason presented to the subject of the interrogation that will make them give you the information you're interested in. The compelling reason must also be enough to ensure that the veracity of the information provided is reasonably reliable. I suppose the last hurdle worth mentioning for someone in my position is that I have no training in interrogation techniques, none of us did, nor did any of us have any specialized training in PsyOps (Psychological Operations). However, I believe this story highlights one of the many reasons that the US Army Infantryman is readily referred to as a "Jack of all Trades". One last caveat of interrogation is that as US soldiers, we have limits to what we are willing and/or allowed to do. We do not harm prisoners.

Early February of 1993 would be a very busy month for us as we built up security in the Merca area after leaving Baledogle. We controlled access to and from Merca with checkpoints, while E-87 patrolled the roadways in both directions. The engineers had begun building us a base from which to operate, though at this point it was still pretty rudimentary, having no roofs on most of the buildings, and only the most basic of facilities. The port of Merca was always a challenge due to the fact that even though it was surrounded by concertina wire and had several fixed and built up positions form which it was guarded, there was also the Indian Ocean to consider. A person could literally swim onto the beach, which was mostly clear of concertina and obstacles due to the nature and purpose of a port: to unload boats. We would rotate approximately two days of checkpoint duty, two days of port duty and three days of other types of missions including: air assaults, ambushes, patrols and QRF (Quick Reaction Force) missions, among others. Then the companies of TF 2-87 would rotate and we'd be given bigger missions. We never got downtime, not ever. I do not ever recall ever getting a complete night of sleep for my entire deployment, nor one full day of rest.

The cargo of the boats was normally unloaded onto the beach; just 15 to 25 meters beyond the where water would go at high tide, possibly less. There were almost always numerous large stacks of rice bags and several dozen drums of oil on the beach at any given time. This provided a challenge because once on the beach, a trespasser could easily maneuver their way around almost freely if left unguarded, which it never was unguarded. Even then it was especially challenging. Especially for a 16-man platoon guarding an area probably best secured by a company of light infantry. We were spread extremely thin to say the least, with just two men responsible for probably 500 meters of beach front access to the port as well as the entire beach for the most part. And it was extremely common at night to catch Somalis trying their luck at swimming in from the ocean and trying to breach our security, sometimes armed, other times not. What to call an armed Somali swimming in from the ocean? A Somali SEAL? I think "Shark Bait" is likely more appropriate, and these waters were full of sharks.

Though "Skinny" is the most broadly known term for the Somali people due to Hollywood, our platoon had a name for them which I preferred much more; Starvin' Marvin. SSG Ferriero and SPC Mangold had coined the term, and it stuck. And on this particular night, Marvin was starvin' enough to take his chances with us. A most unwise endeavor as he would soon learn. Especially when a Ranger happens to be lying in wait on the beach. Marvin would have had better luck with sharks, me thinks, but certainly not as much fun.

It was 0'dark-thirty on this typically windy night at the port. A gentle 60 knot (actually 20) wind in our faces ensured we had to be extra alert while on guard, because right away we are robbed of one sense: hearing. You couldn't hear shit unless you were standing right next to someone, especially on the beach due to the breaking tide. SPC Anonymous, a Ranger, was one of the two people guarding the beach. After watching some Somalis poking around outside the wire (apparently doing their Shark Bait recon), SPC Anonymous and his companion decided to take up less conspicuous positions on the beach and cease their patrolling. To be blunt, they were bored as fuck and had figured out that Marvin was planning some shit and they wanted in on it. While interrogation may not be a skill often attributed to our trade, camouflage and ambush are definitely skills mastered by the infantry, and perfected as an art by the Ranger.

Now disguised as rice, the Ranger and his companion, SPC Dude, lay in wait as two unsuspecting Marvins made their way out of the water. Creeping and crawling like the highly trained Marvins that they were. There's nothing more funny (other than what I am about to tell you) than watching people sneak around, believing they are completely unseen, their eyes as big as baseballs, their movements awkwardly animated as they crept up the beach with their knives at the ready. They had some Mission Impossible shit going on for sure. Like, literally.....it was impossible, there was no hope for success, as they would soon find out.

As the two crept close to the Ranger's rice-clad position, I imagine they were feeling pretty pleased with themselves for having penetrated our security unseen. And now they would reap the pay of their success (what they planned on doing with 50-100lb bags of rice I can only speculate as the rice likely weighed more than they did) as they lightly chuckled amongst themselves. Then suddenly......SURPRISE! You're a pretzel! Ranger and Dude seized their prey simultaneously from behind with a series of hand-to-hand and takedown moves as the pair shrieked in absolute terror. That is, prior to the proper application of some "Ranger Chokeholds" followed up with some 5-50 prussic cuffs. They had shrieked so loudly that I actually heard them from the normally muffled beach and through the ever present gale force wind of the port. My first inclination was that some women were being raped as I headed expeditiously towards the beach when I was then met part-way by the Ranger and Dude, along with two others now, proudly toting their hogtied prey as though they were on their way to a pig roast.

"HA HA HA HA! WTF?" Mangold exclaimed in glee as the two were set down in front of a group of us.

"Caught these fuckers creeping around the beach!" Dude said as he displayed the knives the pair had been carrying.

"There's probably more nearby outside the wire, make sure everyone on guard is alert." Dude ordered.

"Mohammed, ask these fuckers if there's more of them out there." Someone said to our interpreter, who complied.

Neither Marvin answered Mohammed.

"Ask them again and tell them if they don't answer, there's going to be trouble!" Ranger demanded.

Again, nothing, no response. Suddenly, Dude whipped out a chemlight, shook and snapped it, causing it to light up brightly, and then cut the top off.

"Tell this motherfucker to answer the question or I'm going to melt his face off!" Dude said as he demonstrated by splattering some of the glowing Cyalume (which is completely harmless by the way) liquid onto a wall.

Still no reply. Suddenly, Dude grabbed another chemlight and started to repeat the process. Except this time, he positioned himself directly in front of one of the two Marvins as he was fastened to a utility pole and looking a little nervous.

"Tell him that I am going to pour all of this 'acid' on his friend if they don't start talking!" Dude exclaimed before proceeding.

Then, in very dramatic fashion, he began spattering Marvin with the contents of the chemlight as Marvin shrieked in a way that would make you think someone was cutting his balls off had you heard it. As he shrieked, it almost looked as though he had managed to partially climb the utility pole backwards at one point, as his hands were fastened behind it as he danced about the pole wildly as though he were on fire. He didn't even slow down enough to realize that the Cyalume was doing absolutely nothing to him. Suddenly, the Marvin next to him began 'singing' like a bird, talking so fucking fast that it seemed Mohammed even had trouble understanding him.

"He said they have friends further down on the beach!" Mohammed announced as he pointed to where Marvin had also pointed.

"Go check it out." Dude told someone.

Dude quickly turned his attention to Marvin number 2, and began splattering him wildly with the contents of yet another chemlight. As the first

Marvin began to calm down and notice that he felt no pain, and other than glowing in the dark he was totally fine, we sat back and enjoyed another few minutes of a girl-shrieks and glow-stick dancing. I lit a cigarette and offered one to Mangold while the group of us quieted down to mere chuckles. As we smoked our cigarettes, the brothers Marvin soon stood there glowing like a pair of Halloween decorations. Their faces now very solemn with a strong hint of bitterness, like they had just eaten a big bowl of shit, as they realized they were both fine, despite the fact that they were brightly glowing neon yellow and green, like they had just been bukkaked by a Martian. They appeared to be around the age of twenty or so, about the age of most of us in the platoon. We untied them and found something to clean them up a bit before leading them over and handing them to the local MASF for their probable incarceration.

The last I saw of the brothers Marvin they were disappearing into the dark streets of Merca on their way to the local jail. Except that they didn't disappear. They couldn't have, not for the next several hours anyway. Those skinny little motherfuckers led the way brightly into the darkness; their heads still glowing like brightly lit jack-o-lanterns as they walked out of the vicinity of the only street light. I waved goodbye slowly to my new friends, with a sense that we had all shared in something very unique and very special together. And now I could say I had a new skill. Interrogation.

Having no prior training in handling an EPW, no one really knew what was ok, and what wasn't. While no one was harmed in this incident, it's probably the wrong way to have handled the situation. However, the possibility of our lives being in danger existed, further compounding the lack of training. I would also like to add something that our commander was probably completely unaware of; the spooks that frequented the port actually encouraged and taught some of the techniques such as this, though not this specifically. This made it seem legit, though it may not have been even though no one was permanently harmed by the incident.

No Rest for the Wicked

In summary, our mission in Afgooye and surrounding the area, dubbed Operation Phoenix, had resulted in several sporadic firefights, sniper attacks, the confiscation of numerous automatic weapons, rocket propelled and hand grenades, as well as several prisoners. Though it wasn't the first time we had taken hostile fire, nor the last by any means, it was our *first* "close call" and the first time many of us contemplated being killed. Something that tends to cross your mind when bullet rounds come so close that you end up with a mouth full of sand.

The adrenaline rush of someone trying to kill you is something not easily explained, nor can its intensity be matched by anything else in life. And by the time we left Somalia, we had had our adrenaline constantly flowing for months. Our "fight or flight buttons", stuck in the on position, and for most of us, "fight" was always the response. Some people realize its effects right away, while others may take years to fully understand how events like this affect them. In many cases, I believe the effects are permanent. In my own experience, it made me paranoid, therefore more alert. I found that my adrenaline would fire at random, keeping me ready for anything. I constantly examined my environment, contemplating every possible thing that could go wrong and how I would react. I slept lightly, never seeming to find a deep sleep. A whisper could wake me. All of these effects are positive things for a soldier. Both he and everyone around him is safer as a result. However, no two people are affected the same, and there are plenty of negative effects I am leaving out. Some people completely shut down.

On the 2nd of February, 1993, our focus returned southward, away from Baledogle, Mogadishu and Afgooye, and focused on Merca, Barrawa and Kismayo and their surrounding areas. Merca would be the initial focus of our operations. By now, regular shipments of food and supplies were flowing through the Port of Merca, keeping both US forces and our locally recruited Somali Security forces busy when on port security to say the least.

A few days later in early February, 1993, our company had been patrolling through Merca to deter clan fighting and looting. A regular show of force to keep things calm. I remember when we'd walk past the market and marvel especially at the meat that was on display. Fish, goat and various unidentified bush-meats, all laid on tables or hanging by hooks, almost all completely covered in flies. If you were lucky enough to survive starvation in this country, you then had to contend with various foodborne illnesses. I remember wondering what good money actually was in a place like this, a country with no real economy and nothing backing its currency. I suppose trade was an acceptable way to get goods and our American money was worth gold all over the world, internationally recognized and accepted, including here in Somalia.

Also in the market were various, and obviously old or outdated, canned food items, some with rust on the cans, indicating they were likely many years past their "best buy" dates. It was here that Corey, Douglas and Laing bought some ingredients to try and make a real spaghetti as we were so done with eating MRE's, we were willing to try just about anything to eat. Even if it was outdated by a decade like the spaghetti sauce they bought was.

On February 6th the local allied Somali Militia, The Merca Auxiliary Security Force (MASF) was busy providing security in the city, while a truck distributed food to locals near 2nd street when they were attacked by several armed Somalis, who initiated the assault with knives. Food was commonly used as a weapon in Somalia by rival clans who would seize control food supplies and cause starvation among the general population. Many of the MASF personnel carried canes and weapons other than firearms when keeping the crowds under control while the food was distributed, so they were ill equipped for armed confrontation. While severely beating two of the MASF members, a third MASF member who was armed with an AK-47 tried to intervene. Several more armed fighters then opened fire from an over-watch position in the buildings above the street, severely wounding one MASF member in the chest, and severely wounding the arm of another. As shots rained down on the streets below, the crowds scattered in panic.

One MASF member managed to escape the immediate scene and make it back to our company who was already conducting a patrol nearby. I believe it was 2nd platoon they had met up with first as our company was spread out during the patrol. We were only a street over and had heard the gunfire and were trying to ascertain the situation when the panicked MASF member found us.

As our company maneuvered toward the area, we immediately came under intense small arms fire. As we took cover, we were initially unable to return fire due to the large number of innocent bystanders still fleeing the area and filling the streets. A situation we routinely faced in urban combat situations. Not everyone is a combatant, and as Americans, we do not kill indiscriminately. It takes a great deal of restraint and discipline to lay there in the street, taking cover behind whatever you can find, while people shoot at you. It's a helpless feeling. You want to return fire but if you do, you risk killing the people you're there to protect, either with your own rounds, or by drawing more fire toward them. I found that the men in A Co normally utilized an amazing amount of restraint in situations like this.

A woman slumped over in a doorway about 10 meters in front of me, seemingly dead, as several of what I assume were her children sat and stood nearby, some crying, some staring expressionless. I wanted to help her and felt helpless as I looked at the children in the doorway around her who stared back with hopeless expressions. I have no idea how old she was. I hadn't even noticed them until she fell over.

"Slane! Come on!" someone yelled. I got up and moved forward with the rest of my platoon, hesitating for a second, though it seemed like an eternity, wishing I could stop and help. I felt as dead inside as those young eyes that had been peering back at me. What a truly fucked up existence. What a truly fucked up world.

While the lead elements of the company continued maneuvering and taking cover from hostile fire, members of one of their squads, or a squad from another platoon came in from the east hoping to corner the hostiles. As soon as they got in sight of the attackers, they promptly took and returned fire.

After several rounds barely missed one of their PFC's, a SAW gunner I had gone to Basic Training with, and his squad leader, striking a doorway just over their heads, the two returned fire, immediately hitting one of the three gunmen.

As the rest of the company now continued to maneuver forward, the remaining two gunmen took to the rooftops and continued firing down on the lead element of the company as well as the platoon still coming in from the east. They appeared to be heading toward to edge of town, down toward the Mosque near the port. Eventually the assailants made it back to the ground when, one of the remaining two gunmen fell, being severely wounded. The third gunmen then quickly disappeared into the Mosque complex, which was a walled compound that contained several buildings.

Normally the Mosque would be off-limits to us, by since we had pursued an armed combatant into the Mosque, we had justifiable cause to search it, and did so to no avail. He had gotten away.... for now. The entire ordeal had lasted between 30 and 60 minutes. This would not be the last time we would have cause to enter the Mosque in Merca, though as I recall, it was the first. The wounded gunmen were put in the local UNICEF hospital to be treated. If they survived, which I doubt they did, they would likely then be taken to the jail near the port and eventually questioned.

The SAW gunner who first returned fire, was a skinny, wiry guy with a good sense of humor. He was always laughing and always joking around, though I found him to be a bit too much of a loud mouth at times. However, he was a good soldier and a good person. And although there were times I thought

134

he seemed to have a more serious look than usual, maybe a little more stoic, it only took a few words with him to be assured he was the same funny wise-ass as always.

A day or two later, during the day while we were doing a security rotation at the port, Corey acquired some cooking supplies from our little friend, the cookie girl, and then built a fire over which to cook some gourmet spaghetti. The spaghetti sauce had an expiration date of sometime in the 1980's, but everyone was so sick of eating MRE's, no one gave it a second thought. Corey tended to the sauce as though he were a chef in a five-star restaurant, stirring and occasionally sampling it for taste. A fleeting sense of normalcy I suppose.

As night fell, I prepared to man a machine gun nest with Spec. Richard Hughes. And like every other time I was around Hughes, I would once again face death in the dark. In fact, it happened so frequently that once back in the states when we were all deciding where we were all going to and who was going with who, Hughes and I would look at each other and say "Yeah, no thanks. You go with them and I'll go with them. Nothing good ever happens when we hang out together."

As Hughes and I started our long guard shift that night, we quickly got involved in philosophical talks about religion and the meaning of life. After a couple hours of talking, we got a little too complacent with our surroundings, took off our protective gear and helmets, and literally sat in t-shirts on the sandbags that made up our machine gun position. A mistake, I know. Our position was in the middle of the compound rather than in a key location near the perimeter and it just *seemed* like a good idea at the time. We were practically laying down or leaning on our sides on opposite sides of the position, staring at the clear night sky, talking about God, religion and life.

Without warning, one or two gunmen opened fire directly in front of us at the entrance of the port. Almost as though it were scripted, Hughes and I rolled into the machine gun position and reappeared in full "battle rattle" almost instantly. A few of us briefly returned fire after they had fire 30 to 40 rounds at us, each missing us. The gunmen ran away, again in the direction of the Mosque as the entire rest of the platoon which had been asleep, emerged ready for anything. Several illumination rounds were fired, but revealed no one. They were gone, as quickly as they had appeared. Hughes and I spent the rest of the night in full battle-rattle and completely awake.

The next morning, the commander appeared to assess the situation. Several fresh bullet holes lined the wall next to the machine gun position. The commander stared at the wall for several minutes with his hands on his hips like he was counting the holes. SFC Jones and SSG Ferriero eventually joined him when I heard the commander say to them "Observe the wall." I'm not sure why, but I burst out laughing. Yeah, OK, let's observe the wall, man.

I'm not sure if people in combat zones just say weird shit because they're sleep deprived or because they're stressed beyond the limits of normal human capacity, but the command to observe the wall just sounded ridiculous. Or maybe it was me who was overly stressed and sleep deprived to the point that no matter what anyone said during or after a stressful situation, I found it ridiculous. Like I was looking for a reason to laugh so bad, that my mind could interpret anything to be funny. I think all of the above is true. And after talking with several of the people present 20 + years later, it's a consensus that the "Observe the wall" command, complete with hands on hips in deep thought while staring at a wall for about 15 minutes, was indeed a universally funny thing to hear and see.

The next day while cleaning my 9mm, the slide arm spring somehow shot out and landed in the oblivion of sand surrounding me. Great. After trying for several minutes in vain to find it, CPL Schmidt came over to see what was going on.

"What's up, Slane?" CPL Schmidt said.

"I was cleaning my 9mm and the fucking slide arm spring shot out and got lost." I told him.

"Dude, what the fuck? You're not going to find it. Hold on." He replied. "Estes! Can I get a catheter?" He then yelled over to the medic.

After a few minutes, Estes brought him a catheter. To my surprise, Schmidt asked for my 9mm, took out his Leatherman tool and started tinkering around.

"What are you doing?" I asked him.

"Making you a new spring." He said.

"Huh?" I asked, getting no reply.

Within just a couple of minutes, he had the 9mm back together, charging it over and over with a magazine seated in it to ensure it worked properly.

"That should hold." He said as he handed me my 9mm and walked off.

I sat there for a few minutes inspecting his handy work. And I have to say, it was impressive. Though after we returned home and were turning our weapons into the arms room, I got a talking too from the armor as to why the hell I had a catheter for a slide spring. Oh well.

Schmidt had been a scout before coming to first platoon. And he was genuinely a resourceful and amazing soldier. One story that Dirty D relayed to me involved Schmidt during war games in Panama the year before I got to the company. Schmidt had just graduated from Air Assault school and put his training to good work, capturing an opposing force (OP4) helicopter by merely standing in a field and using the standard hand arm signals he learned in Air Assault school. After the black hawk landed, he casually informed them that they had all just been captured before proceeding to eat the pilots bag of chips. Pretty bad ass, I don't care who you are.

A Very Dengue Adventure

Aside from a hostile population that seemed to constantly try and kill us, Somalia had another enemy; disease. We were given vaccinations for everything, including plague, which I didn't even know there was a vaccination for. But it's stamped on my Army vaccination documents in my medical records as plain as day, dated Dec 1992.

Every Sunday in Somalia started out the same for us. We would have the medic come by and watch us take our Lariam tablets for malaria. At some point, we also took quinine, though I am not completely sure about that. Quinine would explain the kidney problems I started having right after Somalia, at the age of 23.

Several studies have shown Lariam to be a dangerous drug that can cause psychotic episodes, and the drug is only widely used by the US Military. Probably on purpose. What's better than a well-trained killing machine? A psychotic well-trained killing machine. The drug even has an unusual nickname in some studies; the kill pill.

At least one of us got Malaria, CPL Schmidt. The list of diseases in Somalia included Malaria, Plague, Yellow Fever, Dengue fever and just about any other nasty-ass third world disease you can think of. I'm pretty sure I got something that never got diagnosed because I don't recall having a solid shit for at least two years after I left Somalia.

One hot afternoon in February, the day had proceeded as routine. I was actually on downtime between guard shifts at the port of Merca. Suddenly, a flurry of gunfire erupted on the beach. I recognized the distinct sound of a SAW (Squad Automatic Weapon) firing, and it was firing a lot. I grabbed an M16 and my Kevlar, and ran toward the beach, expecting a full out firefight. As I got out of the platoon area, the gunfire abruptly stopped and a moment later I was met by Spaceboy and Beem walking up from the beach. Beem's Kevlar was kicked back on his forehead and sweat was pouring down his face like he was standing under a fucking shower. I have never seen anyone look like this. And his eyes were not the eyes of the Beem I knew. Somalis was running absolutely fucking everywhere. It looked like we were in the "shit" once again.

"WHAT THE FUCK IS GOING ON?!!?" I shouted, ready to finish the task on the beach.

"Mother fuckers bum-rushed us." Beem replied in a strange, monotone voice.

"WHAT? WHO?" I asked as I looked to Spaceboy for answers as Beem passed by me.

Spaceboy was shaking his head at Beems reply.

"What, dude? What the fuck is going on?" I asked Spaceboy.

"I don't know. Nobody bum-rushed us. We were just sitting there and he started firing!" Spaceboy explained.

"WHAT? Is anyone hit?" I asked him.

"I don't think so, but I'm not sure how…." Spaceboy replied.

Recognizing something was wrong, Doc Estes was ordered to check Beem out, who was now disarmed. Like, they took his shit and say him down. A command decision. We all knew Beem and randomly shooting at people wasn't the Beem we knew, and he really just looked "off".

"His temperature is 105" Estes announced. "It's like 125 out here, he's got to be cooking his brain in his Kevlar." Estes continued as he got an IV bag out and then proceeded to stick Beem with the IV.

Before long, Beem was taken back to the base and promptly got a medevac to Mogadishu where they might be able to figure out what was wrong with him.

As Beem recalls in my interview with him, like everything else that happened to us in Somalia, his journey was anything but ordinary.

After being medevac'd to Mogadishu, he spent a couple days at the Marine tent hospital at the stadium where he laid in a cot hooked to an IV, and all but forgotten. After a day or two, the Army came and picked him up to move him to the 86th EVAC field hospital. After being loaded in a field ambulance, he got a memorable tour through a familiar city, Mogadishu. As they ambulance moved past the well-known and infamous Bakara Market (Black Hawk Down), a place we were very familiar with by now, the nurse became especially nervous.

"Hey, are you infantry?" she nervously asked Beem.

"Yeah, why...." Beem answered, only barely aware of his surroundings.

As she then handed him what he described as the filthiest M16A2 rifle he'd ever seen, she instructed him "Just keep this aimed at the back door...." as she then moved to the most forward position in the ambulance, putting Beem between herself and the backdoor.

"Since we had been issued brand new M16A2's during basic, as dirty as this thing was I knew we were fucked if the shit hit the fan. It would have fired maybe 2 rounds and then jammed. And here she was supposed to be helping ME, and now I'm guarding her. As we slowly rambled through the city I could hear lots of skinnies outside and nearly feel them brush past the ambulance in the crowded streets. I could have felt more helpless being so far away from my 1st platoon brothers. Take away my SAW, take away my health, but don't take me away from the guys that would protect me when I'm down." ~ SPC Rick "Earl" Beem, January 2016.

After what seemed like an eternity, the nerve racking ride ended without incident when they arrived at the field hospital where he immediately began receiving better care. In the cot next to him, the only guy who was possibly in worse shape than he was; a guy who had been bitten in the ear by a black mamba when he rolled over in his cot. Had the black mamba bit the man in the neck or face, he would not have lived to be in the shit shape he was in. His face was grossly distorted, like the size of a basketball and lopsided. Beem said that the man's ear didn't look like anything that belonged on a human.

"The 86th Evac Army Hospital nurses and doctors were simply awesome; I could kiss those ladies." ~ SPC Rick "Earl" Beem, January 2016.

Now in safe environment and well cared for, Beem felt he could finally let himself sleep and mend. However, while he was able to relax, he still had to wrestle with the effects of dengue fever in the form of several hallucinations.

"I was on the East coast of early America and a large wooden schooner landed at the shore, I asked the captain if this was the first ship to reach America?? The captain replied 'No, this is the first ship to reach America with a 1970 GTO Judge' and then he revealed the shiny orange muscle car in the hold of the ship. In another hallucination, I was driving all over Somalia in an RV with my dad, looking for Malaria pills. Yeah, weird...." Earl recalled to me.

From his vantage point in the hospital, he was close to the emergency entrance where he observed several bloodied Somalis, as well as NATO and US troops coming for treatment. Within the week he began regaining his strength and was well enough to be released. However, he had no gear; somehow all of it had been misplaced, probably left behind at the Marine tent hospital at the stadium.

After arriving at a hangar at the Mogadishu airport, Beem spent a couple of days trying to arrange transportation back to his brothers in the field. As he sat in the hangar for two or three days, he was amazed at the constant entrance and departure of high level pentagon brass, coming into the country and then leaving. "Pencil pusher types" he recalled to me. Anyone who has spent a day in the Army knows why they were doing this. Simply put, they wanted credit for being in the "shit". However, this was our shit, not theirs, and it's something I find beyond insulting and disgusting.

One major issue Beem had was knowing where to go, where to request to be transported to. He was on his own and desperately trying to rejoin us. He first hopped a flight with the Canadians to Baledogle to see if he could find anyone where our brigade CP had been. To his surprise he ran into PFC Paul Dehart.

"Beem! WTF are you doing here?!?!?" DeHart asked.

"I've been in the hospital in Mogadishu. Trying to hook up with everyone but don't know where they are." Beem replied.

"Dude, everyone is in Kismayo now!" DeHart said.

Beem quickly found the Canadians still on the airfield and hopped a ride back to Mogadishu. Next it was the Kiwis (New Zealanders) who would help him. However, Beem had no idea why we were in Kismayo or what he was flying into, and by the time he flew to Kismayo, we were gone. The battalion had fought hard to quell the clan fighting there between warlords Jess and Morgan, and it calmed down just enough for most of the unit to leave. Only B 2-87th Infantry was still in the city, right smack dab in the middle of full out clan warfare. Beem, still unarmed or equipped with anything at all, hooked back up with the Canadians who eventually strapped him to a pallet and flew him back to Mogadishu where he made history by being the only human being to hitchhike through Somalia (through various Army and coalition troops) and live to tell about it, eventually finding himself back in Merca. Outfitted with whatever gear we could scrounge up for him, he was back in the shit and I for one (though I wasn't alone by any means) was glad to have him there. Misery may love company, but we sure as shit loved our Earl. And from then on, the chaplain loved Earl the most, following him as often as he could, making sure it really was just the dengue fever that had caused him to shoot up a beach full of people.

"Got any family back at home, son?" the chaplain said, uttering his famous "I think you're crazy" question to Earl.

How he didn't hit anyone, I will never know, he was a great shot.

While in Somalia, our FO, SPC Farley, was medevac'd when he contracted Malaria. Several others in the company caught Dengue Fever as well as Malaria. Even after coming back home members of our unit contracted Malaria. Disease was another unseen enemy in this country, and death was a constant threat even when there were no bullets flying.

SGT John Wasik one day went to check on our Kenyan translator, who had traveled to Somalia and volunteered to help American forces. It had been two weeks since we had seen him and we knew where he stayed in Merca, so, Wasik made a house call. When he arrived, he was told our interpreter had died more than a week earlier, reportedly from Malaria. The man, though his name escapes me, was a brilliant and articulate man. He and Wasik spent hours discussing everything from world economics to politics and religion. I too remember engaging him in similar discussions, always left amazed at his insight.

As a side note, at this time there were only three strains of Dengue fever in the world. In another year, Beem would become the first person I know to catch 2 of those 3 strains, after we air assaulted off the deck of the USS Eisenhower being the first into Haiti for Operation Uphold Democracy. I suggested he travel to Brazil next and catch the 3rd and final strain. But alas, it would have been for nothing as now there are four or five strains of Dengue fever.

In all, at least as much as 20% or more of A Co 1-87 reported severe illness, including myself. Aside from not having a solid bowel movement for what seems like years after leaving Somalia, I was diagnosed with kidney stones shortly after my return.

Barawe

In mid-February, A Co 1-87 infantry would move to the southern coastal town of Barawe (also called Brava), Somalia, a place that few in the American military can claim to have gone, unless they were in TF 2-87 or members of SEAL team six who raided the town twice during the war on terror. In any event, I was there first with the 87th regiment. Located south of Mogadishu and Merca, but north of Kismayo, it was a logical place to establish a presence as the insurgency in and around Kismayo continued.

While serving as an ROTC instructor at East Tennessee State University around 2014, my squad leader in Somalia, John Wasik (now a captain), was being shown slides by one of his cadets who had served in the Navy in an intelligence position. As CPT Wasik realized what he was seeing, the cadet paused on a slide of the lighthouse at Barawe, saying that they had no idea what this structure was when the SEALs were planning their raid in the town.

"Oh, that's a lighthouse." CPT Wasik casually informed him.

"What? How do you know?" the cadet replied.

"Because I've been there. Operation Restore Hope, 1993." CPT Wasik told the class.

"Wow. We had no idea what that was…" the cadet replied.

"Yeah, and there's the villa we stayed in. And over here is the mosque." Wasik said as he continued to point out structure after structure in the photos.

If I remember correctly, our initial nighttime sweep was something to remember as our M203 gunners fired parachute flare after parachute flare as we swept the town street to street. While we patrolled from dusk to dawn, we ran into no real resistance other than a few rounds of sniper fire as I recall, something that we were pretty accustomed to by this point. No freaking out, just take cover and check the immediate AO (area of operation). We then withdrew from the town's center as the sun rose.

On the outskirts of the town, we manned positions around the outskirts city, Spaceboy and myself in an over watch behind the gun. During the sweep I did my now normal introduction to the young Somalis, telling them I was a Muslim named Mohammed Alibaba. While this set them at ease, I felt it also put them in danger at inopportune times when they'd try and greet me during searches of the city, or when they'd walk up to my position in groups, like they were this day. However, at this time I was running extremely low on cigarettes and decided to pick a courier out of the group to go barter for me.

"Hey, kid!" I said as I pointed to one of the older kids, maybe about 10 years of age.

"Get me some cigarettes!" I said, showing him one of my few remaining cigarettes.

After he nodded, he ran off and returned quickly with a whole carton of "Sportsman" cigarettes, a brand I wasn't familiar with, but whatever, I just wanted some cancer sticks. I began showing him various items for trade until we settled on a cheap pair of sundry sunglasses that they handed out to all of the soldiers, along with some MRE's, which I no longer ate at this point (if I could help it). I believe the cigarettes stated that they were from Kenya. As I quickly lit one up to try them, I was convinced the kid had run off and bought a bag of camel shit and rolled me 100 cigarettes with it. I first thought I had come out pretty good on this deal, but by this point, I was pretty sure the little bastard got the better deal. Whatever, they smoked. I guess.

Soon we had set up a company base in a villa on the edge of town which had a good view of both the ocean and the surrounding valley and rolling hills from the roof. It really was quite beautiful. I much preferred pulling guard atop the roof in Barawe than just about any other duty I had had in Somalia to this point. While I really wasn't lacking in being tan at this point, the roof was sunny and breezy. A nice breeze that contrasted just enough to make the fact that during the day I was standing in direct sunlight while it was well over 100 degrees. Spaceboy and I set up a hooch on the roof and alternated taking turns on watch, while the other got shade under the hooch.

In the backyard we dug a latrine alongside the wall, far away from our sleeping area where we'd spend about five days if I recall correctly. The platoons were rotating guard and patrols in the town and the surrounding area, and I believe may have even gone down around Kismayo from here during one two-day stretch. While we weren't on duty, the beach and swimming in the Indian Ocean was amazing. It gave me a sense of normalcy just to be able to be clean. Barawa had beautiful beaches that rival any I've seen. Or maybe it just seemed that way to me at the time. Either way, I don't care.

February 12th in Barawa was a busy day. By noon the battalion started investigating reports of "bandits" that had stolen a herd of camels. After some investigation it was decided to investigate further. A CO and the Battalion TAC set out to recover the herd. After initially talking to the men who had stolen the animals and letting them continue on, it was decided to take action.

As BN TAC and our company approached the men, the bandits immediately opened fire. One technical threw a grenade which exploded near the BN medical officer and even the BN commander returned fire. After a firefight lasting no more than 20-25 minutes, one technical lay dead, and two were wounded. The remaining men got away, though I am unsure how many. We'd be sent look for them later, aka, we'd sit in ambushes and wait for them. The wounded were treated by our medics, to include the same medical officer they had tried to blow up with a grenade, and transported to a UNICEF hospital (I believe), later to be handed over to the town elders.

Later that night, my platoon set out on an ambush. Though I don't recall specifically why, I believe it was in an effort to get technicals related to the earlier gunfight. Although, men and weapons were also flowing into Kismayo at this time. Possibly both were targets of the ambush.

After we infiltrated to our ambush site, we lay still for some time waiting for our intended prey to come by. However, what actually came by were innocent civilians, which someone in charge had determined in the nick of time. As they approached, a loud explosion rocked the area and things got tense in a hurry. However, what we were seeing wasn't matching up with a group who was out to attack us. It was then that SGT's Wasik, Douglas, Ferriero and Szulwach made a command decision to handle the scene more like a flanking maneuver, taking several fire teams with them, and swung out and around into the road to control the scene up close while the machine gun teams covered them.

Though the scene got pretty heated as I and the other M-60 team covered the rest of the platoon as they searched and questioned everyone, it was much ado about nothing, although enough of a scene to make a bullet on our commendation medals for having acted in a "highly professional manner which prevented the killing of innocent Somalis". If I remember correctly, it was a group of men with sticks. Which can look like weapons at night through a night vision scope.

It seemed to me that "ambush" wasn't the best mission to be carrying out without having confidence that a specific target would be coming by. They almost always turned out to be innocent people just going about their business. So, while we technically did almost everything by the book in everything we did, the ambush would be one exception. This is because the very way we're trained to carry out an ambush requires that we literally kill anything and anyone that enters our defined kill zone; without exception. The result of which would be about a 20% success rate where killing only the intended target was concerned. We got very good at distinguishing "friendlies" from foes.

During another ambush mission in Barawe, possibly the next night, we sat staring at a perfectly clear Somali sky listening to locals singing in the distance. It was hypnotizing, which turned out to be ok. Nothing at all happened other than a relaxing night with beautiful music and scenery, and a shit load of guns, ammunition, and explosives. Just a bunch of very chilled out guys lying in wait to kill some folks. I'm glad it was an eventless ambush. No one likes killing to an easy listening soundtrack, especially one as beautiful as what we were listening to.

On February 15th we conducted a high risk cordon and search just before dawn in a nearby village where we recovered, among other things, what we thought was a modified .50 caliber machine gun. The weapon had been mounted and modified to also be used as an anti-aircraft gun. The house to house search that resulted in this find was mostly uneventful; I don't recall hostile fire, though by this time, if it was light, it's likely that I shrugged it off as quickly as it ended. As the M-60 gunner, my job was to cover my team in an over watch as they went house to house, though on occasion, I got to participate in some door kicking (when it was required).

As one of the fire teams entered the house in question, they were surprised to find a rather young man lying in bed with a much older woman; neither was dressed. It was awkward to say the least. When the team had the house secure, they discovered a modified .50 cal machine gun in what would be the equivalent of the living room.

"What the hell is this?" Schmidt asked the man.

"I have never seen this before. I do not know where this is from." The man replied in broken English.

"So, you have a mounted .50 caliber machine gun in your living room, and you have no idea where the fuck it came from?" someone asked.

"No. It is NOT mine." The man insisted.

The ridiculous reply got the man immediately hogtied using 5-50 prussic cuffs by Schmidt and Szulwach, who then carried him out in front of me, and tossed him into the back of a Humvee.

"Have a nice trip, fucker!" I said, waiving as he was driven away.

As my first squad leader as a private, and a master of all things Ranger, Szulwach had not only given us extensive training on knot tying, but he gave use practical use implementation training for every knot he taught us. End of line bowlines for rappelling, rappel seats, prussic knot hand cuffs, square knots, etc. He truly gave us the practical tools and know-how to be knowledgeable and self-sufficient grunts. Tactics such as infiltration, ambush and patrolling were also among the skills we mastered under his watch.

SGT Wasik was my second & current squad leader at this time, and every bit as competent as Szulwach. The personalities of the two men couldn't be more different on the surface. Wasik came across as softer spoken, yet definitely still in charge. I think Spaceboy took his being soft spoken as him being "nice", which he was, but only if you did what you were told and were squared away. Otherwise, he could be as nasty as the nastiest drill sergeant you can remember, just minus a lot of yelling. He wasn't there to be our "buddy", he was there to lead us and to get us home safely. And he accomplished that very well.

It turned out the weapon was not a modified .50 caliber machine gun, but rather a 12.75mm Soviet DSKA. We killed several shitheads in Barrawe, which is still a hotbed for Al Shabbaab.

While in Barawa, we were getting reports that things were escalating to the south of us, in Kismayo. Men and weapons were flowing back into the city which was occupied by Belgian forces and our own 3-14 infantry. As we were the QRF in Somalia, our number was about to be called.

Walking with Jesus

Like most of this book, the story of Jesus in Somalia isn't widely known. A secret weapon of the US Army, Jesus was in fact a sergeant in my company while we were in Somalia. Unlike the majority of us who held the Military Occupation Specialty (MOS) 11B (infantryman), Jesus had the MOS of 11C. I know what you're thinking, but no, the "C" doesn't stand for Christ; it stands for indirect fire infantryman, eg, mortars. Meaning he could cause the enemy to explode from a few miles away, just like one might expect of the messiah. And the mortar section of an infantry unit really can be a savior of sorts when needed. Why Jesus only held the rank of sergeant, only God knows. And while the ways of the Lord are known to be mysterious, so too were the ways of Jesus of Merca. Perhaps even more so. I won't be using his real name, and for all you know, I've told you nothing else about him that can identify him. It has nothing to do with legal protection for myself, but more out of respect for Jesus that I do this. In fact, I hope that at this point in his life, he can read this story and laugh.

If you grew up or were an adult in the 80's you might remember the anti-drug commercials where the guy says "This is your brain. This is your brain on drugs." as he holds up an egg and then drops it into a frying pan. Well, that's kinda what happened to Jesus' brain. Except the only drug in his system was the anti-malarial medication we took daily, which is known to have side effects that include psychosis and the frying pan was his skull being constantly baked to oblivion by the insanely hot Somali sun. Add in the stress of a combat environment, which in itself can drive people over the edge, and you have one very exciting messianic figure! Who happens to be armed to the teeth!

My walk with Jesus, such as it was, began in the coastal town of Barawa, Somalia, sometime toward the end of February (I think). Unlike born again Christians who can tell you the exact moment their walk with Jesus began, it's hard for me to pinpoint the exact date in my mind. Don't get me wrong, it was a life changing experience for sure. Since I remember the location and that I was there late February/early March, I have something to go on as far as timeline.

SPC Evans was probably the first to tell me that something wasn't right with Jesus. He was in the same platoon and told me that Jesus had been doing weird shit, and saying even weirder shit. And that just like Jesus of Nazareth had twelve disciples, Jesus of Merca was recruiting twelve disciples. And Evans wasn't telling me just to share a laugh. Not only was Evans one of the twelve disciples of Jesus, the lord had sent him to recruit me!

"Yeah, I fucking jump right on that shit, thanks Evans!" I said, thinking he was joking.

"Slane, I'm serious. He sent me to ask you. He expects an answer, and I hope it's yes because I have no idea what he'll do if you say no." Evans explained.

"So why don't you go fucking tell someone, man? Instead of coming after me to recruit me into this shit?" I replied.

"Everyone knows already. I don't know why no one's done anything about it. I don't think they believe anyone about him saying he's Jesus." He further explained. "Just go along with it for fun. It's actually kind of entertaining and I think he's harmless. Except for when he charged his weapon and pointed it at Babbit."

"He did what?!?!?! And no one has done anything?" I asked excitedly.

While in the middle of explaining how Jesus had pointed his weapon at PFC Babbit, I sensed someone walking up behind me as I noticed Evans give a nod as he began to smile and suddenly switched topics. That's right, Jesus was right behind me.

Spc. Evans (left), Spc. Corey (middle) and Spc. Slane contemplating Jesus of Merca in Barawe, Somalia

"Slane, you are my right hand man. You are the beloved John. Will you follow me?" Jesus said, sounding a little like Barry White crossed with Morgan Freeman and then crossed with a Pakistani cab driver (which is how he always sounded).

"Uh, sure…." I said, shocked as fuck at what I had just heard.

"We're going down to the beach. Grab your weapon and come along." He said.

"Ok…." I replied hesitantly.

Almost right after I had changed into my PT (Physical Training) shorts, I turned around and he was there. Nothing creepy about that, I know.

"Are you ready to go?" Jesus asked.

"Yes….Sergeant…." I said, not knowing if I was to now address him as lord or by his rank.

"Bring your M60" he added and then hesitating for a second before saying "But conceal it."

"Do WHAT?" I said, kind of laughingly. "How the FUCK would YOU suggest I conceal the fact that I am carrying a nearly 4 foot machine gun?" I added, standing there in nothing but some pretty small shorts and flip flops. "I think I missed that training."

"What training?" he replied, ignoring the most relevant part of what I had just said.

"The training where you walk around practically naked while fucking concealing a nearly 4 fucking foot machine gun?" I said, growing annoyed.

"Oh. Right. Bring your 9MM. And conceal it." He retorted.

"Yeah, ok on the whole brining the 9mm thing. But again, if I conceal it, I think my appearance is going to be highly fucking offensive to the locals. Like, why is this huge guy walking around nearly naked with a giant fucking hard on? Or if I hide it on the other side, why is this guy walking around with a huge fucking crap in his pants?" I asked in my now very smart a$$ tone.

Expecting some sort of response, I was a little bit surprised when he just started walking as though I had said nothing. Evans was smiling at me, as was Grish, Mangold and Spaceboy.

"Well, come on, Slane! Let's walk to the beach with Jesus!" Grish said excitedly.

I smirked and we started off to the beach, walking just behind the lord. When we got to the beach, it was time for Jesus to give a sermon. At this point, I really wished he could produce massive quantities of fish and bread since I had been eating MRE's for nearly four months. But no, instead he began giving us his famed "Sermon on the Beach", recorded and found only in the gospel of nowhere.

"And now there are twelve. Someday, we will return to this land and rule it. Together. Of course, I will be in charge, but, together we will rule this land." Jesus explained.

"What do you mean?" I asked.

"Slane, the time will come when I shall call upon you to kill for me. And….you'll do it." He said.

"Roger that…. But WTF are we even talking about here?" I asked, with a big fucking smile on my face.

"We will return home to the US and when the time comes, I will call us together and we will return to this land as mercenaries. As warlords.   And we will rule this entire continent, starting with here." He explained. "The CIA are everywhere here. Have you noticed? The Brown and Root contractors are all CIA. There is more to this picture than meets the eye." He continued.

"Uh huh." I said and then hesitated. "So…. you think the 13 of your…chosen…guys or whatever, are going to take on the entire continent of Africa? And win? How would that work?"

"Slane. You have a large body that moves quickly. You'll be my right hand man. You shall carry a minigun as your primary weapon, with a rifle strapped across your front and back, a shotgun strapped to each leg and a pistol on each side." Jesus proposed.

For those who don't know, an M134 minigun is an 85 pound, six barrel machine gun that fires up to six thousand rounds per minute. And is a vehicle or aircraft mounted weapon. What Jesus was describing to us was right out of the movie "Predator" and I was Jesse Fucking Ventura's character "Blain"("I ain't got time to bleed!") Realizing now that he was completely out of his mind, I decided to just have a little fun with it. What else could I do?

"Dude......that all sounds swell, but who the fuck is going to carry all the ammo for me? With all of those guns and ammo I'd only be able to walk a few meters at time and then we'd have to take like a ten-minute break!" I exclaimed.

SGT Jesus completely ignored my rational question. Of course he did. He's out of his fucking mind. He doesn't deal with anything remotely close to rational. I mean, just half an hour ago he was telling me to conceal a nearly four-foot machine gun in my ass. Because that's fucking logical.

Jesus then stood on the beach right where the tide washed across his feet and extended his arms toward the sea. To everyone's surprise, tears were now streaming down his face as he said "This is where my mother the earth meets my father the sea......" It was a real Hallmark moment we were all having now. But it didn't end there.

First he told us his secret, saying "I can blend in here, disappear without a trace. No one would ever find me." Then, without further warning, Jesus dropped "trow" and took off down the beach butt-ass naked, junk flapping to and fro.

Now, maybe it's just me, but I always thought Muslims were a little conservative over things like full nudity? The looks that man got as he sprinted past the locals down the beach was priceless. Now leaderless and our savior out of sight, we all looked at each other briefly, exchanged some nods of "Yep, that really happened." and then began to disperse like disappointed fans at a rained out baseball game.

Beem, Grish and I found a nice little cove in which to go for a swim. God (no, not him, the real one), the water felt amazing. And I was beyond filthy. After swimming around for a little bit, I went back to shore for a smoke where I noticed something I wished I had saw before I went into the water. The shoreline was littered with quite a few jawbones. Shark jawbones to be specific. I then looked back at the cove, surveying its natural design. I realized we were swimming in the one place sharks likely love to come. No more swimming for me, thanks.

But Earl had an idea. How about some seafood? Earl paid a pair of Shark Baits to go get some lobsters. Only one returned of course, but he had lobster. Just kidding about that first part. If only Jesus had stuck around for some lobster. He could have turned our canteen water to wine and made us a few more lobsters and some bread. Throw in some fucking butter while you're at it, Sarge.

Back in Merca Jesus approached me as I stood unaware. In other words, he snuck the fuck up on me. In the dark.

"Slane......eh....how do you feel about....torture?" he inquired.

"Um. Giving or receiving?" I asked.

"Both." He replied.

"Both?" I asked again.

"Well, start with receiving then. How much do you think you can take?" He asked me.

"Uh. Why? Am I about to find out? Because I'm good right up until they drive the nail through the scrotum." I said, starting to feel slightly awkward. Luckily, someone walked up and tried to join the conversation, at which point Jesus became agitated and wondered back off into the night. Thank God. No pun intended.

The last time I saw SGT Jesus even attempt to go on a mission, he showed up for a pre-mission inspection in what could only be best described as "combat casual". He was wearing his desert camouflaged boonie hat, a t-shirt, a reflective belt, PT shorts and flip flops with his rifle slung across his back, all while holding out two canteen cups as though he was expecting some coffee. For the rest of our time in country, Jesus patrolled the interior of whatever base we occupied. To everyone's great relief, his rifle contained no bolt. But he looked sharp. Always in combat casual and never without a canteen cup.

As it turned out, I started to think that nut was right about the CIA. Especially after the events of 19 March. Also, over the years, I've learned there may have been some truth behind many of his theories, like the reasons the US was interested in Somalia. Not really a topic for now, and maybe not for this book. For twenty + years now I have waited in vain for SGT Jesus to "call on me to kill for him". I think he'll call on me when I least expect it. Like maybe while I'm taking a leak and his face pops out of the toilet unannounced. "Slane......the time has come!"

The Gift

In the Lower Shabelle Hoose region of Somalia, outside a small village near the city of Qoryoley, on February 16 of 1993, I would experience what I now refer to as the 'The Gift'. As I describe the events of that evening, I am sure you might misconstrue the meaning of this gift. Who the recipient of the gift is. Who the giver is. Maybe you're more perceptive, and the meaning of the gift is transparent to you. In telling this story, it is my sincere hope that people will get a better understanding of the monumental decisions soldiers are faced with on a daily basis in combat. I want people to see the true nature of the American soldier and that we are unique from most every other military in the world in that we are taught to think for ourselves. We are also taught to do what is right, above all else.

For well over two months now, we have been executing mission after mission, mostly at night. Sleep is something we did in another life it seems. We've experienced our first real combat experiences in the Mogadishu suburb of Afgooye and surrounding areas. By now, we can easily recognize the distinctive *crack* made when a weapon is fired directly at us. It is around this time that our battalion is rumored to have the highest body count in Somalia among the entire Task Force. We eat mostly ramen, crackers, Vienna sausages, Pop Tarts and anything else we can get from home. We've only recently been given access to showers. We are on a rotation of doing five to six days of non-stop missions, and one or two days of down time.

By now I have seen people shoot at everything from camels to donkeys and wild boars. I've been caught in the crossfire of Somalis, as well as my own friends, and I was nearly wiped out of existence by a Marine Cobra attack helicopter. We have captured countless 'bandits' and 'technicals', the latter belonging to one of the many factions fighting for control of this godforsaken country. Even the bandits have allegiances, so that distinction is blurred. We've also confiscated an unimaginable amount of weapons caches of every type, even American made weapons. It is a reminder that the U.S. had once sent weapons here around the time the Soviet Union fell, hoping to court this strategically placed country as an ally.

As daylight began to disappear and the afternoon turned to dusk, Corey, Spaceboy and Eddy and I went to the range and sighted in our PVS-4 night vision scopes. Performing routine tasks like this are key in a combat environment. My scope was sighted in perfectly. It was dead center, about a half or three quarters inch below bull's-eye at 25 meters. The same way I sighted my 270 deer rifle growing up back in North Carolina. The PVS-4 of the early and mid-90's wasn't the best scope at long range at a point target. But, within 200-300 meters it was a pretty good scope, and mine was ready for business. Captain Hamill even took a minute to admire the precision, which, as I would find out later, likely put me in one of the most difficult, intense situations I've ever been in…in my entire life.

The mission seemed fairly simple. Set up an over watch position on the edge of a small town to observe possible technical activity, and engage any hostiles. The objective wasn't very far from our new base in Merca, so we weren't going to air assault by Blackhawks. We were to go by vehicle and then infiltrate on foot to our objective. As best I can recall, it took about an hour and a half to get to our line of departure, where we would begin our infiltration. The area was fairly dense with hills in comparison to most of the country, surrounded by barren desert at its outermost boundary, and dense shrubs and vegetation, which mostly consisted of thorn bushes that could penetrate our flak jackets. This region also had areas dense vegetation where we had previously performed several night missions, including ambushes and reconnaissance.

As we slowly drove to our line of departure, it was easy to forget what we were doing there as we observed the wildlife we'd previously only seen in zoos when we were kids. As the sun began to disappear completely, we could enjoy the cooler temperatures and relax a little as we traveled the winding, rolling hills. Herds of tiny antelopes, called dik-diks run wildly through the bush. Wild boars, too. Baboons and the occasional giraffe remind me just how far from home I really am. I almost feel like we are explorers on a safari. However, once it was completely dark and we had reached our dismount point and set out to infiltrate on foot, it seemed things were going wrong almost immediately.

After dismounting our vehicles we began crossing the road in pairs to move into our position, when suddenly, a large truck appeared out of nowhere. This was the exact type of truck that would likely be carrying the very people we were sent to get. I was trapped on the very side of the road the truck was travelling on, along with less than half of our sixteen-man platoon.

Of course my AG (Assistant Gunner) Spaceboy needed a little coaching almost immediately, as the truck rolled near and suddenly stopped. The truck is cutting the platoon nearly in half, each on opposite sides of the road. The truck is completely obscuring our view of each other. "Shut the fuck up, Spaceboy. And don't move." The sentiment was whispered several times amongst us. "What the fuck are we going to do?" someone whispered. The platoon sergeant, SSG Ferreiro replied "Nothing. Just sit still and shut the fuck up!" I can hear people dismounting the vehicle. My pulse quickens. My adrenaline is enough to single-handedly crush this truck. I can hear the footsteps on the side of the road, only a few feet away, just above me. I have no idea if they can see me or any of the rest of us. For all I know someone is aiming at the back of my head. I am stuck facedown and if I move now, I will most certainly be seen. It is completely dark. All I can do is hope that the rest of the platoon on the other side of the road was ready to deal some serious violence on these guys if we got compromised. I am also hoping that everyone else stuck with me, or at least one of them, isn't stuck in the same stupid ass position I am in…face down. I can't see anything. I just pray one of us can see what was happening. I am lying completely still, barely breathing. It is nerve racking to say the least.

After what seems like an eternity (but was all of about five minutes) we can hear people piling back into the truck. Then, as quickly as it had stopped, the truck was gone. Breathing again, I exhale a huge sigh of relief. "Were they armed?" someone asks? "Probably, but I couldn't tell for sure" someone answers. It wouldn't have been smart to engage them in the compromising position they had us in, that's for sure. Without being able to see each other from opposite sides of the road, we would have most likely have had some friendly casualties in the crossfire.

With our platoon reunited, we could continue to our ambush site/OP (Observation Post), which was only another 100 meters away. Though we were technically conducting an ambush, it was a slightly modified version being that we were in a country where not everyone was an enemy. We moved quickly, silently through the thick Somali brush, keeping the road in sight. Once we arrived at our position I am assigned a sector that pointed down a slight hill, directly into the town. I can see everything perfectly. In a country where daytime temperatures regularly exceed 120 degrees Fahrenheit, it was very common to see a lot of activity at night. This town is no exception. There is a market of sorts, right near a crossroad and down the hill approximately 150-200 meters from me. There is one building that was lit, and there are probably 50 to 75 people, maybe more, gathered in the immediate vicinity. At this range and in this position, I can easily suppress or destroy anything I needed to. I replaced my

30 round teaser belt with a full 100 round belt of 7.62mm, and began observing. I feel some sense of intense seriousness, responsibility…or maybe importance is the word I'm looking for. Perfectly concealed and armed with the deadliest weapon a light infantryman can carry, I feel my senses sharpen as this feeling grows over me. Part of me almost wishes something would inflate the situation. No, not almost, it does. I want something to happen. I need somewhere to direct this intense feeling and the massive amounts of adrenaline that I suddenly feel pumping through my veins. My senses are now so sharp; I can smell the various scents of Somali life I've become accustomed to, coming from the market. Shit being one of those smells, along with a sort of burnt charcoal and incents smell…like everywhere else in this fucked country. People are moving freely in the market, likely high on their narcotic of choice, Khat. It seems as if every male over the age of about 12 is chewing and getting high on this stuff all day long. Especially the fighters. It gives them a feeling similar to that of cocaine, making them feel invincible. This explains why many of those who attack us foolishly often have less than 10 to 20 rounds of ammunition. I am carrying 100 times that much ammunition. Now, I am definitely ready for something to happen. And it does.

I hear radio silence break, and SFC Jones acknowledging over the radio and then telling me "Slane, we've got a guy down in the Market who's got a weapon! Officer in Charge (OIC) wants you to take him out!" "Roger." I reply, as I peer through my scope, scanning the market. "OIC says he's right in the middle" SFC Jones relays. "Roger." I reply, still scanning the market intently. Then I spot him, describing him as best I can, and his location to SFC Jones, who confirms with the Officer in Charge. "Officer in Charge says roger, that's him. He wants you to take the shot. Take that mother fucker out!" "Roger" I reply again. However, as I am studying my target, I notice something. At first, it did appear he was armed. But now, I am not so sure. He isn't handling this like someone would handle a rifle. Not that it mattered, Somalis rarely did anything right with firearms, including carry them correctly, so maybe it is a weapon. I look more intently.

"OIC wants to know what the holdup is." SFC Jones asks.

"I am not so sure that's a weapon." I reply.

"OIC says it's a weapon and he wants you to take the mother fucker out!" SFC Jones relays.

I pause. I am wondering how I can make this shot and only hit the guy in question while he stands in a crowd. I open the feed-tray of the M60 and remove the belt. I then break off one single round, and seat it then close the feed-tray.

"What are you doing?" SSG Ferreiro asks.

"This is a fucking machine gun, not a sniper rifle. That guy is surrounded by tons of people. If I shoot with the belt I will kill him, and everyone anywhere near him. This gun has a nice long barrel and shoots a 7.62. It will function perfectly as a sniper rifle like this and ensure that I only kill him, not everyone else." I explain.

No one says anything. I go back to studying my target while the Officer in Charge grows more agitated.

"OIC says shoot the mother fucker!" SFC Jones relays.

"NEGATIVE. HE'S NOT ARMED." I reply, adding, "IT LOOKS LIKE A FUCKING STICK!"

At this point, I can hear the Officer in Charge screaming into the radio. I feel like the entire planet is crushing me into the dirt...I continue to refuse the order. The ordeal carries on for another fifteen minutes while not ONE single person in my platoon utters a single word. No one. At this point, SFC Jones is ignoring the Officer in Charge, laughing nervously, clearly frustrated.

"SHOOT THAT MOTHER FUCKER GODDAMN IT!" you could hear the radio echo.

"NEGATIVE. FUCK THAT. HE ISN'T TAKING THE GODDAMN SHOT. HE SAYS HE'S NOT FUCKING ARMED, OVER!" SFC Jones replies, repeating it exactly as I said it.

Now I'm shouting and cussing at an officer while refusing his direct order. In combat. I haven't even been out of basic training for one year yet. Who the fuck am I? I am sure the Officer in Charge is asking himself the same of me at this point. I studied the target one last time. Nothing. There is not a single weapon in sight anywhere in the market, especially not on this guy.

I am now technically guilty of violating Article 92 of the Uniform Code of Military Justice (UCMJ) for failing to obey a direct lawful order. And also Article 90 of the UCMJ for failing to obey the direct lawful order given by a superior officer in my chain of command, an order appearing lawful on it's face, while in combat, which is punishable by death. But I am sure he is unarmed, therefore any order to kill him is illegal, so I stood my ground.

I raise the feed-tray again and slide back from my weapon a little. I am expecting something to happen now. I am wondering what is going through the minds of everyone with me. Do they doubt me or my judgment? My mouth is so dry I feel like I'm eating sand; I doubt any amount of water can quench my thirst at this point. I almost start to question myself. But, I *am* sure. I *know* I am right. He didn't have a weapon. You hear stories like this where people get killed in combat for refusing orders. Is someone going to put a bullet in the back of my head? I did honestly wonder. Briefly. Then, I realized. Not one person has said anything contrary to me. Still. Nothing. I look over at Mangold, who had relayed some of the shouting match between the Officer in Charge and I at first, before SFC Jones just took the radio from him. He's got that "Fuck yeah!" smirk on his face. Mangold believes in me. He knows if that guy had been armed, he'd already be dead. It is reassurance that I really needed at this point. I shook my head and try to smile. Under my breath, I try to explain myself.

"It's an illegal fucking order. I have the right to refuse an illegal order. I'm not about to shoot some unarmed mother fucker. Fuck that. Throw me in jail, execute me, I don't give a fuck. I'm not killing an innocent man." I say, talking into the air.

I didn't have to explain myself. And I am being a little dramatic it seems, though quietly. But I would come to realize, that no one there wanted to be in my position, and they trusted my judgment. I didn't have to explain myself to anyone. Yet. And if I do have to eventually, it won't be to these guys. They have my back, and I have theirs.

"OIC says he's sending a squad in to take the guy down." SFC Jones relays.

Ten more minutes pass and radio silence is once again broken.

"Roger!" SFC Jones says, and then tells us "Officer in charge said it was a cane! The guy didn't have a weapon. He had a fucking cane! Good call, Slane!"

I don't know if I've adequately conveyed the immense pressure I had felt to this point, or the atmosphere to you. But if I could have, I would have laid there and cried for a few minutes. I'm pretty sure a tear of relief fell from my eye, unnoticed by anyone but me. It's not because I didn't know I was right. It's because until this point God and I were the ONLY ones who knew that I was right. And now, finally, everyone else knew I was right too. Maybe a few in my platoon doubted me, but I will never know. If they did, they were at least respectful enough not say anything out loud. However, I honestly don't think any of them doubted me. This highlighted to me the immense amount of trust and respect we had built together as a group. I felt safe in this moment, with these men, in a way I cannot describe. That respect and trust endures to this day.

Twenty-one years later, a one-time platoon leader of mine would come to tell me that he used this story as an example of moral courage and ethics in war.

He said he had always hoped my actions were the norm, but that he found out that wasn't always the case. As I read his email to me, I was amazed at what I was reading, almost dumbfounded by the magnitude of what he had told me. I replied that I wished I had been with him later in his military career, but it appears that I actually had been. I realized the truth in what I had replied, because I too have carried with me all of these people through all of these years. I think of them like brothers, and I recall their stories, their deeds often. I realized how much we each impacted each other in the military, and as it is now apparent, generations of soldiers to follow. The military is like a family. No, it IS a family. A family with an ongoing lineage of honor and courage. It is full of parents and siblings, teaching each other, learning from each other, taking care of each other. Each lesson is passed down to the next generation and one man's actions can shape soldiers he will never even meet or know. I don't know exactly who Lt. Kreyling may have passed this story on to, or to how many, but I hope it served a good purpose for whoever he told the story to, because it obviously impacted him enough to tell me after all of these year.

Have you decided what exactly the gift is? Who its recipient is? It is clearly a gift to the man that I didn't kill that night and to the people that might have died with him. His life almost ended abruptly and violently. His life could have potentially ended with several other lives in one violent act at the hands of someone 'just following orders'. However, the gift is actually mine. The gift is my own soul. I can live with myself knowing that when it counted most, I was true to who I am, to the oath I took, and to the ethos I live by. If I ever need reminding that I was born with a purpose in this life, all I need to do is remember this night. A night when I saved at least one innocent life, without that person ever knowing how close he came to dying.

As the Somali sun rose the next morning, I could feel its warmth bringing me back to life. While we were loading back into Humvees to go back to the base in Merca, this incident had become all the talk. The entire battalion got to hear about it-because Mangold had dropped his hand mic in the back of the

Humvee as people were talking about how dumb it was of the Officer in Charge to insist on my killing this guy. They called him a dumbass for not just taking my word that he wasn't armed. They praised me for having large balls, and doing the right thing. A few minutes into the celebratory talk, Captain Hamill strolled over to the Humvee and asked that Mangold remove his foot from the hand mic so he could stop broadcasting the fact that the captain was a dumbass to the entire battalion. This moment, for an instant, became the second most intense moment of my life. But, Captain Hamill just walked away seemingly not to care. Someone had made a mistake, and I nearly compounded that mistake. A mistake that could have ended our careers, or worse. A mistake that would have embarrassed our county, and our unit. A mistake that would have taken innocent lives. A mistake that would have had dire consequences to the mission and made it harder to achieve that mission.

Shortly after this mission, our battalion killed three Somali militants in the same area. All three were armed.

Spaceboy

I'm sure many have heard of the term "1,000-yard stare", a term used to describe the blank expression some get after experiencing war. And I will never forget the first time I knew for sure I had seen it.

Though it would have been nice to have a tougher, more physically impressive, AG (Assistant gunner) than Spaceboy, I could not have possibly had a nicer, more decent human being by my side in Somalia. And he actually was a pretty good soldier in that he usually did what was required of him and almost never let me down.

He had a rough beginning in life and had been in and out of foster homes as a kid growing up. He wasn't a troublemaker; he was just someone who'd been kicked around through the system, trying to find his place in the world. Why he had chosen the Army, none of us knew. To those of us who knew him, though we genuinely liked him, he didn't belong in the Army. He didn't seem to have a "mean" side, a side that he could show in bad situations, one disconnected from his inner, truer self.

I believe it wasn't long after the events described in the chapter "The Gift", in early March, that two Somali technicals were killed by our battalion in the same area during a similar night mission. After the sun rose the next morning, our battalion HQ wanted soldiers to go on what I dubbed "brain detail". That is, they wanted the bodies our dead enemies collected and brought back to base where they would perhaps be turned over to their families for burial. I'm not sure why Spaceboy was picked for this detail, or if the person deciding even knew upfront what the detail was, but it was something that changed Spaceboy forever. Something that probably still haunts him to this day, as I know it did the day he left the Army.

The older I have become in life, the more guilt I feel for trying to laugh things off with him, or being hard on him, though I honestly didn't realize how broken he was at the time. In many of the several ambush missions we performed, he and I would often be up and manning the M60 together, and he would ask philosophical type questions or say strange things while using his vivid imagination.

"Slane. Why are we here?" he asked me one night while sitting in an ambush.

"Um. We're waiting for the 'bad guys' so we can kill them...." I replied.

"No, I mean, in Somalia. Why are we here? What are we doing here?" he said.

This cycle repeated itself several times until I decided I had had enough.

"I don't f*cking know, Spaceboy. And, if you ask me that one more time, I will kill you myself." I replied harshly.

While training in Death Valley at the National Training Center in June of 1992, Spaceboy had surprised us all when he suddenly started talking about how it looked like we were underwater, swimming or walking along the bottom of the ocean. He demonstrated doing the breaststroke through the water. We were all kind of in shock at first, but that soon turned to laughter when one of the NCO's (non-commissioned officers – Sergeants) said something that I would often repeat to or of Spaceboy.

"Look! Its Space Boy and his dog Zoom!" SSG Pippen said.

Anyway, this particular task was something that started out very wrong from the beginning. You'd think the most traumatic and horrible part of this story would be the part that won't be discussed in detail, nor the focus here; the killing of these individuals. But, no, that really was just the beginning of a much, much darker story. At least that is my opinion.

It's hard enough for people to see another human being who is dead. But the sight of a human being who was killed in combat can be exponentially worse. And in this case, it was. They had been shot so many times that they were little more than gruesome bloody sacks of flesh with brain matter all over on the wrong sides of their skulls. It's difficult to look at what was once a living, breathing human being and reconcile that with what you're seeing.

As a group of soldiers waited around for instructions on what to do with the bodies, the person in charge, who we will not name, said possibly one of the most shocking things I have ever heard given the circumstances. Apparently he felt that rather than move the bodies somewhere and have them buried or turned over to the families for burial, that using the remains of the recently deceased to send a message was the right thing to do. As if it wasn't bad enough that the bodies sat in plain sight of their family and friends for hours already. He wanted to hang the bodies from a tree near the center of town.

"I want to take these bodies and hang them in the center of town to set a warning for anyone else who wants to make trouble!" the anonymous person in charge conveyed to the group.

At this point, everyone stopped moving around and quit making any noise at all. Everyone was completely still, not quite sure if they heard him correctly. It was so quiet you could have heard ants fornicating from 100 meters away.

"What did he say?" someone uttered below his breath.

"He wants to hang the bodies up......as a warning" another replied.

It's one thing to go half way around the world and kill people. It's quite another thing to then decorate their villages with the corpses you produce. The already horrified Spaceboy was just slipping further into whatever confusion was racing rampantly through his mind. His face bearing a nervous grin of disbelief, his mouth partially open. He wasn't alone, or if he was at first, he wasn't now. Stringing up bodies to scare people isn't part of our training, nor is it something we would have come up on our own. Mr. Scary guy in charge must have had some really special training in psy-ops (psychological operations) and counter-decency.

The confusion, or rather the shock, of this scary order was short lived as he explained over the radio to whom I believe was the battalion commander, what his master plan was.

"[insert name]. Listen to me. I want you to load those bodies up and get back here to my location, ASAP. With the bodies." The voice on the other end of the radio ordered.

"Roger." Mr. Scary guy replied.

Spaceboy now had the wonderful task of picking up the bodies, and loading them into a waiting five ton [truck].

"Ewe, gross. It's all slimy." He said of the body as he tried to wipe blood and brain matter from his hands.

After the bodies were loaded, Spaceboy was given one additional shock, one I believe sent his mind into a rat race of confusion from which he wouldn't soon recover, if ever. He had to ride back to base with the bodies. Not only did he have to ride with them, there wasn't enough room left in the back for him to put his feet anywhere other than......on top of the bodies. It would be about an hour long scary amusement park ride for him with his feet on top of these corpses. Spaceboy was in shock. Emotionally, spiritually and in any other way imaginable. He was in complete shock.

By the end of the detail, Spaceboy was a different person. For a few days (it seemed) he couldn't stop talking about how the bodies felt and what they looked like or how he had to put his feet on them for the long ride back to the base. He couldn't understand how someone could order him to hang the bodies in trees. He didn't ask any philosophical questions like whether or not they had deserved the fate they met. He only questioned everything that followed their deaths. He questioned the person who gave the craziest and darkest orders we had ever heard. He questioned the Army and why he was in it, not being able to distinguish between the Army and the lunatic who wanted to hang bodies in trees. I presume to know that he probably felt betrayed and tricked into service in a twisted military, not being able to separate the Army from Mr. Scary. I get it. But Mr. Scary isn't the Army, nor is he even a majority.

I have no training in psychology and at the age of twenty-two, was the last person on earth who was equipped to help Spaceboy deal with this incident. My replies were dismissive and harsh. Not because I wanted to be mean, but because the whole reality of it overwhelmed me. For me, the best way to deal with something like this was to just cut it out completely and to not try and understand it. To just act like it was like any other day and that the events were just part of that normal day. In other words, bury it and any opinions, thoughts or emotions concerning it like it never happened.

For the rest of our time in Somalia, I would routinely see Spaceboy's blank stare, his eyes like a window with no light. He had the stare that we had always heard about. The 1,000-yard stare. His questions of why were there and what we were doing never stopped, and ultimately, I never killed him for asking, though I kept threatening for the sake of my own sanity.

Spaceboy was also chosen to be one of the few soldiers to get R&R (rest and relaxation) leave in the Kenyan city of Mombasa. Mombasa was notorious for being one of the prostitution capitals of the world. However, I'm not sure Spaceboy had even ever had a girlfriend. And he didn't drink very much, so his time was spent buying worthless trinkets at premium prices. Something he did a lot in the states as well. He was mostly uncomfortable while in Mombasa because he didn't understand why they wouldn't let him take his rifle. Like many of us would feel once back in the states, he apparently felt naked and vulnerable without his weapon.

Back in the states after Somalia, Spaceboy tried to get counseling and help to cope with his overloaded mind and soul from this and everything else he had experienced. Apparently the Army psychologist he dealt with on the base was even more ill equipped than me to help Spaceboy, something he was extremely frustrated about.

"They just keep telling me that nothing is wrong with me…. it's pissing me off" He would tell some of us.

"Well, did you tell them that you're coo coo for Cocoa Puffs and you shit Fruit Loops?" I jokingly asked.

"he he he, whaaaaat?" he replied, seemingly proving my point.

I've always regretted saying that to Spaceboy, even though he knew I was kidding. It's just the way we all were with each other. Like a bunch of brothers always picking on each other, but the first to step up and defend each other from outsiders. And, I too have felt a bit coo coo for Cocoa Puffs and shit plenty of

Fruit loops over the years. On one hand they were right. There was nothing "wrong" with Spaceboy. His feelings and reactions were a completely normal response to a completely extraordinary and a very not normal circumstance. His trying to deal with it was also healthy. He recognized the need to deal with it, which is more than I can say for myself or anyone else who just buries terrible things that bother them. No matter how deep you bury them, they will eventually resurface. And when they resurface, they will likely cause ten times the amount of issues they would have had they not been buried for so long. However, it is a survival mechanism for a soldier to bury things he's uncomfortable with, usually after he's made or heard a few uncomfortable jokes.

Spaceboy gave counseling an honest try and it failed him. Not long after I made sergeant, I passed Spaceboy as he was walking to the parking lot with boxes of his possessions.

"Hey, bud, how's it going? What are you up to?" I asked.

"Hey, Slane. I'm leaving. I'm going home." He said.

"Ok, man. Take care of yourself...…." I replied.

I was pretty sure he meant he was going AWOL, though I could technically deny "knowing". Maybe he was just going on leave and I was unaware. I had plausible deniability. And I hoped Spaceboy could find the answers he was looking for. As I thought about the type of discharge they would ultimately give Spaceboy, I got angry. He had served about 75% of his enlistment and had served in his country in combat. He was wounded in a way that they couldn't treat and left to find his own treatment. It didn't seem fair that he would be given anything less than an honorable discharge. I hoped that something would happen and he would be helped and given an honorable discharge, but I was pretty sure that isn't how things would play out.

"I was pissed off about Spaceboy for going AWOL……. But, I wish I could find that little bastard and give him a hug." Interview with Spc. Rick Beem, A co. 1/87 Infantry, 1ˢᵗ platoon SAW gunner, December 2015.

We received letters from Spaceboy for the next year, asking the commander to forward his mail. Apparently he was clueless about going AWOL and then telling the military where, exactly, you are AWOL at. Might as well end each letter with "PS – send some MP's to come get me whenever you're ready!"

For his time in Somalia, Spaceboy did his job and looked out for us while we looked out for him. He was a good soldier and he never let me down as my assistant gunner. Though I will always feel that I somehow failed him in return.

Christopher Grish (on the left) and I with Spaceboy on our shoulders during hurricane Andrew relief in Florida, 1992.

Michael Jackson is Gay

Before telling you about this incident, let me first be clear that I have nothing against Michael Jackson or gay people, nor is another human being's sexual orientation anything that I have ever concerned myself with caring about. As a teenager, I listened to Michael Jackson quite a bit. I guess. As it turns out, everyone in Somalia listened to Michael Jackson. I would venture to say that in Somalia, Michael Jackson was second in popularity only to the prophet Mohammed and Allah himself. Insulting someone's religious beliefs is definitely something that is off limits to me. However, insulting their taste in music? Well, I think that is something that can be insulted, torn up and burned without boundary. Especially when it's 130 degrees outside, its noon, and you're

173

wearing body armor, Kevlar, carrying a weapon and you're really, really bored. And your target of insult is a volatile crowd of hostile and potentially dangerous people in another country. And honestly.......maybe I snapped a little.... for my own amusement. And I would love to tell you about it.

This incident took place at the port of Merca, in the lower Shabelle province of Somalia. I have no idea what the date was. All I know is it was hot, I was really tired, I was bored, and a crowd had begun to amass at the gate leading to the port. The gate I was guarding on this fine day, which is what we did during our "downtime", the time when we weren't doing Air Assaults, raids or ambushes. We would guard things. I had always heard that the man that measured the pyramids, Sir William Matthew Flinders Petrie, was able to do so by wearing a tutu so the locals would think he was insane and wouldn't stone him to death. I have no idea if that is historical fact, or if I risked my life believing something that wasn't true. But after three days without sleep, I was pretty sure it must be historical fact.

As Steve Mangold and I manned our post and the afternoon sun grew to its highest point in the sky, workers toiled to unload shipments of rice, oil and other goods from a large boat out in the harbor. Doc Cooke from 2nd platoon came by as a small crowd had started to gather, a crowd of maybe forty people, when a young man in the crowd tried to strike up a conversation with me by exclaiming "Michael Jackson!!!!" and pumping his arm in the air, then asking me "You like Michael Jackson?"

"Michael Jackson?" I asked. "Michael Jackson is gay!" I exclaimed as I performed the internationally recognized gesture for a blowjob in every imaginable angle to make sure he understood what I was saying.

"NO! Michael Jackson NO gay!" he screamed frantically, waiving his finger in my face.

"Oh yeah, he sucks dick!" I replied, continuing my crude gestures as more people in the crowd began to concentrate in our immediate vicinity, their grumblings becoming increasingly noticeable.

Mangold looked over at me as he took a puff from his cigarette, a mischievous smile on his face, slightly shaking his head as he smirked and exhaled, turning his head back out toward the crowd as he leaned up against a shipping container. He was relaxed and cool, as though he was hanging out on a street corner back home in California, a smile on his face. The look he gave me was almost as though he knew what was coming, though I doubt for a minute anyone could have predicted how this day would play out. It was also a look of approval, almost saying "Yeah, I'm pretty bored, too. Entertain me."

Doc Cooke gleefully helped fuel the fire by echoing my sentiments about Michael Jackson. After about 10 minutes or so of dick sucking gestures and back and forth screaming about whether or not Michael Jackson was in fact gay, the crowd had become increasingly agitated and had now tripled in size. And they were getting closer to us. Almost like we were being boxed in as we sat there smiling, smoking our cigarettes and performing simulated fellatio en masse. Their discontent began growing exponentially with each gulp, slurp and stroke of a gigantic air-cock. The group closest to me was furiously pumping their fists and repeating "No! Michael Jackson NO gay! No suck dick!"

"Hey, Slane......I think this is about to get a little out of hand, dude...." Mangold chuckled, still smiling, though maybe through a hint of growing apprehension.

Mangold then charged his weapon, which made the crowd closest to him jump back and become startled. Things quieted down for all of about 2 seconds, and then got even louder. The startled people becoming more and more furiously animated, the look in their eyes was pure hatred. I had defiled what they apparently held most sacred, second only to The Prophet Mohammed himself. Some in the crowd tried to reason with me through pleas of broken

English, begging me to recant. "Sticks and stones may break my bones"…. and these mother fuckers were looking for both…..and they wanted to do more than just break my bones.

I slurped away. Stroking and gulping. Holding firm, as it were, to my claim that Michael Jackson does, in fact, suck dick. And he likes it. And just when I thought things couldn't possibly get more heated, one of the people in the crowd grabbed my arm. I quickly pulled out my 9MM and pointed it at him, the crowd moving back just a little, but not seeming very much calmer. In fact, they seemed like they might be getting even angrier with each passing second. What I did next was only previously known by a handful of people, all of whom were very close to me. Only people in my inner circle, so to speak. But there really is no way around telling this story to the entire world, and it is a story I think worthy of telling, and not divulge the fact that did something completely and utterly…..insane. I am sure many of already think what I've described thus far is insane. But you never really know how insane a person can actually get without pushing the envelope. As if I hadn't already done that to this point.

I was pointing and waiving my 9MM, demanding people to step back and calm down, while simultaneously holding to my initial statements about Michael Jackson and his oral love of all things phallic, and shit was out of hand. Suddenly, like Cleavon Little in his famous scene from Blazing Saddles, I charged my pistol and quickly swung it up to my own head, exclaiming "Nobody move!!! Back up! Shut the fuck up!" I looked over at Mangold. He smiled and relaxed a little.

"No! No! No!" begged one man directly in front of me.

"Don't fucking move or I'll do it!" I shouted, and being as animated as possible.

"Do not do this!" another pleaded.

At this point I pulled the thumb safety on the 9MM, which when cocked causes the hammer to slam forward, as though I had pulled the trigger.

"CLICK!!!!" as the crowd gasped and ducked.

"NOOOOOO!" many protested as they ducked down to avoid the inevitable infidel brain mass they were allegedly nearly splattered with.

"What the fuck!" I said, acting confused and examining the pistol for the reason for its malfunction before charging it again and returning it to my head.

The crowd pleaded for my safety. They begged me not to do it. Just three minutes ago they were ready to tear me apart with their bare hands and scatter my remains across their city. Now, they pleaded for my life as it rested in the hands of a madman. Me.

After several minutes, I was talked down. Dissuaded from harming .... myself. A unanimous sigh of relief could almost be heard coming from the more than one hundred defenders of Michael Jackson and his manliness. Several of those closest to me in the crowd were visibly relieved, expressing their gratitude at my decision to let myself live. Until, that is, I restated my original claim.

"Michael Jackson IS gay! Michael Jackson sucks cock!" I quietly said to those who were comforting me.

"NO! NO! NO! Michael Jackson NO gay! No suck cock!" they replied.

Again, I cocked my 9MM and held it to my head. The crowd gasped and backed up, the pleadings for my life began anew. I shouted the same demands for the crowd to calm down and back up. And again I pulled the thumb safety, causing the same reaction as before. "CLICK!!!!"

Mangold was quietly laughing, though maybe a little disturbed and a little worried for both of us. The situation repeated itself a few times, though I don't recall exactly how many.

An older man, maybe in his 30's which would make him an elder in a country where people don't live past their forties, approached from the crowd and pleaded with me in broken English, for some time.

"You must not do this thing." He said calmly.

"But, Michael Jackson....he's gay. He really does suck dick." I said quietly back.

"No, my friend. No gay." He said quietly.

After a few minutes of calm talking, during which the crowd was almost reverent it was so quiet, I holstered my sidearm and expressed gratitude to the man and a few of the people closest to me, and waived to the now dissipating crowd. Shocked and amazed at what they had witnessed. Maybe Michael Jackson is gay? Fuck no. He is not gay. And if you say he is gay? They will kill you. That is, unless you or someone else tries to kill you. At which point, they will intervene and plead to save your life. For me, it proved two things: 1) I actually might be crazy. Or at least, I am very convincing at being crazy. 2) I had always heard that Muslims extremists, though they might rape your goat and kill a random infidel for fun, will not harm a crazy person.

This incident highlighted how absolutely overworked we were, how totally deprived of sleep. And how giving us guard duty when we weren't actively out on missions, really did nothing for this lack of sleep. I had also been keeping lots of company with Sgt. Jesus Christ. No, that's not his real name of course. But he really thought he was Jesus and that I was the mercenary version of the Apostle John. He had gone through the trouble of recruiting 12 disciples from amongst the members of our unit. No one understood how he was still here in Africa with us. It seems only me and the rest of the disciples, along with anyone else he spent five seconds talking to in the company, knew how absolutely out of touch with reality Sgt. Jesus was. As you read, Walking with Jesus is a story of faith, insanity and the emotional toll that a combat environment can exact from a soldier. His real name isn't important because I have no interest in embarrassing him or causing him unwanted attention. I don't believe its fault that he lost his marbles and hopefully by now, he found them all and is able to read this and laugh about it.

Lieutenants

I have had good lieutenants and I have had bad ones. Most were good. Nothing is more annoying than a bad one. Lt. Scott Walker, our FO (Forward Observer – for artillery and air support), was a great lieutenant, though he was only attached to us rather than being our platoon leader. He was a Ranger from Kentucky and like me, had played football in college. He was in charge when the situation dictated, and just one of the guys when it was time to fuck off. He was a 1st Lt. so I can't say for sure if he ever acted like some of the 2nd Lt.'s who walked around over compensating for their lack of large genitals and experience by over-exercising their authority as officers. Lt. Kreyling, a platoon leader of mine later in my military career, was another example of a Lt. Walker type. He didn't just demand and expect respect, he earned it. And he listened to his NCO's (Non-commissioned officers: Sergeants and corporals).

Lieutenant Al Toon, a temporary attachment to our platoon for a short period, was not a great lieutenant. He reminded me of a lieutenant who had stopped a group of us at the Merca base and yelled at us for not saluting.

"Why the hell didn't you salute me?" he screamed.

"Sniper check, sir!" one of us said as we all saluted with glee.

He then turned about 18 shades of red and hobbled away angrily. Our response was not original or unique. We didn't invent the sniper check. I believe the sniper check is as old a tradition as 2nd lieutenants in the US Army itself. Dating back to at least 1775. We had just carried on the then 218-year tradition with pride. Saluting in a combat zone is a no-no. I'll let you figure out why this is funny if it's not immediately clear to you.

While pulling a two-day rotation guarding the port at Merca, Earl (Rick Beem) was having an exciting time with our local Somali police force in the wee hours of the morning, at around 2 AM. His position was down on the beach, which was relaxing because there was an ocean to look at and a gentle and ever constant 60 knot wind. (Seriously, the wind near the coast at Merca was always like 20 knots)

As Earl pulled his watch this night, shots rang out down the beach. Quickly he readied his saw and scanned the direction of fire. He radioed the platoon CP where Lt. Al Toon was manning the radio. No response. More shots rang out, sand flying in his face. They were getting closer but he couldn't quite pinpoint the origin of the shots. He again radioed for help.

After Earl had had enough sand flung in his face from rounds hitting so close, he IMT'd (crawled and ran in a tactical manner) from his position, and kept maneuvering toward the direction of fire. As he got closer to what would be the front gate of the port, he noticed the local police chief and several of his men firing down in the direction where Earl had just come from. Again he radioed. Again no response. Earl looked back at where he had come from, trying to determine if maybe he was missing something. Was someone down on the beach near his position and these guys just saved his life? After a few minutes Earl realized that these guys were high, probably on Khat (a narcotic), and shooting at shadows on the beach. He maneuvered close enough to grab the police chief, manhandling him like only a good ole boy from Iowa could.

Earl held the police chief out in front of him and made his way back toward the platoon CP, still not sure what was going on. Were these guys turning on us and actually trying to kill him? He wasn't taking any chances. As Earl came around a corner, a Somali armed with an AK-47 popped out in front of him. And as quickly as he had popped out, he disappeared, hitting the ground HARD thanks to all those vitamins one gets from growing up in the "corn belt" of America. Even more impressive as that Earl, now using the police chief as a human shield of sorts, didn't miss a step and didn't let go of his new friend.

180

After arriving at the platoon CP, Earl was more than just a little dismayed to see Lt. Toon fast asleep, the radio in his hand and up against his cheek as though he was on duty. What happened next is not something that anyone can admit to openly. Not Earl and not Lt. Toon. Earl released his prisoner and proceeded to choking the Lieutenant after he woke up and gave Earl the wrong answer as to why he hadn't answered the radio.

"You know you wrong, Beem!" Lt. Toon pleaded as Earl choked the living shit out of him.

"I might be wrong, but you're fucking wrong, too!" Earl replied.

"You're wrong, Beem, you're wrong! And I'm wrong, too!" Lt. Toon reasoned.

Earl released his pray, his adrenaline still rushing. He had just spent the last 20 minutes dodging bullets, calling over the radio for help, taking a prisoner, and beating a man with his own gun. Not to mention giving the Lt. a lesson in "Buddy Fucking". That's one thing that is not tolerated in a combat zone, by anyone. It doesn't matter if you are the lowest private, or a colonel. You fuck your buddy and chances are he's gonna fuck you back. Hard. Sleeping on guard or radio watch is buddy fucking to the nth degree.

The Lt. didn't try and impose any punishment on Earl, and Earl being in a bit of a pickle for choking the Lt., didn't report the Lt. to the commander. It was a good ole fashioned stalemate. However, in my opinion, Earl won. He choked a platoon leader (who deserved it) and walked away with his rank and his dignity. And Lt. Toon probably a lot more respect for Iowan corn fed Earls.

One side effect of choking the Lt., however, was Earl being harassed by the chaplain.

"You have family back at home, son?" the chaplain would ask Earl, trying to see if this Lt. choker was stable.

The incident highlighted a serious problem with the local police. Whose side were they on? Why the hell were they shooting at Earl? Or was it just drug fueled shooting? If they ever did shoot at a legitimate target (other than us), they certainly never coordinated it with anyone.

A couple of days after the band aid incident, Doc was on top of a shipping container, or connex as we called them, down at the port in Merca, standing tall and letting all the snipers in the area know he was there (by default because he was standing on top of a giant box in the open) when some local fuckhead apparently decided Estes should die today. So, they did what every brave man would do; they sent a child up to Estes with a grenade.

"CLUNK! CLUNK!" followed by "GRENADE!!!" as Doc Estes flew off the top of the connex, landing face first in the dirt, the grenade still on top of the connex.

The child then began running away quickly, right out in the open, when the person next to me (I honestly don't remember who it was) raised their rifle as though they were going to shoot him. I instinctively hit his rifle upward, not knowing if he actually intended to shoot the child or not. None of us took cover and wouldn't technically need to since grenades explode up and out and we were at the base of an 8 foot connex. After a few seconds had passed, it was apparent that this grenade wasn't going to explode. Estes had huffed sand for the last 5 or so seconds without any wounds other than his pride, so we decided to begin chuckling. Ok, you're right. Grunts don't chuckle, they fucking laugh their a$$es off. Especially in situations that are uncomfortable and even more so once we found that the grenade still had its pin snuggly and safely in place. In other words, it wasn't armed.

"Fuck you guys" his famous response to us as he chuckled nervously.

"Dude......that was awesome!" Mangold (I think) said.

Since no one was hurt, we now had yet another prize of a story we could tuck away for when we might need a laugh the most. I offered Doc a smoke and a smile, and we went about our business. Nothing was off limits when it came to laughing in this shithole of a country. And no one was beyond getting picked on.

We all genuinely loved Estes and we all genuinely flipped each other shit and we all bitched and moaned and crossed several lines with each other at times, so, I really am not trying to pick on Doc Estes. He earned his shit just like the rest of us, and he deserves it. However, this is my fucking book. If he wants to write his own and explain himself, then he's free to do so. I owe you $20, Doc. I imagine with 22 years of interest, it might be a lot more.

One night at the port while manning a machine gun position with SSG. Ferriero, we decided to make some International Foods Swiss Mocha that my mother had mailed from home. Our position sat right on top of a connex and was built up heavily with sandbags. We were able to shield the light from my stove long enough to boil a couple of canteen cups of water and mix our coffee.

"Mmmmmmm, that shit's good…..." SSG. Ferriero said as he took a sip. "Sllllluurrrrp"

"Yeah, I love this shit." I replied.

Our International Coffee moment ("Celebrate the moments of your life") was soon interrupted by several bursts of gunfire from at least two separate positions on the beach in front of us. One position up near the city, and one down by the water. I could see at least 5 distinct muzzle flashes. I quickly manned the 60 and traversed the beach, picking out my potential targets.

"Should I open up?" I asked.

"Sssssllllluuurrrrp. Nah. I can't tell who is who. Sssssllllllllrrrrrppp. Might be friendlies down there. Sssssllllluuurrrrp. Let's finish our coffee. They'll be fewer of them when we're done." SSG Ferriero said.

"Sssssllllluuurrrrp. Ok." I replied, relaxing the M60 and picking my coffee back up.

As I sat and contemplated what was happening before my very eyes, I came to the conclusion the SSG. Ferriero was indeed a wise mother fucker. He's right. There will be fewer of them once we're done with this delicious fucking coffee. This truly was an International Foods Coffee moment. And we were definitely celebrating the extraordinary moments of our lives. Besides, why shoot a whole bunch of people when you can just let them shoot each other first? After checking on the radio, there were no friendlies outside the wire near us, so, they were all Somalis, shooting each other on the beach. The only thing missing from this scene was a fucking soundtrack. "Staying Alive" by the Bee Gees might have fit.

Because of the ever changing rules of engagement, all we could do at this point is report the incident and wait for the QRF. We couldn't return fire because they weren't shooting at us and we weren't sure if our own troops were involved. The only thing I'll add in finishing this chapter is that the coffee was absolutely superb.

Best fucking cup of joe I've ever had.

Bloodtrails

Most people, including people who served in Somalia, are only familiar with combat in and around the city of Mogadishu, which is a main source of motivation for my writing this book. Furthermore, most people, excluding the aforementioned who served in Somalia, see Somalia as a single combat or war-type incident; "Black Hawk Down". I want to correct the version of history as "someone" saw fit to present to the public while also vindicating, if you will, thousands of my brothers and sisters who served in Somalia as members of the Army, Air Force, Marines and Navy.

While no engagement can match the duration, size, ferocity or valor of the battle on October 3rd and 4th 1993, Somalia was a dangerous place where our military was continuously engaged in combat with "enemy" forces. Though we really weren't sure who, exactly, our enemy was. At a time and in a place where the press wasn't regularly, if ever, embedded with American forces, the only people who can set the story straight are those of us who served there.

Enter two opposing warlords you know nothing about, in a city you've never heard of; Col. Ahmed Omar Jess who was aligned with Aidid's Somali National Alliance (SNA), and General Mohammed Said Hersi Morgan, head of the Somali National Front (SNF), who battled each other for control in the southern port city of Kismayo, Somalia. Both of these men were responsible for the deaths of hundreds of thousands of Somalis through outright genocide, forced starvation and armed conflict. In my mind, the two men represented everything as to why we were in Somalia. On and off in February of 1993 through March 1993, we fought them in and around Kismayo where TF 3-14 and Belgian forces were situated.

Prior to our arrival in 1992, General Morgan, locally known as the "Butcher of Hargeisa" for atrocities he had committed there, commanded a force of approximately 54,000 fighters. Morgan and Jess both where originally part of the Somali Patriotic Movement (SPM) until the SPM split along clan lines. Morgan's group supported the old establishment and Jess supported Aidid. While Aidid was focused on Mogadishu, Jess and Morgan were focused on carving out their own piece of the pie in the south, using Kismayo as a capital.

The operation, dubbed Condor Titan, occurred from 24 February to 15 March and is described in the combat action log as "Stabilization Operations as part of QRF" (Quick Reaction Force). The combat action log lists the task organization (units present) as BN Control, A 1/87, A 2/87, B 2/87 and TM

Hawk with the duration of contact described as "Continuous" and the type of fire received as "Automatic rifle, grenade and pistol". While there was no single, definitive battle, Kismayo was a nonstop shooting gallery. While my platoon had already been conducting several ambushes southwest of Merca and Barawe that were aimed at disrupting the return of the guerrilla fighters of the two factions as well as the flow of weapons, the most dangerous operations occurred within the city itself. To give you an idea of how much of a hellhole Kismayo was at this point, just looking at two pages of logs for the 3-week operation, there are about 20 entries of contact, some containing as many as 3 separate events. A book could probably be written on this engagement alone, so I will try and summarize as best I can in a way that will convey just how much was going on in Kismayo while also "representing" all of the companies involved.

As previously discussed, A Co 1-87's Spc. Rick "Earl" Beem had been getting treatment for Dengue fever in Mogadishu when he was flown straight into Kismayo to be reunited with our company and platoon. It truly was a "Welcome BACK to Somalia" in the harshest way after spending 10 days watching top pentagon brass fly to and from Somalia to earn credit for having been in theater. He flew to Baledogle first, then to Kismayo with Canadian and New Zealand soldiers. Arriving with no helmet, weapons or protective gear of any kind, he was a bit out of place and underdressed.

Kismayo was a city at war and our forces (and the Belgians) were just third and fourth parties being thrown into the mix, giving the warring clans a common enemy. Because we were "neutral", our operations were aimed at stopping both sides. In the city, this meant cordon and search operations as well as roadblocks/checkpoints on the main routes leading to the city. As our QRF started cordon and search operations, some of the militia fighters had left the city and were gathered in an extremely large group when Smith and the rest of the scouts arrived just outside Kismayo. When the group spotted the scouts, a large crowd started toward them while a couple of the militia were busy mounting a .50 caliber machine gun. As the scouts pulled back toward the bush, they began taking fire from the .50 cal. Though it was a few hundred meters away, the .50 cal is devastating at any range against both troops and vehicles. The scouts returned fire and ultimately broke contact, which was a smart move. Our Cobra attack helicopters made short work of the .50 cal mounted vehicles, destroying six in all (I believe).

In the city on the first day at around 1023 hours (10:23 AM), A CO. 1-87 took fire from several buildings and alleyways across from OP3. After a brief firefight, they militiamen broke contact and took to the streets where they couldn't be immediately located having blended into the crowds as they typically preferred to do. In other words, they were complete chicken shits once bullets started flying back their way. No problem, they would eventually run out of places to run and blend in as the task force tightened its noose around the city by sweeping it a section at a time. Later that evening at 2045 hours (8:45 PM), E-87 took and returned fire at OP1. The rounds originated in the Belgian sector and though no one was injured, their vehicles were struck. Approximately two hours later, the BN TAC (command element) came under attack near a mosque and subsequently engaged in a firefight for approximately 20 minutes during which one militiaman was wounded, and the rest escaped.

At 1131 hours the next morning, A CO 2-87 was unexpectedly caught in the crossfire of opposing militia and immediately engaged. As the action was punctuated by several grenade explosions, the A Co soldiers fired and maneuvered toward the enemy positions when they then took and returned fire from several sniper positions. The snipers immediately broke contact and withdrew amidst several grenade explosions. Five or six minutes into the fight, the Belgians came in on A Co's flank and joined in the fight, as E-87 also joined from the south. One Belgian soldier was wounded in the fighting as were several militiamen. Though only one of the enemy wounded was recovered, there were several blood trails leading away from the scene.

Just one minute later, B Co 2-87, who was just to the north of A Co, made contact. As the gunmen tried to break contact, B Co pursued them and immediately came under sniper fire. After the firing ceased, several locals aided B Co in locating the gunmen who had fled and after again engaging nearly a dozen of them, they were able to capture two at around 1438 hours. As the BN TAC element moved toward B Co, they began taking sniper fire from 3 distinct locations. One of their attackers lobbed a grenade, the explosion of which was buffered by a wall. As the TAC was effectively pinned down, A Co flanked the sniper positions, at which point all 3 snipers were captured. An hour and a half later, B Co again came under fire from a nearby meat factory. Alpha and Bravo Co swept the area later than night, but found nothing.

The next morning at around 0800 hours (8 AM), A Co 1-87 was targeted with several grenade attacks. In one such attack, Spc. Evans, one of the mortar-men and a fellow disciple of Jesus of Merca, had been in one of the OP's (Observation Posts), when a Somali tried to throw a grenade into the OP, through a window. The grenade was deflected by the camouflage netting the OP was covered with, which saved the lives of roughly 8 soldiers. Though they got their bells rung by the subsequent blast, no one was hurt nor were they able to stop the perpetrators of the attack as they disappeared into crowds of Somalis, making it impossible to return fire. Even the Somalis who weren't part of either militia were being aggressive towards the American and Belgian forces by rioting in the streets and throwing rocks.

In the worst of the attacks, a couple dozen Somalis were the only casualties as the militiamen continued to hurl grenades. Though our medics and soldiers did their best to help treat the wounded, there were simply too many and most were taken away in carts to a nearby hospital. At around 0845 two more grenade attacks took place against A Co 1-87. One of the attackers had his arm blown off as his grenade detonated in his hand. Though the log states that soldiers attempted to stop the bleeding I can assure you those "efforts" mostly consisted of words of encouragement.

After the Belgians then reported spotting a vehicle from which grenades were being lobbed from as it drove through the city, E-87 pursued and captured the vehicle and its occupants at around 0854 hours. At 1037 hours, TM Hawk and the BN TAC engaged in a firefight with several gunmen, capturing five in total.

After several more incidents throughout the day, at around 2050 hours, the Scout's Smith and Peterson initiated a firefight with several armed militiamen which resulted in one killed and two critically wounded, with the rest breaking contact. I believe it was here that Doc Cooke treated one of the two men for a penetrating or sucking chest wound by giving him a chest tube.

The next day, A Co 1-87 and the Belgians were interrogating approximately 23 prisoners collectively captured by noon. As they were lined up on their knees with their hands on their heads, the Belgians moved down the line trying to get information. The Somalis were being less than cooperative as usual so it was clear that some creative interrogation was about to take place. Since it was daylight, chemlight dancing was clearly out. However, our Belgian friends came up with a pretty good substitute in my opinion. They started again at the beginning of the line and when a Somali refused to answer a question, that Somali was immediately grabbed and taken around the side of a building behind the prisoners where a single shot would then ring out. To their credit, the bastards refused to talk until just three of them remained. Though I am not sure we got much useful information from them, one thing was for sure.....they sure were more than a little embarrassed and angry when they were then taken around the side of the building and saw all of their friends there. Alive and well.

After most of the battalion left Kismayo, one of the most heroic events of our time in Somalia took place when B CO 2-87 was left behind in the city. At this point, the battalion had already recorded 23 kills and probably at least 10 times that amount in wounded enemy fighters. It was then that 4 soldiers from the mortar section of B CO 2-87, were caught in a crossfire with militants, they fought their way through, killing nine and wounding several more. As this isn't a firsthand account of their actions, I can only hope to do the story enough justice to correct an overlooked incident that involved enormous valor.

As it was relayed to me, the mortar section sergeant, who was only armed with a 9mm pistol, killed the Somali nearest him and took his weapon, before continuing the fight. He then personally killed 3 or 4 more fighters, and the rest of his men killed the remaining 4 or 5. None of the Americans were wounded in the fighting. When the four made it back, a LT in their chain of command threatened to court martial for breaking the Geneva convention for having used the enemies weapon to kill them. Yep, that's actually illegal. Go figure. However, since they couldn't get medals for valor (true story) because the US government position was that they aren't at war, then the rules of the Geneva convention also don't apply. In any event, I don't think anyone would be prosecuted enforcing such a ridiculous "law".

The medals for "Operations other than war" was an issue for almost everyone who served in Somalia, most notably for those who served in the initial phase, and especially for the men I just described. This topic will have its own chapter in the prologue.

In support of Condor Titan, 1ˢᵗ platoon and A Co 1-87 also conducted several night ambushes to stop the flow of arms and militants into Kismayo and surrounding areas, something I am sure many of the companies also did. On these ambushes, our normal combat loads included something we had only ever simulated in training, and never done in combat to this point; live 60mm mortar HE rounds, one round carried by each man. Oh sure, an ambush is certainly one type of mission I would most associate with "peacekeeping" or describe as "humanitarian". For a mission described by the Clinton government as peacekeeping and "Operations other than war", it sure seemed like a fucking war to us.

Kismayo changed very little for most the three-week period until Jess and Morgan pulled back into Kenya and Ethiopia. It stayed pretty violent and bloody before the killing moved into the countryside. By this time, 3-14 infantry had returned home and the Belgians controlled the city until their withdrawal in December of the same year. As they withdrew, the fighting again commenced between Morgan and Jess, with Morgan ultimately capturing and holding the city until 1999.

In February 1993, Private David Conner of the 10th MTN Division 57 Transportation Company lost his life.

A Humanitarian Ambush

Wikipedia defines the ambush pretty well, stating: "An ambush is a long-established military tactic, in which combatants take advantage of concealment and the element of surprise to attack unsuspecting enemy combatants from concealed positions, such as among dense underbrush or behind hilltops. Ambushes have been used consistently throughout history, from ancient to modern warfare."

Peacekeeping is defined by Wikipedia as such: "Peacekeeping refers to activities that tend to create conditions that favor lasting peace. Within the United Nations group of nation-state governments and organizations, there is a general understanding that at the international level, peacekeepers monitor and observe peace processes in post-conflict areas, and may assist ex-combatants in implementing peace agreement commitments that they have undertaken. Such assistance may come in many forms, including confidence-building measures, power-sharing arrangements, electoral support, strengthening the rule of law, and economic and social development."

Last, let's define humanitarianism from the same source: "Humanitarianism is a moral of kindness, benevolence, and sympathy extended to all human beings."

While we weren't under UN control (the only US Forces that were never under UN control other than TF Ranger) and subsequently never awarded a UN Service Ribbon, our government had sold to the world that we were on a peacekeeping mission. While reading the definition of what peacekeeping entails, I fail to see any of the military operations we conducted, least of all the ambush. None of us had considered our mission in Somalia as peacekeeping, not since about the first few days in country. Likewise, our mission clearly wasn't humanitarian, though the goals of the mission were said to be humanitarian with the end result being peace.

The way we were trained to conduct ambushes required that we establish what's called a "kill zone" and then kill anyone who comes into it. Obviously being in a country involved in a civil war we couldn't just kill anyone who happened into our kill zone. Nonetheless, we participated in nearly a dozen ambushes. The goal of which was to disrupt the movement of militants and arms into the major cities. As the situation deteriorated in Kismayo, we conducted several ambushes in an attempt to quell the fighting. When you carry out an ambush, you are going to kill people, plain and simple. There's neither anything peaceful or humanitarian about it. Unless you want to consider it a form of euthanasia where we're putting poor, suffering souls out of their misery.

On this night, we were to conduct an air assault and be inserted several miles from our objective, *somewhere* in the Lower Jubba province, maybe somewhere in the lower western Shabelle. Unlike much of Somalia, the area had dense almost jungle like vegetation, and even swamps, which meant mosquitos. There were many farms and plantations in the area, similar to what you might find in Bardera. In fact, we may have been near Bardera (for the second time I believe). In preparation, we sprayed our uniforms with bug repellent that is so toxic, the uniform has to remain untouched for 48 hours. I believe we were given 24. We also learned that we would employ a new (to us while in Somalia) tactic on this mission; our mortar teams would air assault with us and set up a firebase from which they could provide indirect fire support. Mortars are extremely heavy and their ammunition weighed about 7-10 lbs per round. If memory serves, danger close for 60mm mortars is about 300 meters. Meaning, as long as we were at least 300 meters from whatever location we called for mortars to fire on, we were "safe".

Picture taken of us departing on an air assault mission.
Specialist Mcahenney and myself (right).

Our air assault mission commenced just before dusk. Have I mentioned how much a fucking love air assault missions? Everybody on an air assault mission gets a sense of "shit just got real", especially when your mission is going to be an ambush. After performing a few false insertions (the helicopters pretend to land in a few different places) to throw off anyone who might be watching, we were inserted into a clearing. Aside from goggles, wearing something to cover your nose and mouth is also a good idea unless you want to eat sand and camel shit. After clearing our LZ, we proceeded to our first checkpoint or line of departure to being our infiltration into our ambush. Due to intel that a very large caravan of camels was in the area, we had to take extra precaution while infiltrating to not be detected. Caravans of this size indicated wealth and they would likely be armed to the teeth to protect their wealth. Our fight wasn't with them so we didn't want any accidental encounters with the caravan.

The vegetation was something to behold, and it felt like it added substantially to the humidity as we walked to our ambush site. Along with my insanely heavy load, I now had a mortar round added to the weight. 7 to 10 pounds extra might not seem like much, but it sure felt like it. Especially since we walked for around 4 hours, easily covering 12 miles, probably more. My squad had won the squad competition for the 12-mile road march back in Fort Drum by completing it in 1 hour and 53 minutes with full combat load (which is considerably less weight than an *actual* full combat load I might add). Though our winning pace had been impressive considering infantry and Ranger standard was 3 hours, while the Army wide standard was 4. However, I highly doubt we were setting any records this night.

Spaceboy's back started giving him an extra bit of trouble after he lost his footing and slid down into an empty irrigation ditch through some thick brush. Corey and I nearly did the same but caught our balance. Spaceboy asked to stop several times, and nobody on the M60 teams was going to complain if he asked for a break. Though we got no real break. Several times we stopped while waiting for lone vehicle to pass by, or to check the map. Our route was a combination of breaking brush and skirting the main road.

Suddenly as we walked, word was passed back to get our mortars ready for drop off. I remember being so delirious that I didn't actually understand what was said until I got to the mortar position and someone stopped me and removed the mortar from on top of my rucksack for me, apparently able to tell I was a bit zoned out. It wasn't just the strain of the walk; it was the fact that we almost never slept. I felt like I was sleep walking, and with a car on my back no less. From this point, I believe we were within a kilometer of our ambush site.

As you might imagine, setting up an ambush is an quiet affair. You must set up near and far side security, rear security and put everyone in position without being seen, and without making a sound. My M60 was position directly in the middle of the ambush. It would be my job to initiate the festivities by opening fire first once something got into the kill zone. However, keep in mind that we're basically in someone's backyard. Civilians live all around here and to open up with the M60 and kill whoever came by would likely be a tragic mistake.

There is no talking on an ambush, no anything except stay alert and wait. As we lay in wait, the mosquitos became an extreme nuisance. Not only did I have the super-toxic shit on my uniform, I had that other super-toxic nasty shit all over my face and exposed skin. While I have no idea what's in that stuff, I know that I have skin problems on my face to this day where the area around either side of my nose dries up and gets blotchy. Something that wasn't an issue before Somalia.

Whatever these mosquitos were accustomed to eating must have been pretty nasty because the protection we had bothered them not one bit. I was repeatedly bit through my uniform, especially around the cuffs and even on the thighs, and all over my face to the point that my face got numb. At one point I remember thinking I was being bitten, but wasn't sure and put my hand on my face and felt blood running down my cheek. I heard Forde whispering something under his breath next to me. I couldn't make out what he was saying, but I could see his gold "grill" shining back at me as he smiled in the moonlight.

"Dude. Quit fucking smiling." I whispered back. "You're going to give our position away!"

He lightly laughed in response and our wait continued. It must have been 0400 hours by now (4 AM), and we hadn't spoken for many hours aside from the smallest whisper during the grill incident. Suddenly, one of the NCO's signaled back to us.

"Get ready!" SSG Ferriero said. "Someone's coming!"

I could now hear several people talking at a pretty high level and the sound of some kind of cart or something. I steading myself behind the machine gun and readied the weapon. I could feel my heart rate pick up in anticipation. The sounds moved closer and closer. I looked up and down the line to see whoever I could see. Everyone was ready for business as they entered the kill zone. I exhale. 15 more meters. 10 meters.

"STOP! HOLD YOUR FIRE!!" SGT Douglas said as he, Szulwach and Laing jumped into the road in front and to the side of the group of people behind a donkey cart having determined this likely wasn't a legitimate target. I felt a sigh of relief having had the same feeling the closer they got as I wondered what kind of a bad ass weapon could be mounted on a donkey. Though, in this country, you could never be sure.

SSG Ferriero followed quickly into the road, grabbing Hughes and Forde for additional security. Once they quickly established control of the group, they began searching the cart and people for weapons. After a few minutes, it was apparent that it was nothing more than a family. A man with three wives and a donkey cart. Pretty rich by Somali standards. But certainly not who we were sent to kill. As the group was sent on their way, we regrouped for what to do next. Technically our site was now compromised. We couldn't stay, so we picked up and moved, opting to do a recon of a nearby village. As we set up a perimeter in a wood line next to the village, we spread out as some of us walked around the houses nearest us, and the rest kept watch over the area, including a field in front of us.

Suddenly, a man appeared on the road. He started walking towards us. Everyone held completely still as he got closer and closer. I may have previously mentioned that we're good at camouflage. When the man stopped, he was no more than 3-4 meters in front of me with his "skirt" pulled down as he squatted to take a shit. I had the "best" view in the house. Or the worst, as it was.

"Oh HELL no!" someone slightly behind me whispered, followed by SGT Wasik shining as red-lens flashlight at the man which freaked him out.

"AAAAAAHHHHHHHHHHHHHHHHHH!!!!!!" the man shrieked as he darted back toward the road, tripping over his "skirt" as he ran. And probably shitting, I imagine.

"RUN, BITCH! Pull your dress up!" I quietly added as the man disappeared into the night, shrieking for what had to be a mile down the road.

After a good laugh, it was obvious that our ambush was over. Time to withdrawal for some rack time. After an hour or so of walking, we found our way into an area we could set up as a patrol base. We were still laughing about the mad shitter we had encountered just before dawn. In a place where a laugh really was the best medicine, we always seemed to find the best. And this time while we were lurking about with every intention to kill. Later that morning we linked up with other elements of the company and did a sweep of the nearby town. As I recall, nothing was found.

On the air assault back to base, we put the commander's Humvee on a sling load, just as it had been brought there for the mission. Somewhere short of our Merca base, the vehicle began oscillating, which causes drag that pulls the helicopter down; as in, to the ground, you're gonna crash. After exchanging a few brief smiles, the load was "released", sending the Humvee crashing down about 300 feet, which turned it into a toy car at best. I cannot tell you the joy that was shared among the troops in that moment, and I'm not even exactly sure why it made us happy. Feel free to guess. Our feet hurt......

A Co. 1-87 Infantry catching a ride home with a black hawk during air assault operations in the Somali bush

After being radioed by another nearby element, we moved to another area. Eventually we again set up an ambush later that night. In the morning, we exfiltrated to our extraction point, picking up a mortar round each as we passed the mortar section. After a short flight back to the Merca base, we exited the Black Hawks and struggled to make our way back to the company area. As we passed over a concrete slab near where the helicopters had landed, Mangold adjusted his rucksack in such a way that his mortar round flew from the rucksack, and bounced and skidded across the pavement.

"TINK TINK TINK" as it bumped along, stomping a foot or so in front of two communications "POG's" who appeared to be setting up a SAT-COM. The two looked at the mortar, then briefly at each other before hauling ass out of the area as Mangold walked over and picked up his rogue mortar round.

"Fucking dumb asses. It's not armed unless you hit the primer in the bottom!" he yelled as he tried to taunt them.

"What's the point, dude?" I said. "They don't know any better."

"Did you see the fucking look on their faces! HAHAHAHA!" Mangold followed up.

We laughed until we reached the company area where we realized sleep was within our grasp. After some weapons maintenance, we crashed pretty hard for the rest of the afternoon. While the mission was technically a bust as far as the military was concerned, we had a few good laughs along the way. Sometimes at night, I can still see Forde's gold teeth smiling back at me in the dark and I laugh. And, we had a real "No shit!" story we could tell forever, as I am sure that Somali is doing to this day if he is still alive. Even though we did nothing humanitarian, the only thing we technically killed on that mission was a man's most sacred time with nature. Truly, we had messed some shit up. Our first ninety days in Somalia are now behind us.

To the Soldiers of
TF CONDOR

Your performance during the last 90 days of Operation Condor Guardian has been outstanding. You are demonstrating once again the unique versatility, flexibility and discipline of well trained, highly motivated light fighters. You are the lead elements of a changed American security doctrine that seeks to change the face of fighting for liberty by defending the rights of mankind to the same sense of hope our nation enjoys.

Though we have seen much death and destruction, this is still a humanitarian mission; maintain the edge you have shown in force protection and compassion. We must continue to relate to the Somali people in a positive manner. They are not a population we subdued, they are a people we are here to save. The Somali people are tired of the suffering and look to UNITAF elements to improve the overall security situation in order to begin the long road to normalcy. We are getting a great deal of information from the Somali people on the movements and actions of the hostile forces and bandits that continue to take advantage of the helpless. While this means our operations will be more dangerous, and we will be more vulnerable, we must continue the positive interaction we have developed with the people of Marka and all of Somalia.

The ROE has not changed.

·Control your aggressive tendencies. The vast majority of the population only deserves to be treated with dignity and respect.

·Understand the tactical environment so that you are familiar with potential trouble spots. Approach with caution. Your chain of command will lead you when the potential is higher for direct hostile fire.

·Engage targets discriminately. Fire on anyone who raises a weapon or attacks you with intent to injure (knife). Fire on anyone attempting to steal a sensitive item. Detain anyone with a visible weapon and confiscate the weapon.

·Vary operations. Patrol times, start points-routes-end points, size of patrols, and method of patrol. Remember, this is a hostile situation!

·At checkpoints, show courtesy. Smile as you search. Ask the driver to show you where the weapons are and inform you if he has registration forms for the weapons. If he volunteers to show you the weapons and registers them, tell him he can return to the checkpoint when he concludes his business in MARKA and claim the weapon.

Keep up the good work. Your performance in KISMAYO was simply brilliant! As US forces withdraw, the hostile forces may grow more bold and we will surely be involved in more dangerous, direct action missions. As you correspond with your loved ones, remind them you are skilled in your tasks and will be safe. But, false hopes of a return home prior to June would be unfair to them. We may well be sent to Mogadishu once a coalition force takes over here in Marka. We continue to work hard to get home in April, but tell your loved ones the truth.

Again, you are demonstrating great Lightfighter skills, your Nation salutes you. Drive On!

CONDOR SIX

From LTC Jim Sikes, TF 2-87 Commander

An American Sniper

When I hear the word "sniper", one person instantly comes to mind; my "battle-buddy" (or battle for short) in basic training, Eric L Smith. Smith was a great soldier and a true badass, and among the finest the human beings I have ever known. I feel privileged to be his friend. As soon as we met and were made battle buddies in basic training, we realized we were twins. The resemblance is uncanny, though somehow he got caught using my ID card in basic training while trying get into the chow hall, something that still puzzles us both to this day. You can probably only tell me from Thomas due to my eyes being green. We were also the same height, weight and build and also both played football in college. We also both left college early after hearing that same patriotic call to duty. Today, we are both college graduates and also both work in IT.

When A Co 1-87 deployed with TF 2-87 to Somalia, we brought along one other 1-87 asset, our scout platoon. They can be best summarized as a battalion level "special ops" type unit. Almost everyone in the scout platoon was Ranger or Sniper qualified, many were both.

My twin and I (in the back row) at Ft. Benning GA in 1991.

In December I had been introduced to their platoon sergeant while at Baledogle as a potential candidate to become a scout, and I was genuinely excited about the prospect. I was to follow up with him once we returned state-side (though I never did). One obvious advantage I saw to being a scout is that they got higher priority in the battalion for all the best schools. Some of them had even attended SERE School (Survival, Evasion, Resistance, and Escape) which was a tough school to get (and pass). Smith had gone to Sniper School while still a private and within less than a year of being in the Army. It would be well over another year before I had the opportunity to go to Sniper School, which is a highly competitive and highly sought after school to have on one's military resume.

The scouts typically operated in small teams, sometimes as few as 2 men would compose one of their teams, especially when they were deployed on missions to act specifically as snipers. Sometimes they even worked alone. Being in a firefight, and *usually* at night in my case, many people never have actual knowledge that their bullets ever found their mark. Which is a luxury or a comfort in some ways in my opinion. A luxury never enjoyed by a sniper. He only fires when he has a target acquired in his scope, and he fires one shot, hence their motto "One Shot, One Kill", making each and every kill an entirely intimate affair. One of his main purposes in life is to harass the enemy in a way that they become demoralized, by randomly picking them off at will, while never being discovered. Another major function they have is provide an extra layer of protection for guys like me who might be on a patrol or kicking in doors, unaware of danger that may be lurking nearby. In this role, he acts as our guardians.

Many of our missions in Somalia reminded me of the stories I had read about the LRPS (Long-range reconnaissance patrols; pronounced "Lurps") in Vietnam in that we operated in such small numbers while performing air assaults, reconnaissance missions and ambushes, and the way we lived day to day was also very similar. In the dirt.

Many times we would break down into teams of 8 men or less during missions. With the scout platoon, this was even more true and applied to almost every mission they did, with very few exceptions. Occasionally they would patrol in the streets like the rest of us might do, but usually they were in concealed positions as snipers or doing reconnaissance. Also, their engagements were usually more equally matched than our typical engagements seeing how there were probably never more than four of them operating together at any given time. At this time in Somalia, *most* engagements were with 5 or fewer Somalis at any given time.

On one particularly dark night in March in the Lower Shabelle region of Somalia, outside one of the smaller towns in proximity to Merca, Smith had laid in wait for hours alone in a well concealed sniper position. He wasn't far from where I had been during the events of "The Gift", but the circumstances and outcome of his mission would be much different. He was monitoring the area for guerrilla or militant clan activity when he suddenly acquired a target. As previously stated, the night vision of the day wasn't particularly clear, and like I had done in "The Gift", he took his time and studied his target cautiously.

Once he was sure his target was armed, he prepared to take the shot. He steadied his breathing as he dialed in on his target and began to apply steady pressure to the trigger. When properly done, it should almost be a surprise to the shooter when the weapon discharges. At this point, as romantic as it might have sounded to say that in this moment he pondered the weight of taking a human life, it just simply isn't true. Having a legitimate and identifiable target, training takes over and you do what you're trained to do as though it was second nature. Because it is.

At the instant the shot rang out, his target being just over 100 meters (the approximate length of a football field), the armed man fell instantly in the dark. It was a headshot. But, before moving an inch, Smith radioed in a brief sitrep to higher and reported the action, and then scanned the area for some time to ensure there weren't more targets. Being alone, he'd have been foolish to have gone anywhere away from his position.

After a brief wait of about fifteen minutes it seemed clear. Just then, a Humvee which had been hastily racing to the scene, pulled over on the road near well his target had fallen, where it then stopped. Several soldiers got out and then secured the immediate area as Smith made his way toward the Humvee.

The officer in charge walked over with Smith to examine the body when he realized his target may not have been armed.

"Are you sure he was armed? I don't see a weapon. Did someone take it?" the officer in charge inquired.

"No, sir, no one has gone anywhere near the body until just now. Yes, sir, I'm positive he was armed." Smith replied.

The officer continued to ramble on until Smith himself began to doubt that the man had been armed and that he may have made a mistake.

"Hold on" the officer said as he walked quickly back toward his Humvee and dug around in the back for a minute. He then returned with an AK-47 and positioned it near the body.

"I've got you covered, son." The officer said.

At this point, Smith was thoroughly confused at what was going on. Before any more discussion could take place, another Humvee pulled up that carried this officer's superior. He began to get the details from Smith and the group about exactly what had transpired. Since it was clearly evident that it had been a headshot, and that the man had been armed (due to the AK-47 lying next to him), the new ranking officer on site offered Smith his congratulations on a job well done and then ordered that the body be turned over onto its back.

"Let's roll this body over" he told a couple of the soldiers nearby.

As they rolled the body over everyone was more than a little surprised to see yet another weapon which had been lying under the dead man.

"This man had two weapons?" the ranking officer asked if Smith.

Being in an even more awkward position at this point and not wanting to lie, Smith just sort of shrugged his shoulders and stared in silence as they continued to examine the scene. The first officer on the scene who had placed the weapon was the same officer that had previously ordered a group of us to hang the bodies of three dead Somalis up to serve as a warning. I had also later learned that it had been this same officer that had created so much tension during the events described in "The Gift", and why I had to repeatedly refuse to take a shot on unarmed civilians, while he remained adamant that at least one of them had been armed and therefore persisted with my commander that I take the shot. Now he's placing weapons by bodies where he believed the deceased had been killed by mistake. I see a pattern, and one that I don't like, and one that Smith was deeply troubled by as well.

Having done his job and done it well, Smith returned to Merca where we discussed the event in great detail. A few days later, a formation was called and he was awarded The Army Achievement Medal, a medal at the time normally given in training or while garrison stateside. Certainly not a wartime medal at the time, and something we joked about. Given the amount of danger he was in while sitting there alone all night in a combat zone, taking that shot and remaining calm and collected, and oh, for having INTEGRITY, I would say that AAM felt more like a slap in the face than it did an award.

Real soldiers don't do anything with the idea that they will be earning a medal. Medals are never a motivation for one's actions. People who are motivated by the prospect of medals don't belong in the military in my opinion. However, giving an inappropriate medal to recognize what a soldier has done, or failing to recognize a soldier at all, demoralizes a soldier. Smith never voiced an opinion one way or the other about receiving a lowly AAM. But I voiced mine when he told me that he was getting one, and he laughed at my comments, so I know he thought it was silly as well. In my opinion, the act itself was probably best suited as a bullet point in a long list of bullet points for a higher award, and one that was a "wartime" award rather than a training award, that encompassed his service and achievements in Somalia.

That's Life

SFC Robert Deeks, a green beret, was killed on 4 March 1993.

A short time after in March of 1993, we caught a 15-year-old Somali boy sneaking through the wire at the Merca base. I say boy, but being armed with a sterling assault rifle, he was in a man's world, and a dangerous one at that. And he was lucky to be taken alive.

As the morning transpired, I loaded our captive in the back of a Humvee as we prepared to do a rotation at the port. The makeshift jail at the port that was run by our local security force was to become his new home. Curious as to what the hell this kid was thinking, I asked the interpreter to communicate between us for me.

"Mohammed, ask this fuck why he was carrying a rifle and sneaking into our base." I told the interpreter, and he complied but got no answer.

"Tell him to answer the question!" I said, making a fist at him, angry that this kid had risked his life, and ours, by his actions.

Suddenly, a woman on the side of the Humvee began crying loudly and holding her face.

"What's her problem?" I asked Mohammed.

"She is his mother…." He said, after asking the woman what was wrong.

It was enough to quiet me down into quiet contemplation. I felt bad for making the woman so upset, if I had contributed to it at all. I told Mohammed to tell her that her son would be ok, and not to worry. I didn't know that I was telling her a lie.

When we got to the port and were unloading him, Tom Corey was in the Humvee helping the prisoner down, and I was on the ground, assisting him out of the back, when he fell. Though I partially caught him, it was still enough to draw a rebuke from SGT Laing about safeguarding prisoners. I told him that it was an accident, but agreed that he was right. And he was. Unlike the people we were fighting, hurting prisoners is neither something I do, nor the Army does. I brushed him off and smiled at him, trying to let him know everything would be fine. That would be the second misleading thing I did that day.

We walked him over to the jail and gave him to our Merca police force, and they led him over and introduced him to his new home. Though I don't technically know what the process was, I assume that even though we caught him breaching our wire while armed, that he would be tried under local law. In other words, he wasn't a prisoner of war, and I technically was a policeman as far as international law was concerned. The technical term is "Operations other than war", which is just a clever way politicians found to send troops to war under the banner of the UN, though we didn't answer to them, nor do we have UN medals. We had no idea that was the term used to describe our presence there. What was clear to us is that we were in combat, therefore, the only operation we were involved in was war. The political distinction kept us from proper recognition for our service in Somalia, including a campaign streamer on the Army colors, right up unto the writing of this book. And it partially continues to this day, a topic for later discussion.

SGT Laing in Merca

As the day continued on, I remember the people not on guard doing maintenance, writing letters, doing personal hygiene and messing around in general. SPC Adams, a member of our Scout/AT platoon came into our sleeping area with a surprise; a hedgehog. Quite an interesting creature and something that provided us some distraction for a while. I'm not sure how he caught it, but it was pretty cool. Adams was a quiet guy and reminded me of a granola of sorts. A warrior for sure, but one with a dash of hippy, albeit one that would kill you if need be.

Spaceboy was quite interested in the hedgehog and spent some time trying to hold and a pet it. As much as the guy irritated me at times, I was genuinely glad to see him smile about something. Anything. And it was something he could get lost in for a bit without anyone noticing he was lost; unlike almost any other time for him there.

CPL Jason Adams and Spaceboy with a hedgehog.

Even I spent some time admiring the hedgehog. As I remember, though they look prickly, they are actually kind of soft. Quite different from all the other exotic animals I'd seen in this country to this point. It didn't appear to have the means of killing me.

Around this same time, I found a couple of other guys playing with a snake, poking it with a stick, and laughing. Curious about what the commotion was all about, I went over to have a look.

"What's so funny?" I asked.

"Check out this little snake!" Chico said.

"Little fucker is mean for a garter snake!" Hughes said.

"You guys are fucking idiots." I told the pair.

"Why?" one of them asked.

"That's a fucking asp!" I informed them.

"What the hell is that?" Hughes asked.

"Only one of the deadliest snakes in the world. They call it a 3 step. It bites, you, you take 3 steps, and you're dead." I told them, kind of excited by this point and lying out of my ass (It was a burrowing asp I think. Not quite that deadly, though they can be quite toxic and even fatal in rare cases).

"Holy shit!" Chico said as he threw the stick and jumped back.

I went about my business mildly amused with myself. But, shit. It's Africa. Playing with random snakes isn't wise. And it actually was a poisonous snake, just not quite as bad as I made it out to be.

Life in Somalia was improving quite a bit in some respects. At the port, we now had a tent and hot chow was brought to us every night, as well as to the checkpoint. The only complaint there is the cooks seemed to bring us the same fucking meal every day, Chicken cacciatore. A dish that I will not eat to this day. I don't care if it's a five-star restaurant, I won't touch it. That may be my perception of the food, but it's probably mostly dead on. While the cooks kept the "good" food for themselves back at the base (apparently) and brought us this crap, we'd wait for them to unload it and steal the huge cans of fruit off the back that they carried, though mysteriously never gave us.

I didn't eat MRE's at all at this point, relying on shipments from home containing ramen, cheese wiz, crackers, coffee, cigarettes, and various canned foods. Apparently my mom thought "light" infantry meant I didn't have to carry much so canned food would be appropriate. Her first shipment was two 75lb boxes of food containing can upon can of things like ravioli. Fuck my life.

Spaceboy eating hot chow. He had that look on his face for the whole last half of the deployment.

However, it was worth the extra weight to my already insane load. If we were going out on ambushes, I'd take just enough canned food and ravioli to last the 2 – 3 days, knowing my load would be much lighter during our exfiltration. Bonus.

After we left the port this time, we were sent out on what was supposed to be a high profile ambush. Weapons were being brought in to the country, as our scouts had actually captured a plane load of them, and we were sent out to sit in an ambush for three days. Intel was allegedly high that the weapons would be transported down a particular road and we would be waiting for them.

Our platoon was airlifted by black hawk quite a ways from our base. I have no idea exactly where to. As was typical, we performed an infiltration through the bush, staying off the main road, finally identifying our objective, and setting up a patrol base in the scrub. The area here was thickly covered in thorn bushes and other beautiful and pleasant plants with not a human dwelling anywhere in sight. After the leaders identified our objective during a leader's reconnaissance, we quietly moved through the bush and into position overlooking a road which was our objective. Now we wait, not knowing when our friends might happen by.

As the sun began to make itself known over the horizon, but not quite risen, we quietly withdrew from our ambush site and made our way back to our patrol base, several hundred meters away. The patrol base was totally isolated from the world. There was no way anyone would be able to spot us. After having been awake all night, we set up hooches and prepared to catch some sleep after the NCO's made up the guard roster. Except, it was unimaginably hot.

It was so hot that sleeping seemed impossible. I got up several times and examined my hooch, looking for ways to improve my shade, or anything that might make me more comfortable. Nothing I did worked. The issue wasn't just the shade itself, it's that it was so hot and there was absolutely no breeze whatsoever. Some people managed to sleep, though I have no idea how.

Unable to sleep, I sat up and made myself some coffee and ate. Talked a little, though we weren't loud by any stretch of the imagination. We exercise stealth and silence in the patrol base as though we were expecting someone to happen upon us at any time. Which is completely possible. Especially if someone in the general area would have heard a bunch of talking and grab-assing. Instead, talking was at a minimum, and people generally whispered or talked pretty quietly. I think Chico and Hughes might have played spades, while most everyone else kept to themselves with little exception.

The day seemed to last forever but finally it was getting dark. Between dusk and total darkness, I thought I'd catch a few winks because by now, I have been awake for around 36 hours. Nope, time to gear up and get ready to move out.

We quietly crept back into position and waited for our prey once again. And again, with the same result. We repeated everything I just described one more time. Except on the third morning before the sun was completely up, the leaders did a recon a bit further down the road in both directions. I'm not sure exactly how far they went, but they were pretty pissed off when they got back, especially after comparing notes. Apparently the road was completely washed out within a click (kilometer) in each direction of our objective, something that really makes one question the term "intelligence" when referring to "military intelligence". What a cluster fuck. And I was so damn tired and angry by this point, I was about to start yelling.

So after not seeing another living thing other than snakes, spiders, millipedes and scorpions for three days, we exfiltrated to our extraction point, grumbling the entire way. Yep, we could have just as easily walked on the road the entire way in like a bunch of clowns and found out for ourselves that our objective was pointless, but, we relied on the intelligence we were given and went tactically as trained.

Once we were back in Merca and recovered after half a day, we went to the port to start a routine patrol through the city. Something that was done every single day by any given platoon in the battalion. As we rode through the gate at the port to do our pre-patrol inspections, I noticed something pretty disturbing right at the entrance; a human body, wrapped in a rug just sitting there with a pair of feet hanging out the end. Obviously this is something we would inquire about.

As it turns out, the young kid we'd taken to the port jail several days earlier was now dead and wrapped in the rug. I watched the people walking by, no one paying any notice to him lying there. None at all. Not even the platoon on guard at the port was paying him any mind. Everyone was just going about their business like everything was normal, Somalis and Americans alike. I didn't ask how he died. One of our interpreters had just up and died one day from Malaria and it could have been anything at all that killed him. It didn't matter, he was just dead.

As we patrolled that day, I was distracted, I admit. I couldn't stop thinking about that kid. I also thought of his mother, and my trying to convey to her that her son would be fine. And I didn't understand why we would be here supposedly helping people who valued life so little. It's true, they seemed to place no value on human life in this country whatsoever. This, among other things, ultimately tore apart the perception of the world that I had that our parents and teachers spend so many years trying to give us.

The reality is, the world by large is a cold, dark fucking place. And your life likely doesn't mean shit to anyone else but you, and those closest to you. For me, that would be my family and the 15 men I was with in Somalia. They are my family.

As I recall, that kid's body rotted there in the sun for several days, if not a week or more. Tough shit, kid. That's life.

Illuminating

Aside from the combat action log for this incident, I have something much more detailed; signed statements by myself and my platoon leader, dated shortly after the incident. I'm not sure about everyone else who served in Somalia, but not only did we log everything, we had to submit statements about each incident.

The M-60 machine gun is one of the most feared and successful weapons when employed in a defensive position. It's range, power and rate of fire up to 650 rounds per minute are enough to scare the living shit out of anyone; it's distinctive noise alone demands immediate attention.

It was the 19th of March at 0145 hrs (1:45 am) when several Somalis opened fire on yours truly as I sat atop my perch at the port of Merca, in a heavily sandbagged machinegun position on top of a connex. After several rounds struck the connex, they had my full attention. However, I didn't immediately return fire because I didn't see where it originated. It's probably one of the smartest things

I think I did during my entire tour. Not sure if it had just been probing fire, I waited several seconds before doing anything. Behind the gun, I scanned the entire beach and walkways in front and to the side of me trying to identify a specific target.

Suddenly, several distinct points opened fire on me, specifically me. Spotting the muzzle flashes along the walkway wall, I immediately began suppressive fire on two positions near each other. I'm sorry that I can't report exactly who else was firing and at what, but I was kind of busy tearing up the beach and walls along the walkway.

According to the SFC Jones' statement, everyone else not tied to a specific position was awoken and joined the fight on my flanks. Who specifically that was, I can't say. But I owned that fucking beach now.

Without warning during a momentary lull, I heard a mortar round's distinctive "thud" from the mortar position and after several more seconds, night became day as an illumination round lit the area up and I felt even more adrenaline shoot through me. Now not only could I see the areas they were firing from, I could see those skinny little fuckers casting shadows along the wall. Another illumination round went out before the first had fallen, taking away all hope for the assholes along the boardwalk.

"Along the wall!" I yelled out as several others began opening up and several Somalis began scurrying around fully illuminated.

Every time one popped up and tried to fire now, we immediately suppressed them. They didn't stand a chance.

However, as their luck would have it, there was a lull between the second and third mortar round, although only slight. But it was apparently enough for our skinny little targets to disappear as quickly as they had appeared.

After several more minutes of our sporadic fire where they had been, it was apparent that they had taken the opportunity to break contact. I wasn't even aware until this point that the front position on the port had been in contact as well.

"CEASE FIRE! CEASE FIRE!!" SSG Ferriero yelled out.

Not that I hadn't been awake when the shooting began, but I was way more than awake at this point. I snapped an extra 100 rounds onto what was left of the belt still in the gun as another illumination round went out. SSG Ferriero and SFC Jones then rallied the NCOs.

"100% security, no one sleeps! I want a patrol ready to go get these fucks!" SSG Ferriero said in his "let's whack some fools" voice.

Luckily the guard shifts were due to change at 0200 hrs (2 AM), so no one was actually asleep when the shooting started. But shit, I had been on guard since 2200 hrs (10 PM) on the 18th and had been only 15 minutes away from getting some rack time. I hadn't slept since I had woken up probably 18 hours earlier. Now, we were going to all be up for the rest of the night.

Immediately the squad leaders formed a make-shift squad out of everyone not manning a position, did a quick ammo and equipment check, and headed out of the wire near my position as another illumination round went out. I was pretty sure that they'd find at least one corpse out there during the sweep. As they moved tactically out of the wire and along the boardwalk, bounding by fire teams, alone in my machinegun nest, I traversed the area searching for targets, but saw nothing. I tried to keep my traverse path all along the front of their direction of movement and also above them, knowing that Earl and Chico were covering the flank with SAWs.

It was really quite the scene as another mortar round illumination round continued the appearance of an early dawn. The shadows caused by the falling parachute illumination round can also trick the eyes a little, making you think you see movement at times. I don't recall being particularly worked up during this incident. I was definitely high as hell on the adrenaline rush, but I was calm and focused. My senses seemed so sharp that I could have probably walked around like a bloodhound smelling the ground and air until found them. I wouldn't say that anyone in my platoon ever seemed "out of control" while taking fire, but I can definitely say by this point, it was just *different*. It was business as usual after having been "there and done that" for the last four months. And by all accounts, we were true professionals in these situations by now.

Not only were we forever changed by now, but there wasn't a "cherry" among us. At just 1 year and 1 month out of basic training, us younger guys had the genuine respect and trust of everyone senior to us. As equals in most regards. Sure, rank still got the respect it demanded, but we were just treated much differently than we had been over the previous year prior to coming to Somalia. Everyone was hard. Though we had a few brotherly spats here and there, when it came to business, we were swift and exact. And you know how brotherly spats work. I can beat the shit out of my brother, and he can beat my ass too, but if anyone else tries to beat either of us? It's on. We will end you.

After at least six or seven rounds of illumination from the mortars, our M-203 gunners took over popping up parachute flares over the beach. Though they didn't last anywhere near as long, it works pretty well. The squad continued maneuvering along the boardwalk over the next couple of hours, eventually taking a slightly more relaxed approach to their movements. By this point, they were pretty sure the skinnies had gotten away. Though I am pretty sure one or more of them had to be wounded. And without proper care in this country? That's a death sentence. But who knows? These people were MUCH tougher than the analysts were touting on CNN and to the rest of the world.

What they lacked in basic soldiering skills like marksmanship, they more than made up for in toughness. Think about it. They had endured years of famine. Every day of their life was a struggle. To be alive as an adult, which was pretty much anyone over 15 it seemed, you had to be pretty fucking tough.

As an example, SGT Wasik and SGT Douglas had taken a zodiac out into the harbor and manned a position on a barge for several nights as a large ship was anchored nearby, unloading more and more of its load each day. The ship's captain, who could have been the twin brother of Robin Williams, had requested the security fearing the Somalis would swim out to the boat. At first, Wasik and Douglas, along with everyone else, thought that was ridiculous. The swim from the beach to the boat would have been difficult for even a US Navy SEAL. The water was rough, it was full of sharks, and it was a pretty fucking far swim there and back.

However, much to their surprise, Wasik and Douglas actually caught two Somalis who had managed to swim all the way to the boat and board it. At first they hogtied the pair with prussic cuffs before freeing their feet, realizing it was probably a bit much seeing how neither had been armed.

As another example, CPL Schmidt had tried to wrestle one of the MASF members one evening after a mission. Schmidt had wrestled in high school and outweighed his skinny Somali opponent by at least 80 lbs. As the pair began grappling, Schmidt quickly went from offense to defense, nearly losing to this half-starved opponent. If Schmidt had started with any reluctance, maybe fearing he would hurt the frail man, that reluctance was quickly gone. I believe the pair ended on a draw, which was pretty shocking to everyone.

My only point is that to underestimate your opponent in battle based on things like them being extremely skinny from starvation, is an extremely stupid thing to do. The Somali people are without a doubt the most naturally hard individuals I have ever encountered in my life. The analysts who had downplayed the opposition here should have been forced to come fight alongside us as a way to eat their words. Somalia isn't considered the one of the most dangerous countries on earth because of disease or famine; it's because of hard, tough and ruthless individuals who will kill you that it's one of the most dangerous countries on the planet.

After an hour and half, maybe two hours, the patrol operation ended and everyone came back in the wire. It was between 0400 and 0500 hrs and I wasn't quite as excited as I had been between 0145 and 0230. I believe SPC Eaddy came up and relieved me in my position so I could at least make some coffee and try and wake up a little. Though the guard shift had now officially taken place, the sun would be up soon and we were staying on 100% security at least until then.

As I sat and drank my coffee, the morning call to prayer began to echo out across the land. Personally, I found it to be quite beautiful to listen to. Before long, the sun began to break the horizon and people could be seen on the beach, facing Mecca, and praying. It was peaceful and I was tired. I had now been awake for at least 24 hours, had been the center of attention of the Somali affections in the middle of the night, and really just wanted to find some sleep.

By 0600 or so, we were officially off 100% security and our camp became normal again. People began doing hygiene, weapons maintenance and eating some chow. After trying to find some sleep and getting disappointed, I eventually went and swapped myself back out with someone on guard. I took my coffee making gear and some food and knew myself well enough by now that I would have just laid awake for the rest of the day. So, might as well make myself useful and have someone to talk to.

I honestly have no idea who I spent the first four hours of the morning on guard with that day. I went back to my M-60 and performed some maintenance on it while the other guy remained on watch. Occasionally, talking about the night's activities and sharing some food, but it's pretty much a blur. I can promise you I probably drank at least three canteen cups of mocha and smoked two packs of cigarettes now that the sun was up. Yep, like a freight train. I had actually given up smoking before we deployed here. And had I known what the rest of the day would bring, I would have gotten some sleep.

Knights and Pawns

The infantry is called "The Queen of Battle", referencing the unrivaled power of the queen on a chessboard; her ability to move in any direction, and kill any other piece on the board. This day was a checkmate. Everything I have written about to this point, with few exceptions, is 100% verifiable in the official combat action log that was painfully maintained in Somalia by the battalion and brigade headquarters. Many of the things are also listed in the bullets on the Army Commendation Medal (ARCOM) that I received for my service in Somalia, as well as my orders for the Combat Infantryman's Badge (CIB) which specifies the date I first engaged in active ground combat. This incident, however, is conspicuously missing from the combat action log, yet it is the only incident that takes up an entire bullet block on my ARCOM recommendation. The bullet paragraph only tells part of a story that is now official military record per permanent orders #11xxxx, but leaves out the details that only I and less than two dozen other people can verify. The bullet remark reads in part as follows:

After receiving sniper fire and maneuvering in the direction of fire on 19 March 1993, Specialist Slane assisted first platoon in the seizure of a large cache of weapons that included: Rocket propelled and hand grenades, automatic rifles, pistols, mortars, lanti-tank missiles, claymore mines, crew-served weapons and large amounts ammunition..........

As magnificent as it sounds that I ran the "wrong way" (as some people might say) while being shot at and that my actions resulted in the seizure of a huge volume of weapons, this bullet point doesn't tell even a fraction of the story. I'm probably lucky that it tells that much of the story, or mentions this action at all. Also, it doesn't specifically mention any of the other men who also ran the "wrong way" while taking fire and also seized the weapons. Szulwach, Douglass, Schmidt, Eaddy, Ferriero, Forde, Beem, Lainge, Mangold and Jones to name a few. It also doesn't tell you anything about where this took place or any other specific detail other than I'm a wild-ass who, with a group of wild-asses that I just partially listed off, charged someone who was shooting at me and took his guns. While it inherently describes some good degree of danger that resulted in a "win" for our side, the entire truth of our deeds were stricken or omitted from the official log my battalion kept of everything that happened and everything we did in Somalia. And, it is no accident that it was omitted.

Aside from the firefight at o'dark thirty, the resulting patrol, and staying awake all night, I don't recall anything particularly extraordinary about the day to this point aside from the obvious aforementioned. Late morning, we were settling into our daily routine that we had perfected while on port duty. Those who weren't on guard and had given up on sleeping played cards, did personal hygiene, ate or found other ways to pass the time until their shift started. The NCO's cleaned up their make-shift quarters, which were basically a dilapidated fraction of a building, and made their rounds to each position to make sure their soldiers were where they were supposed to be.

Around noon, a flurry of activity caught the attention of SSG. Ferriero at the front gate. People in the streets seemed hurried and anxious, moving around like something had happened. There was lots of noise and commotion. He learned through an interpreter that there was some sort of altercation up the street to the west, which led up a hill and fed into a series of intersections and crossroads. Being somewhat bored by now, SSG. Ferriero decided to put together a patrol to investigate. Volunteers were taken or made, and we set out for a patrol of the surrounding area.

Some of the local MASF (local Somali militia) members accompanied our patrol as we followed the narrow, winding streets toward where the flurry of activity seemed to be concentrated. We then heard that someone may have been stabbed or shot. Some people appeared frantic or anxious as we got closer to some sort of medical clinic. As we entered the clinic, we found a table covered in fresh blood, but no apparent patient was present. Was this from the firefight we had just hours earlier? The crowd seemed anxious and urging us like they wanted us to go into some walled off compound near where we were. It was a mosque, though not everyone was readily aware of that fact.

The hastily wiped and bloodied medical table in the clinic.

Everything seemed pretty calm as everyone waited for the NCO's to decide our next move. After a few minutes of discussion, we were going to open one gate to what appeared to be a large villa and see if anyone there was in need of help. Again, we found nothing interesting, though on the way out Beem spotted a couple of hand grenades on our way out and something just didn't "feel" right. As we opened the gate to exit the villa, we started taking immediate fire from just up the street. We immediately kissed the wall closest us.

As we took cover against the wall, SFC Jones accidentally discharged a tracer round that missed Mangold's foot by inches as it lay there smoldering in the sand. Mangold had a somewhat comical, yet extremely disapproving look on his face. Again, Mangold's comic relief in the middle of a Somali shit storm, curtesy of SFC Jones. When I think of this today, I can hear SFC Jones' famous phrase echoing through eternity. "If the shoe fits…...!" How perfect. And if the shoe doesn't fit, what then? He will blow your foot off and make it fit, that's what. No disrespect intended, SFC Jones is one of the finest human beings I've ever known. And that is funny shit.

"Sorry about that!" SFC Jones said with a nervous smile.

"You're a fucking dumb ass…" Mangold calmly but sternly said.

The shots were now coming at us from at least two positions, one definitely on foot on the ground, the other was fixed and up high. Several rounds were quickly exchanged downrange with our new friends in an effort to suppress the area where we believed the sniper rounds were coming from; up the alley and toward the only structure that had a vantage point that could see over the walls to where we had been in the street. Having only started with a "teaser belt" (a partial belt of M60 ammo, usually 15-30 rounds of a 100 round belt) in my M60 and with no assistant gunner, I hastily tried to retrieve a full belt of 7.62mm from my butt-pack where I kept another 200 rounds.

With little warning, Eaddy and Forde were the first to take off in a sprint toward an attacker after his weapon jammed as the rest of us followed close behind, hauling ass through the narrow, winding street, shots ringing out from all parties. I felt as though I had tunnel vision as we sprinted up the street and closed in on our attackers.

As Forde and Eaddy followed an assailant through one door into a compound, he discarded his weapon while the rest of us "rang the doorbell" on another door. That is, we kicked it the fuck open. Szulwach, Douglas, Laing and Schmidt breached the entrance and the rest of us followed in a hurry. Our entrance was followed up with a flurry of butt-strokes (striking an opponent with the butt of your rifle).

Since I carried an M60 rather than a rifle, a butt-stroke was not practical. So I offered one Somali who got up too fast what I will now dub a "Rooster Tap" (In Vietnam, the M60 gunner was called "the Rooster") with the barrel of my 23lb weapon. He "sat" the fuck down in a hurry. When another Somali went for a pistol on his hip, Rick "Earl" Beem said "Cute Toy" and then knocked him straight upside the head sending him to the ground.

"Exactly as I remember it! And I still have no idea why they dropped their weapons either!" ~ 1st Sergeant(RET) Daniel Ferriero, after reading this chapter, December 2015.

Inside the gates were several armed men, Somalis as well as Arabs (maybe even from Yemen?), who were surprised and perhaps a bit overwhelmed by our apparent zeal to send them to Allah to retrieve their virgins, which caused them to immediately drop their weapons, almost in unison. (To this day I do not know why.) It looked like they were gearing up for a party, and we were a little more than pissed off at our invitation, though it appeared their colleagues that were now being man-handled by Forde and Eaddy, had invited us prematurely. Grunts do love to party. And this was just our kind of party. I guess in actuality we had crashed this party before it really got good. Shit was extremely tense to say the least, but we were chilling the situation out expeditiously.

We then gathered the immediate twenty or so partiers to the center of the courtyard not far from where we had surprised them. This walled in complex isn't just their villas, it contains the mosque where almost two months earlier we had chased an assailant who got away by disappearing through it's gates. As Earl watched over the rowdy party goers, I went back outside to watch our six (guard our rear) with the machine gun, and then ultimately guiding the commander to our location, while everyone else started looking around the compound. I then met linked up with SGT Wasik in the road to get a water resupply. It was Africa. It was really hot and we just got running through dusty streets exchanging gunfire. It makes you thirsty, something I previously mentioned about in "The Baptism" chapter. When I ran up the street and returned to the compound, things were getting even more interesting.

"WTF is this shit?" Schmidt asked aloud as he observed an awkward piece of wood sticking out from where it shouldn't.

Our friends were growing a little agitated as our curiosity led us further into their dwelling. Their apparent leader, seemingly an Arab, who was standing in the very center and completely surrounded by his friends, tried to step out like he was going to intervene before we got any further. Earl and 22 years of eating Iowa corn quickly ended his plight, as Earl grabbed him and put him back in order. Now shit got REALLY heated again, as his colleagues became irate. At
222

this point Sgt. Douglas, SSG. Ferriero and I came over with our interpreter, Mohammed, who had come with the commander.

"Slane, keep an eye on the pricks." SSG Ferriero said in his strong New Jersey accent.

"My pleasure, Sergeant." I replied eagerly.

"Mohammed, tell that guy, I'm going to his house and fuck all of his wives tonight if he doesn't chill the fuck out." I said to Mohammed, as I pointed at their highly agitated leader.

"No." Mohammed quickly but quietly replied.

"What? Tell him what I said!" I demanded.

"I cannot." Mohammed said quietly.

"Why the fuck not? Tell him what the fuck I said." I replied to him.

"If I tell him this thing, this man will kill my entire family. Everyone. And everyone I know." Mohammed said with a worried look on his face.

"Oh, alright, dude. Can you at least tell him I think he's pretty?" I asked.

To my surprise, Mohammed complied or at least I think he did. My Somali is a bit rusty. Everyone in the group of prisoners seemed pretty pissed off but quiet, so, whatever he said did the trick. I pointed at the leader who was glaring at me like his head was going to explode and held a fist at him. He was staring at me so hard that I think he actually thought he could make me die. The same look he was giving Beem. He was not afraid of us one bit.

"The way their leader was looking at me.... I had never encountered that level of hatred in my entire life." ~ SGT Rick "Earl" Beem, December 2015.

While Stare Wars Episode I was playing out between me and my new friend Ahkmed the Shithead, Schmidt and Laing were down in some hidden room under the floor exclaiming "Look at all this shit!" as they pulled weapon after weapon out. Szulwach and Douglas had also found plenty of party favors, as had everyone else who was searching the compound. There were weapons everywhere.

"Look at this fucking shit. Fucking claymore mines and mortars? They would have wiped us the fuck out if we hadn't popped in here!" SSG Ferriero said.

"And what the fuck is this shit? SAM's? So if we called for help the QRF would fly in here by Blackhawks and get blown out of the sky?!?!" SSG. Ferriero continued in full form, like a Jersey mob boss about to whack some fools.

There were several shelves of various mortars and grenades.

That's right. **Surface to air missiles**, anti-armor missiles, crew served weapons, grenades of every type, piles of assault rifles, pistols and ammunition for all of it. They had enough hardware to arm the entire city it seemed. And weapons just kept getting found, in every corner, underground, behind doors, absolutely everywhere.

Corporal Christian Schmidt and Sergeant John Lainge as they began
pulling huge amounts of weapons from hidden under false flooring
that had been covered with a rug.

Specialist Rick "Earl" Beem with weapons found behind a false wall.

By this time, the commander had arrived with Spc. Jovino, the company
RTO and a guy us younger soldiers had gone to basic training with. The
commander was getting the scoop from SFC Jones and SSG Ferriero as Jovino
gave me the "what's up nod" with his usual southern California wise-ass smirk,
like he knew something really, really big was going on. The commander listened

intently, hands on his hips as usual. I could still hear "Observe the wall" echoing out, except this time he was observing a shit pile of weapons, some of which we hadn't yet seen in Somalia yet, like surface to air missiles. The commander then walked around while continuing to ask questions about what led us here and who did what. I could see the genuine look of concern on his face as he walked by the piles of weapons we were laying out, and still carrying out from various buildings. He was thinking everything that SSG Ferriero had pointed out earlier. These guys were going to mess us up, and could have. We were actually outgunned by these guys. And we got another surprise, a PRC-77 military radio, and it was on our unencrypted frequency. They had been listening to us and our radio chatter, possibly monitoring our movements. Where did they get this radio?

SFC Jones (foreground), SSG Ferriero (background) and
Sgt. John Douglas (right) smiling in disbelief
as we began emptying the buildings of weapons.

Jovino continued the radio chatter back to HQ while more and more weapons piled out. Suddenly we had unexpected guests. A "spook" (I know his name but whatever) appeared uninvited, though they really didn't need an invitation. One of them said a few words toward the shithead who had tried to kill me with his eyeballs, and then continued over to the commander. Mr. Shithead was smiling now. Why I did not know, but I made sure his smile disappeared quickly. I was quite charming when I really, really tried. All 6'4" 230 charming pounds of me.

Our interpreter Mohammed (left) watching as we brought the weapons out.

Our spooky guests were speaking with the higher ups and it apparently wasn't going well. There was yelling and I distinctly heard the spook say "This never happened. You're not supposed to be here. You were never here."

"Are you fucking kidding me? Are you serious?" someone in charge (maybe everyone) replied, appearing extremely agitated.

They then took the "leader" off to the side and I could hear the SF officer scolding him.

"What are you doing? I thought I told you.... [couldn't hear]" the officer was saying.

"We had an agreement! And you're fucking shit up!" he continued.

What the actual fuck was going on I wondered. They know each other. They REALLY know each other. And before I knew it, he was telling our commander that we were letting them ALL go. The group we had fought this day was called "al-Itihaad al-Islamiya", they were Islamic fundamentalists who were added to the United States list of terror groups in 2001, and were the precursor to the Islamic Courts, and a known ally of Al Qaeda. Today you know them as Al-Shabaab, or, Al Qaeda in Somalia. In short, they ARE Al Qaeda.

"Keep the weapons, but we're letting the prisoners go and you were never here!" the officer informed us.

"This is fucking bullshit!" someone in charge replied.

"Call whoever you want and confirm, but that's what's happening!" the officer told him.

The rest of us were standing there in amazement, not sure if what was happening was a really bad joke, or what. It became apparent that it actually WASN'T a joke as the officer started picking out some of the weapons we had confiscated, and handing them to the prisoners he was now freeing.

"Stand down!" he said to me.

"Your wish is my command…..." I uttered angrily.

"Are you kidding me? You're giving them weapons?!?" someone screamed to no avail as they tried to listen to the radio.

"The way I see it is that at that time we were conventional infantry performing a conventional infantry mission and we are not bound to keep it a secret." ~ Senior Special Forces Sergeant (MSG RET) Brian Szulwach, December 2015.

"GOD DAMNIT!!" someone was heard yelling as they slammed down the hand mic on the top of the Humvee. We had apparently received the confirmation we dreaded. We were not here. And this did not happen. We apparently just found an entire arsenal of weapons lying around in the road I guess, and with no explanation.

"What the fuck is going on, sir?!?" SSG Ferriero asked someone in the command group.

"We're letting them go and we're leaving. This never happened." A reply came.

"That's bullshit, sir! And not only are we letting these mother fuckers go, but we're arming them?" SSG Ferriero yelled.

"FUCK!" SSG Ferriero exclaimed.

Eventually, we grudgingly left the compound and headed back to the port. Obviously we spent the rest of the night, if not the rest of our lives, discussing the significance of the Arab ring leader of a group of Somali Jihadists who was camped out approximately 100 meters from where we were about to catch some sleep.

SFC Jones standing where he never was, looking back as we
heard we were never there.

You know the story; my enemy's enemy is my friend? Our government has played that game for a long time, and the soldiers are the pawns in that dangerous game. And on the 19th of March, 1993 less than a dozen proved that we aren't just pawns. In fact, we're knights. Though we talk can like pimps and mobsters when we're pissed, it's ok because our hearts are in the right place.

Saddam Hussein was a guy not unlike the leader we encountered on this day. A bad guy we used as a friend when it suited us the most. Then we had to fight him several years later. Twice. And lots of American blood was split because of him. The same can be said of the Taliban and Al Qaeda, who we now know was building a presence in Somalia since the fall of the Sid Barre regime in 1991, and it was with this group, al-Itihaad al-Islamiya, with the goal of building an Islamic State in Africa. Who these guys are specifically, I cannot say for sure, though I have my suspicions. But they kept bad company, like the CIA, and I can judge them by that. An Arab in the middle of an African Civil War, just hanging out, looking for some rental property I suppose. I don't know. And I likely never will. And I will never forget how absolutely every Somali was terrified of their ringleader. Because they knew something about him that they weren't telling us.

I guess that's it. I'm obligated to secrecy and I can never tell you this story. And you will never know what the spook was doing, or who they were. Except no one ever specifically or directly told ME that I was never there or it was a secret. In February 1993, we were all briefed that Israeli intelligence had warned us that known terrorists were operating in our area. And I guess we found them.

In December 1992 as troops moved to Somalia, Bin Laden and Al Qaeda are known to have carried out their first attacks directly on US troops by bombing hotels the non-combat troops were staying at in the middle east. After a remote detonated mine killed several MP's in Mogadishu in August, 1993, it was theorized that Al Qaeda provided the hardware to carry out the attack. And in a Federal Indictment in the United States, Bin Laden was specifically indicted for his involvement in Somalia. However, the US analysts at the CIA didn't consider al-Itihaad al-Islamiya a real threat in the 90's because they thought they were idealistically different than Al Qaeda. And by the evidence I provide you today, it appears the CIA was actively involved al-Itihaad al-Islamiya with the good, but misplaced, intention of stabilizing Somalia.

The Last Patrol

Today is 29 March, 1993. As 1-22 infantry began arriving in Merca to take over operations, I was informed by the scout platoon snipers that they had been told we would be doing a battalion run through the streets of Merca and that they would be positioned around the city to cover the route.

"Are you fucking kidding me?" I asked Smith and Peterson.

"I know, right? Hahaha" Smith replied.

"So, they're bright idea is that we should run through a city wearing nothing but PT shorts and reflective belts? Completely unarmed? Who the fuck came up with that?" I said.

"Someone in the battalion command staff, maybe the Colonel, I'm not sure." Peterson laughingly replied.

This is without a doubt the most asinine thing I believe I'd heard our whole time in country. Heading into our 5th month in country, possibly just weeks from heading home, and we're going to do a chicken run through a Somali city, unarmed. A city where we have now fought several technicals, extremists and bandits. Just the thought of it was giving me a bit of a panic attack. Can you imagine? After all the hostile fire we'd taken in this country, the grenade attacks and all the death we'd experienced, someone has the big idea that we can do a farewell run through the city. While Merca was without a doubt much safer than Mogadishu, it wasn't safe by any stretch. Having spent considerable time in both, I wouldn't have opted for a hooah farewell run through either. And having arguably been to more parts of this country than anyone other than Special Forces, there isn't a single place I'd been where I would have felt ok with this.

"There is no way in hell I'm doing that." I said to the group.

"Dude..." Mangold said with a chuckle. "I'm all for it! I'll carry the colors!" he continued as he imitated running and holding the colors.

"hahaha, right." I told him.

"I hope we sing cadence while we run!" he laughingly said, sputtering off a few words to a cadence.

Around 1000 hours, SGT Douglas was taking volunteers for a mounted patrol in the city. Grish, Mangold and I had been hanging out joking about the big run when Mangold suggested that we go.

"Hey, SGT Douglas, I'm going!" Mangold said.

"Come on guys, let's take a ride into town." He told us.

"Alright, I'll go." I told Douglas.

"Grish! You know you want to go, too!" Mangold encouraged.

"Yeah, right. Because I've got nothing better to do other than relax." Grish said.

"Ok, so Grish is going too!" Mangold told Douglas.

"No, he's fucking around, Sergeant. I'm good with staying here." Grish told Douglas.

"Ok, Girsh is going too." Douglas agreed as he walked around gathering more.

"Estes, you're going, you're the medic." Douglas informed him.

"Great." Estes replied in his dry, monotone "Doc Cheetah" voice.

"Thanks, a lot, Mangold. Dick." Grish laughingly said to Mangold.

"It will be fun! What could happen?" Mangold replied.

After a few more minutes, the patrol group had been picked. SGT Douglas, Mangold, Grish, myself, Mcenaney, Spaceboy, Forde, Schmidt, Estes and Chico Perez. By this time, Perez had been given to the CO as the company driver,

233

something he was not happy about. But at least he was with us once more and he was more than happy to go.

"Let's get this show on the road, you big country bumpkin!" Perez said, directing it toward me.

"Yeah, maybe you'll luck out and find a Taco Bell in town, Chico." I retorted.

"Fuck that shit. I want to go to Pizza Hut, homes." Perez replied.

After a pre-mission inspection, we load the Humvee and prepared to head out of the gate. As we stopped at the front gate of the base, the guards, who were part of the newly arrived 1-22 advance party, came over and started talking to SGT Douglas, telling him the new rules of engagement (ROE).

"SGT, just making sure you and your men know the ROE. No one can be locked and loaded until you take fire." The pasty guard informed SGT Douglas.

"What?" SGT Douglas laughingly replied.

"No one can be locked and loaded, sergeant. I can't let you out of the wire until you all clear your weapons." The guard told the group.

"Whatever. Clear your weapons, men." SGT Douglas told the group.

"You need to clear yours, too, big guy." One of the guards told me as I stood with a teaser belt of ammunition conspicuously hanging out of my M-60.

"First of all, I'm not part of the UN, bud. Secondly, how fucking long have you been here? A day? Two?" I replied.

"I've been here for a few days, why?" he said.

"Because if you'd been here long enough, you wouldn't be telling us to go outside the wire with our fucking weapons unloaded, that's why." Mangold informed him.

"I have my orders and you're not leaving until you clear your weapons." The guard replied.

"Ok, you pasty ass fuck. I'll tell you what. I'm going to clear my weapon. And then I'm going to have the driver stop five feet outside the wire, so I can reload. Does that make any sense? Because I'm not going to wait until I'm taking fire until I even bother loading my weapon. Unlike an M16, I can't just charge a round if you're making me remove my teaser belt." I told him.

"Whatever you do is your business, man. I'm just following orders." He replied.

After we pulled outside the wire, Chico stopped the vehicle and we all locked and loaded. In plain sight of the guard who had just held us up for several minutes.

"What a douche." Mangold laughingly declared.

"Fucking idiot." I said.

"Everybody good to go?" Chico asked the group before heading off as we waived to our pasty gate guards.

As we drove toward the city, everybody took opportunity to rip on the "cherries" we'd just encountered.

"They just have no idea, do they B.C.?" Mangold chuckled to me.

"That's the dumbest shit I've ever heard. Wait until I'm getting shot at to load my 60. WTF?" I replied.

"Wait until he figures it out, dude. They just don't know what it's like here yet." Mangold replied.

The conversation continued as we drove toward Merca. I remember the breeze from the ocean and how cool it felt in the back of the Humvee as we made our way down the winding roads. Like every other day here, it was hot as hell, but clear and beautiful. And the breeze and the view of the Indian ocean were amazing.

After a few minutes, we were at the Merca checkpoint, just a mile or so outside of town. The guards at the checkpoint talked with Douglas and Chico for a few minutes and had a laugh about the ROE. They thought it was pretty hilarious as well. And, they didn't tell us to clear our weapons. They just waived us through after a few minutes of small talk. They knew the deal. And the deal was that we weren't going anywhere with unloaded weapons any sooner than we were going to throw some shorts and tennis shoes on and have a nice run through the city.

As we approached the edge of Merca, we noticed a crowd of people centered to the upper left of the main road. As we got closer, we could see that it appeared to be some kind of mob beating the hell out of some people, robbing their donkey pulled cart. By the time we pulled up, all hell broke loose.

"CRACK! CRACK! CRACK! CRACK!" rang out in several successive bursts as a man emerged from the crowd with what appeared to be an AK-47, immediately followed by our Humvee stopping, Mangold literally jumping over the side, giving a loud battle cry, and returning fire. Being in the back of the Humvee, I literally rolled over the tailgate just as the Humvee was finishing it's stop, somehow landing on my feet. The first thing I saw as I got my bearing, was Steve Mangold charging the crowd, simultaneously firing.

The rest of us followed suit, returning fire and causing the crowd to fly in a million different directions. We gave all immediately gave chase.

As Mangold headed to the right and up an ally at about our 10 o'clock (the vehicle facing the 12), Forde and I sprinted off to the left at about a 7 o'clock. As I now couldn't see any weapons in the open, I made sure my rounds went into the wall at about the 8-9 o'clock. As I looked over toward Mangold, I saw him issue one of the best butt-strokes in the history of butt-strokes, as the butt of his M-203 struck a man upside the head, causing the man to fly completely parallel to the ground.

"Let's get these motherfuckers!" Forde yelled as he resumed sprinting toward an alleyway.

As I followed Forde up the winding alleyway, I was reminded as to why Mangold had nicknamed him "Wheels", and although I wasn't exactly slow having run a 4.8 40-yard dash, it was a challenge to keep pace with Forde who ran around a 4.4 40, I admit. And we were running uphill, the winding narrow roads filled with dust from the dozens of people who had gone this way.

After about 100 meters, we approached a split in the road. I followed Forde's lead as he split off to the right, and I headed left. As I ran down the street, my prey suddenly stopped running and began walking. I did the same now that I was completely spent and out of breath. I swung the machinegun around my side on its sling, and pulled out my 9mm. Just as I got it out, the guy I was chasing was now joined by several dozen people. And they were no longer headed away from me, but towards me. Unsure if any were armed, I suddenly had a sickening feeling in my stomach as I realized I was completely alone and now outnumbered 40 to 1. As I slowly walked backwards, making sure to keep my eye on the mob, Forde suddenly appeared behind me.

"Yo, man. Let's get the fuck out of here. I can't believe I couldn't catch that skinny little motherfucker." Forde said.

"I'm with you, dude. Let's get out of here." I said, feeling sense of relief that Forde had returned and found me.

Though completely spent, we moved expeditiously back toward the Humvee where SGT Douglas was waiting with CPL Schmidt and Mangold, talking to someone. Alongside of the Humvee, Mangold and the others had six prisoners they were searching and binding their hands. Mangold was furious as his adrenaline now had no outlet other than binding the prisoners.

"Stupid assholes." He said as he bound one man's hands.

In the middle of the street was an elderly couple with their donkey and cart. Bloodied and bruised, they looked stunned, but thankful that we had happened along. On the cart I saw the center of all the commotion; a 100lb bag of rice. In Somalia, food was money. That's all it was. They weren't killing these people over food, they were killing them over money. And lots of it.

After Douglas gathered some information about the probable whereabouts of the gunmen, some of us now headed up the road towards a house. After we took up positions around the house, Schmidt and Douglas breached the door, the rest of us, minus me, followed behind. I then watched our six as the group searched the house. Looking over at Spaceboy, I could tell he had no idea what the hell was going on. I just told him to face a direction up the road and watch for anyone coming by.

After a few minutes of searching the house and surrounding area, we found nothing and returned to the Humvee to take our prisoners to the jail at the port. As we unloaded our prisoners, SGT Douglas gave the sergeant of the guard at the port a report of the incident. And as he did, things started to look nasty outside the wire.

One individual was yelling and screaming, causing the crowd around him to grow larger and angrier. As we postured ourselves, preparing for more violence, Schmidt and Douglas leapt into the crowd and grabbed the troublemaker who was inciting everyone. At first, the crowd got even angrier, but after the MASFT members talked to them, they began to calm down and dissipate. After handing over our last prisoner, making a total of 7, we loaded back up in the vehicle and started the drive back.

As we drove, we smiled and regaled the battle cry and fierceness of Mangold, reliving every second of our adventure from each man's perspective. But always circling back to Steve Mangold leading the charge. This wouldn't be the last violence we were a part of in Somalia, but it was our last patrol, our last hoorah. And I believe it was a good one. We had saved two innocent people from an angry mob that undoubtedly would have killed them, and we had a lasting memory of each other that would endure for the rest of our lives. Steve Mangold is no longer living in this world, at least not in the literal or technical sense. But, in me, in the rest of us who fought alongside him, his brothers; he is everywhere. As I have always relived our adventures every second of every day for the 23 years preceding this book, I am always with him, as well as the rest of them.

Now, my friend, you are immortalized before all the world, never to be forgotten. We'll join you soon enough.

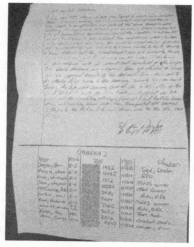

The handwritten statement of SGT John Douglas, dated 29 March 1993.

The Long Road Home

Our last few weeks in Somalia were extremely busy, though unproductive. After first getting intelligence that reinforcement's from Aidid's SNA were flooding to Kismayo, A CO 1-87 was ordered to hold a "blocking position"; basically consisting of numerous Observation Posts (OP's) and ambush positions. If you'll remember, the US government's official stance is that we didn't "hunt" warlords until August of 1993. A complete fabrication. I've already discussed several missions in which we actively faced the SNA and SNF. Most notably in and around Kismayo.

After moving to the areas surrounding Barawa, we spent four days conducting tactical missions aimed at thwarting the insurgency. We spent this time hidden in the Somali bush, once again living in the dirt. Those of us in 1st platoon "humped" (walked quietly and tactically carrying massive amounts of gear) deep into the bush and set our patrol base. As Corey and Grish were getting setup, Mangold noticed what appeared to be a Slane sized baboon sitting in a tree approximately 100 meters from our patrol base.

"Hey, Slane! Let's go check it out!" Mangold said as several joined him to go get a closer look.

"Fuck that. I have the biggest weapon in the platoon and I'm not going anywhere near that thing. It looks as big as me from here. How many grenades are you bringing?" I jokingly asked after turning down the opportunity to go "check it out".

By now, we were used to living in the bush. Few things captured our attention as being anything other than ordinary. But this area and the baboons were unique enough to intrigue us. Not being very far from the Indian Ocean, there was an area that look like it was right out of prehistoric times with its black rocks and packs of baboons. It was truly one of the most unique and beautiful sights we'd seen in this entire country. Though when I stop and think about it, much of this country was stunningly beautiful and wild.

Tom Corey and Christopher Grish after a long movement in the bush.

Later in an OP position as we lay in wait looking for suspicious movement, a woman walked by carrying a large pot of water on her head. This wasn't unusual to see in itself as it seemed that it was always the women who did the work and carried things. Water, wood, large loads of miscellaneous items; usually atop their heads. But this particular woman had a surprise in store for her in the form of a pack of baboons who were also lying in wait for their prey. And as luck would have it, it was her.

As the woman got just underneath the pack of baboons that lined the high ground above her, they attacked as though their tactics came straight from the Ranger handbook, waiting for their target to get into the middle of the "kill zone", past the point of no return. Once she was there, they leapt from their perch and attacked in full fury, battle cries and all. As the woman screamed, the pot of water went airborne before crashing to the ground as the woman fled in terror. The baboons swooped in around the broken pot and salvaged as much of the water as they could as though it had been their mission all along. A rough reminder of the life we take for granted back home in the states. Something as simple as getting water was dangerous here, and clean water hard to find.

One of the more ridiculous aspects of this particular mission involved being perched upon a ridgeline overlooking the ocean looking for insurgents who might be heading to Kismayo by boat. Fucking seriously? Half the United Sates Navy, along with the navies of several countries, sat clogged in the port of Mogadishu and not one vessel could be sent to patrol these waters? We're resorting to Army Infantry troops watching the seas? And what exactly might an insurgent vessel look like from at least a kilometer away from our ridgeline? Your guess was as good as mine. But, we did as we were told and did so without having any clue at all what we'd do if we did happen to spot anything worth investigating. Swim?

In all, the mission was a total waste of time, though a waste of time I can't readily complain about because I don't recall any incidents of hostile fire. And if there were, they must have been light, therefore not memorable. Aside from a lot of "walking" and living in the dirt in the hot African bush, the mission was reasonably easy in comparison to many we'd done to this point. As it turned out, the insurgents never came our way from Mogadishu. They continued to come from Kenya as they had done all along, where, it appears they may have been receiving training and supplies from America's new enemy; Al Qaeda. In Merca, we had fought their allies, "Ali Tahid", the predecessor of Al Shabaab and found weapons we hadn't seen in Somalia prior to that point. Weapons that I believe made the difference in the climax of our involvement in Somalia. And, for some strange reason, it had appeared our government was "friends" with them.

Back in Merca, we were given another "high profile" assignment in the Bush. This time to the north between Merca and Mogadishu, and also near Afgooye. Military "intelligence" said there was some sort of "bandit" camp in the bush and A CO 1-87 was dispatched to locate it. We knew this area fairly well having been "baptized" in Afgooye. For one last hoorah we were in the bush on a 3 day seek and destroy mission. Find them, and kill them. I laugh now as I recall how often we heard the word "bandit" and try to reconcile what it meant to me. In a country in a civil war along clan lines, every person in Somalia belonging to a clan, and every clan robbing and murdering the other, it makes every person in Somalia a potential "bandit", "murderer" and "guerrilla fighter. So there really was no distinction between a "bandit" and a "guerrilla fighter"; they are one and the same, the title depending on the specifics of a particular point in time.

The objective of a seek and destroy mission is pretty clear. We were looking for people and when we found them, they were likely going to die. By this point we knew we were leaving the country soon, though I don't recall if we knew precisely how soon. So, this mission was a good distraction to keep our minds off of the obvious constant thought of getting the fuck out of this hellhole.

For three days we swept endless miles of Somali bush, looking for something to kill, finding only baboons, wild boars and dik diks. And as usual, the spiders and millipedes were bullet worthy in size and aggression. But we found no "base" of any kind, nor any trace of guerrilla fighters or bandits. And while I'd like to say it was our last "hoorah", we weren't done hooah'n by a long shot until we were wheels up and out of this fucking place.

Upon our return to the Merca base, we were kicked out of the barracks that had originally been little more than walls until the engineers and contractors had put roofs on them. As we picked up our personal belongings and packed our gear to head home, we moved out in the dirt in the surrounding area. Listening to the pale, well fed looking replacements from TF 1-22 Infantry bitch about their new accommodations as they evicted us.

It was around April 10th and we'd been here since around the 11th of December, mostly living in the fucking dirt, eating next to nothing, dodging bullets all over this country, and at times even having little water to spare for even a cup of coffee. Barely enough water to even brush our teeth with. We'd gone about six weeks without a shower, our uniforms literally rotting off of us. I doubt any of us ever got more than 3 continuous hours of sleep in any 24-hour period. We had to learn to be resourceful to have any luxuries; learning to cook with C-4 explosives, making bottle rockets from det-cord, buying goods at the local market and cooking a decent meal, smoking cigarettes rolled in camel shit. And these fuckers were whining about living in clean buildings with roofs from the sun in a nice, safe and secure base as they expelled us back into the shit and dirt. They had no idea what sucking was, though I was confident they'd find out.

The road back to Mogadishu was tense, mostly because we all just wanted to get the fuck out of Somalia, and do so before anyone changed their mind and made us stay longer. In my own humble opinion, sending us home at this point was a huge mistake. Though TF 1-22 Infantry was every bit as competent, well trained and tough as us, they were lacking something in Somalia; our experience. Yes, they would learn everything firsthand and maybe even learn to handle things better than us in some situations. But it would have been much wiser for us to have stayed at least two more months and assisted them. In fact, we could have actually stopped the insurgency and escalation that was occurring by increasing our force, keeping the experienced force in country, and doing what the US Army does best; fight and win.

Instead, we were getting the hell out of dodge, and from a personal standpoint, it couldn't happen fast enough. As we drove to Mogadishu, the M-60 machine gunners manned positions on top of the cabs of the five ton trucks for what seemed an eternity, as our gunship escorts periodically circled past to let us know they were watching the way. As we entered Mogadishu, I felt myself become instantly more alert, though I had been alert for hours at this point already. The size of this city with its much taller buildings than most of Somalia, along with its dense population just seemed like a nightmare waiting to happen. After what seemed an eternity, we entered into the main compound near the airfield. I exhaled a sigh of relief as we unloaded the trucks.

We were immediately setup in some tents with cots where we then cached our weapons into a make-shift armory, setting up rotations for guard over them. To our surprise, we were free to shower and if I remember correctly, roam the immediate area without weapons, something that made me extremely uncomfortable. I kept my 9mm with me at all times.

For two or three days we were in limbo, roaming the base and buying trinkets from the various vendors that were allowed in to sell their wares. We marveled at what a huge and built up complex these troops had here in Mogadishu, but still felt awkwardly insecure at all times. My assistant gunner Spaceboy and I went to buy a couple of ridiculous Somali hats and a few other trinkets. He seemed glad to have the distraction of buying worthless shit, something he always seemed to do no matter where the Army sent us, even if we were just sitting in our barracks. Every night, we were lulled to sleep (though I really didn't sleep) by the sound of gunfire, most conspicuously, the lull of the Pakistani .50 cal machine gun.

Though we had showers, I had absolutely no clean uniforms to wear. We had done missions right up until we were ready to depart and unlike some people, I hadn't stashed one away to wear home. I didn't really care. I just wanted out of here, and after 3 days or so, it was time to go.

To my surprise, we were flying out on civilian airliners after having flown to Africa nonstop until we got to Egypt for ammo and supplies. I honestly couldn't believe that they were willing to risk this sort of endeavor. I really wasn't comfortable with the idea, knowing they'd take off in broad daylight, having no counter-measures or toughness of a military troop transport. Before going we had one last stop. Customs.

We had to have all of our possessions rifled through, looking for weapons and contraband, to make sure we didn't take anything "fun" back home with us. Also, anything like local foods that might spread disease. And, we had to turn in all of our ammo.

While handing in our ammo, there was some tenseness going outside the main base in the form of firefights and mortar attacks. And just like the medical staff who had med-evac'd Earl through Mogadishu armed the delusional Earl as he roasted with a 106-degree temperature after finding out he was infantry and giving him the responsibility of defense of the field ambulance, the people who were clearing us through customs and accepting our ammo actually tried to tell us that we were no longer leaving. They even tried to return our ammunition to us, expecting that we'd go out and just jump in the middle of whatever shit-storm was taking place.

Luckily, we were given the order to stand down and once things calmed down, we boarded the air craft. Not only were we flying civilian air craft, there were actual stewardesses on board. Pretty ones who looked and smelled nice. I laughed after considering that I was one of like 300 guys on this plane, and that my uniform smelled like shit. As the plane began its movement down the runway, I remember being panicked.

"Please don't let this plane crash, God. Please don't let us get shot down. Please let me make it home." I prayed silently to myself, feeling as though I was having a heart attack.

As the plane started to get airborne, only then did I start to calm down. Spaceboy didn't look any happier than I was until now, but everyone cheered as the plane soared to its cruising altitude. So, I know I wasn't alone in my nervous paranoia.

At some point in the flight, I finally accidentally let myself sleep for about two hours. Almost exactly two hours. I would later find out that you could set your watch to my two hour intervals of sleep. When I woke up, we were about to land in Ireland. Being Scottish-Irish, this got me a little excited. Although, we were landing in the wee hours of the morning. Somewhere around 2 AM I think. But anyway, I thought who knew? Maybe there's lots of shit to do here at 2 AM.

After landing, we were first told we wouldn't be allowed to depart the plane before the commander decided us to get out and wander the airport for a while. Though we were told "No Alcohol". In any event, I was in my motherland now, and maybe I could walk to Slane Castle from here and claim the throne. As I walked the airport, it was nearly empty except for us. I considered stopping and buying some ice cream, but it seemed everyone else on the plane was doing that and the line was beyond ridiculous. I also found that I couldn't stop looking around continuously, as though I was expecting something to happen. I went back to the plane.

Some many hours later, we began our descending to land at Griffis Air Force Base. Again, I got anxious.

"Please don't fucking crash...." I silently said over and over until the wheels touched down.

As we began to deplane, I was surprised to see the 10th Mountain Division Band playing for us. Yay. Can we get the fuck out of here, please? We then loaded onto buses and began the approximately two-hour drive back to Fort Drum. This couldn't go fast enough. I felt claustrophobic, though I am not. And I was anxious. For me, I felt maybe it would finally be over once I got to my barracks room.

Once we arrived at Fort Drum, we went to a gymnasium full of the family members of the guys who were married. Again, I couldn't give a fuck. I just wanted to be dismissed. I was thankful for my married friends, but seriously, let me get the fuck out of here. But we weren't done yet.

Once we were finally back at the barracks, we had to hand in our weapons. I was even more agitated than ever. I was so close to being "done", but now we had to turn in weapons. Luckily, the armor was extremely organized. Smithey was efficient, which was his usual. However, when I handed in my weapons, we had a little bit of fun when he did a quick inspection of my 9mm.

"What the fuck?" he said as he noticed something peculiar and took the weapon apart.

"Oh, yeah.... I lost the slide arm spring." I informed him.

"So what's this?" Smithey asked.

"That? That would be a catheter...." I replied.

"And it worked like this?!?!?!" he asked excitedly.

"Yep! Go outside and find out for yourself if you want." I laughingly replied.

After turning in our weapons, SSG Ferriero and SFC Jones were pretty quick to release us after giving us a "safety briefing" after us having been away from society for so long.

"Men, wear a fucking condom, if you drink, don't drive, etc etc etc. See you Monday." SSG Ferriero said as he dismissed us.

When I walked into my barracks room, I was disappointed to not feel as relieved as I thought I would, but, I definitely felt better than I had. I stripped off my filthy clothes and took the longest shower of my life, after which I sat down and drank a beer. I knew I wouldn't be able to sit around the barracks all night; I was too anxious. So, I went out into the hallway where everyone was gathering to figure out who was going where to drink and pick up some friendly company. As everyone was discussing the where they were going, Hughes came out of his room and he and I hesitated when we were asked where we'd be going.

"Who are you going with?" Hughes asked me.

"Uh, I'll go with them...." I said.

"Ok, then I'll go with these other guys......" he replied back with a smile, to which I laughed.

"Yeah, every time you and I hang out, someone starts shooting at us. Probably best we don't hang out together." I said, laughing. He agreed.

I don't remember where I went that night, or precisely who with. I believe it was with Earl and Grish and a few guys, though I honestly don't recall. I got that drunk. I couldn't relax any other way, and I don't think I was alone with that issue.

The Summer in Hell

On Monday, April 19th, 1993, we gathered for our PT (Physical Training) formation, as though life in the Army was back to normal garrison activities. However, to our surprise, we were given a PT test. At first, I thought it was a joke, but it wasn't. After spending December 11th to April 16th deployed, the Army wanted to make sure we were still physically fit. Awesome. I believe they were pleasantly surprised by the results as I personally scored over 290 on a scale of 300, even after chain smoking two to three packs of cigarettes per day during the daylight in Somalia (smoking at night was a no-no due to snipers), followed by as much coffee as a person could humanly stomach, and chewing tobacco. I weighed 45lbs less than I had before I left, looking much like the skeleton-like human beings we had been sent to "save".

For the next month after our departure, which was 16th of April, 1993, TF 1-22 Infantry operated in Merca, just as we had done, running many of the same missions. And just as we were, they were made the QRF (Quick Reaction Force) for all of Somalia. However, the United Nations decided they wanted them centralized in Mogadishu. So, in May of 1993, Merca was handed over to another UN force and TF 1-22 picked up and moved to Mogadishu.

Also in May, Major Gregory Alderete arrived in Mogadishu, Somalia with the 43rd Combat Support Group, believing that he was in Somalia to "help" people. To be a humanitarian, with much of the same thoughts that I had running through my head when I arrived in December of 1992. He too would become disillusioned with America's goal in Somalia, and after his departure home, also end up carrying with him similar scars that I bare.

At this time, back at Fort Drum, I was on leave in Seattle, WA visiting my family and friends. On what would have been my first or second day in Seattle, I went on a date with my one-time girlfriend whom I had dated on and off since being a freshman in high school, Jessica. She had reconnected with my family while I was in Somalia and had started sending me letters and pictures for my last few months there. Nothing serious or romantic, just friendly.

She picked me up around 7 PM from my mom and step dad's house in Mukilteo, WA, a small bedroom community near Edmonds. Close to the Puget Sound, they had a beautiful view from their house which sat atop a hill in their neighborhood. It was picturesque for sure; tall Douglas Firs on each side of a perfect view of the Puget Sound where the sun would set in the evening, often producing a beautiful orange and red skyline.

Jessica was friendly and seemed genuinely excited to be going to dinner. We went to a Black Angus Steakhouse in Lynwood, where I eventually met up with several of my schoolmates from my 6th – 10th grade years. I had lost contact with them from 11th grade on into college after going to live my aunt in North Carolina, and was surprised to see everyone remembered me. Most of them even knew I had gone to college on a football scholarship, which surprised me. As Jessica and I ate dinner, we were eventually joined by one of my neighbors and classmates, Michelle Key, and possibly another friend. Jessica explained to her where I had been and that I had just returned home on leave. By now Jessica could tell that something wasn't right with my mood or demeanor and she and Michelle tried to break several moments of uncomfortable silence.

We then went to Casa Guillardo's where we met up with several more classmates, where one rubbed my head and said "OOHHHH! I LOVE MARINES!". Of course I corrected her in a way that would put an end to either of us exploring her love of "Marines". I really was no fun at all and I felt out of place as I constantly looked around to examine my surroundings. It was an awkward feeling I really cannot adequately describe.

After about an hour, Jessica suggested we go dancing and she proceeded to drive me to a very loud, very crowded club where I was frisked at the door. Once inside, we got drinks and I stood at the very back of the club, refusing to budge an inch. I felt paralyzed as I stood there as I looked for all exits and examined every single person as though I was looking for something. And the noise had me completely disoriented. She asked me to dance, which I declined. After a couple of hours, she drove me home. After a few minutes of uncomfortable silence, I thanked her for taking me out and got out of the car. It was the last time either of us ever saw each other.

My mom knew that I was struggling to feel normal and called my best friend growing up, Kevin Rhoades, who had also written me while I was in Somalia. He took me to a club I believe that was called "Pier 70" in downtown Seattle. Working the door were several young hot chicks my age who groped me and rubbed my high and tight haircut as I entered. I believe I said "We must be in the right place...." Determined not to feel awkward, I got drunk as hell, even eventually dancing. I even made several "friends", issuing several shoves and threats after random guys would bump into me in the tightly packed club. Even groups of guys, lots of whom were in the Navy. I wasn't intimidated by anything or anyone and they could all tell, leaving me alone.

Eventually I spotted an innocent looking 25-year-old girl sitting by herself at a table away from all the chaos and walked over and introduced myself. Her looks were deceiving, though not in a way that disappointed. I basically woke up the next morning married to her. Technically, we were married in June, much to the dismay of my family and friends. Jessica even flew back from a vacation in Mexico in an attempt to intervene, thinking that she and I should marry, though she had given no indication prior to now. She tried in vain to dissuade me over the phone. I admit, I wasn't looking for "Mrs. Right"; I was looking for Mrs. Right-Now and for some reason I thought marrying her would just work out.

In Somalia, the situation was becoming increasingly chaotic, something those of us in TF 2-87 predicted because we had experienced the escalation firsthand between January and April of 1993. On June 5, 1993, scores of Pakistani peacekeepers were killed by Aidid's militia when the Pakistanis had attempted to shut down a radio station which was broadcasting Aidid's propaganda throughout Mogadishu. As several Pakistani's sat in the back of an

APC (Armored Personnel Carrier), they were killed by a well-placed RPG into the back of their vehicle. I believe 25 Pakistani's died in the attack.

Being the QRF, it fell to TF 1-22 to respond to the situation where they fought Aidid's forces for some time before the guerrilla fighters broke contact and withdrew. Unlike TF 2-87, TF 1-22 was being utilized in a capacity far less optimal for light infantry. Mechanized infantry, yes, absolutely. But flying around Mogadishu in Humvees in response to every critical situation was a dangerous place for a light infantryman to be. During our deployment, we did textbook small unit missions, utilizing small unit tactics, usually able to pick the time and place for our engagements, under our own initiative. We operated in small units, in sparsely populated areas (though sometimes not), even operating in the bush, doing what light infantry forces do best; skirmish, ambush, raid. Mogadishu, where'd we had been quite a bit in December, January and again in April, was a dangerous fucking place and we knew it all too well.

The day before the attack in Mogadishu, on June 4th, 1993, we had an awards ceremony for our deployment to Somalia where serval of us were presented with the Army Commendation Medal (ARCOM). Myself and SPC Richard Hughes were the only lower enlisted to receive this decoration, and though well deserved, it was much to our surprise (and dismay). Curiously, our ARCOM's did not have a combat "V" or valor device, as no awards for valor were authorized for Somalia at this time. We laughed as we read the recommendation bullets for "merit" rather than "valor", trying to figure out how one "meritoriously" charges snipers. We theorized to meritoriously charge a sniper, one must possess, among other qualities, shiny boots and a sharp salute, as well as a keen sense of punctuality.

In Mogadishu, Nathan Warshaw was a door gunner aboard a black hawk helicopter involved in the June 5th incident. He received an Air Medal with V Device (for Valor) during the incident, when he directed the pilots to a safe vantage point where they avoided damage or loss of life.

By this time, SGT John Wasik had ETS'd (Exited the Service) and was long gone, missing having his own ARCOM for "combat merit" presented to him. Out of our sixteen-man platoon, I believe four of us received ARCOMs, the rest received the Army Achievement Medal (AAM), which at the time, unlike the ARCOM, wasn't even authorized for combat. I was a little more than offended for all of us given what we had gone through together. AAM's especially seemed to be a bigger slap in the face than the conspicuously missing "V" device we all believe our ARCOM's should have had. In any event, I was disappointed to not be able to share the event with Wasik who had been my squad leader in Somalia. I felt like we all were missing something by his absence, and for me, I guess it's like a parent missing the graduation of their child, though he wasn't much older than me. I considered Wasik and Szulwach my "tactical" parents as far as soldiering went. Jones and Ferriero were my role models as leaders as well. Jones was a great leader in my opinion, who always stood up for his soldiers without regard to the repercussions. Ferriero was the same way, just more vocal and animated. I considered all of these men my family.

To my surprise I was informed I was going to the E-5 selection board to be considered for promotion to sergeant the following week. I had now been out of basic training for 15 months. I believe the average to E-5 was around five years at the time. In any event, 15 months was fast by any standard and I wasn't sure what to expect. As I stood in line one of the other guys in line turned around who had been in for at least four years and tried to cause a scene.

"What the fuck are you doing here?" the anonymous individual asked.

"Me? What the fuck are YOU doing here?" I replied in my typical Slane-esque fashion as my new squad leader, SGT Christopher Williams laughed.

SGT Williams was a squared away Ranger who had come to 1-87 shortly after I got back off of leave in May and been assigned first as my team leader with SSG Eddie Campos as our squad leader, before eventually being assigned as my squad leader. He was at the promotion board not only to sit with me during my own board, but he was going through the SSG selection board.

When my time came to appear before the board, I was nervous, but also confident, which was my norm. Though I didn't believe the nervous showed through, SGT Williams would later tell me that my right leg bounced the entire time, something I am known for doing to this day. A trademark of Steve Fucking Slane I guess.

"SPC Slane, what's the maximum effective range of the M-60 machine gun?" one of the first sergeants asked me.

"1,100 meters or as far as the eye can see, First Sergeant." I replied without hesitation.

"What are the five principles of patrolling?" another first sergeant asked.

"According to the Ranger handbook, the five principles of patrolling are Planning, Recon, Security, Control and Common Sense, First Sergeant." I replied, again without hesitation.

The questions only got harder from there as I answered question after question correctly with confidence and without a shred of hesitation. It was now that I understood why I was here before the board; I ate, breathed, shit, laughed, cried and smiled Light Infantry god. I wasn't just a guy in the Army anymore, I WAS the Army. It didn't immediately occur to me that I wasn't that much fun as a human being anymore, unless you wanted to get drunk and fight, or pick up some girls. I didn't miss a single question or draw the ire of anyone on the board. In fact, at some point, they seemed amused by what was occurring in the room.

"SGT Williams!" the Command Sergeant Major barked.

"Yes, Sergeant Major!" SGT Williams answered as he came to parade rest.

"Get this man a stick and make him a team leader!" the command sergeant major ordered.

"Roger that!" SGT Williams replied.

I was then dismissed and congratulated by the board. My score for the promotion board was a perfect 200, the only soldier that went before the board that day to ace it. I was immediately given a date to attend the Primary Leadership Development Course (PLDC), these days called "The Warrior Leader Course". I would be going in August with SPC Roderick Forde, who also passed the board for promotion. I was also told I'd immediately attend the Fort Drum Light Fighters school for the beginning of my training to attend Ranger school, and after PLDC, sniper school, another goal I had. I passed Light Fighter School with one no-go at the very end, which I was given opportunity to re-do, and did so successfully.

My whirlwind marriage was already pretty much gone by this point. I flew to Seattle every weekend I wasn't in the field and we genuinely had fun together, but it was apparent having a weekend husband who startled her in her sleep every two hours wasn't enough for her, and I knew it. She had even stated that having grown up with a father who was a veteran of the Battle of the Bulge, she was more than done with dealing with PTSD, something at this point I still didn't know I had. I thought maybe I was just an extremely good looking asshole who never slept and she should just get over it. No dice. And no hard feelings.

In Somalia, the situation was only getting worse by the minute. On my birthday, July 12, 1993, American forces, including TF 1-22 Infantry, carried out a raid turned full-fledged assault on an Aidid stronghold, the result of which was scores of Somali dead mostly at the hands of those Cobra gunships I had come to admire in Somalia. As the situation in Somalia deteriorated, elements of C CO 1-87 were preparing to depart to Somalia as part of TF 2-14, which already had their advance party preparing to leave and take over QRF duties from TF 1-22.

As I attended PLDC, on August 8th, Aidid's forces remote detonated a mine under an American Military vehicle carrying four Military Policemen (MP's). All four were killed. As Greg Alderete contemplated the fate of the four during a ceremony in Mogadishu, he found himself questioning what they had actually died for, rejecting the notion that they had died for their country. He theorized that while we in the military recognize the heroic sacrifice of our brothers and sisters in war and celebrate them as "American's Finest", that in fact, we are the bottom of the barrel in many cases where society is concerned. And, having died in a war no one still knew was going on, they didn't die for America or for freedom. They died for? What they died for didn't seem like it was much of anything in the young Major's mind at this point. By now, he knew "the deal" in the Mog. It was hell on earth, and we weren't there doing anything to save anyone other than each other. What did they die for? Each other. That's all. If there is any meaning at all to their deaths, it is in that they died side by side, true to each other to the very end. The epitome of true soldiers. While as romantic and fascinating as that sounds, it's little consolation to those that mourn their deaths, myself included. With no defined purpose in Somalia, every drop of American blood spilled there seemed wasted.

After two weeks in PLDC, I was approached by a female sergeant who complained of her back hurting. This was my first time ever being around females in uniform and I was young and naïve. How naïve will become apparently straight away. After she invited me into her room and shut the door, she explained her situation.

"My back really hurts. I hurt it doing an airborne jump a few years ago and it really acts up from time to time." She explained.

"Oh, I'm sorry." I replied, having no idea why she was explaining this to me.

"Would you mind rubbing my back?" she asked.

"Uh…. sure…I guess…" I hesitantly replied, a little confused by the request.

As I turned around, the full gravity of the request became immediately apparent as she stood disrobed, in nothing but the glory she had been born to this earth wearing. Still confused, but now for different reasons, it was at least apparent that this "back rub" was going to be more interesting that originally imagined.

"WHAT THE FUCK!?!?!?!?!" the SFC standing in the doorway exclaimed as he had flung the door open, witnessing our…. back rubbing process.

"She said her back hurt!" I quickly replied, not realizing how asinine my explanation must have sounded.

"Well, I'd say it doesn't hurt anymore! Get the fuck out of here!" the sergeant commanded as I promptly obliged.

The next morning, I was told that being the ranking person in our "back rub" situation, she bore the brunt of the responsibility per the way the Army and military worked in general. She would be kicked out and I would be allowed to finish the course. Though I must admit, I wasn't exactly a baby who was tricked into anything, though I had been pleasantly surprised. However, within an hour I was told the situation changed and the sergeant major was going to kick me out as well.

"Whatever you do, don't say the word 'hooah'." One of the cadre explained as he led me to the sergeant major's office.

"He's artillery and hates us infantry, all of us…" the SSG further explained. "Got it?"

"Hooah" I replied, as he looked at me in surprise.

After several minutes of humiliation and my explaining how I had just been helping a fellow soldier out with a sore back, the sergeant major informed me that his decision was to kick me out because the female had threatened to file an

Equal Opportunity (EO) complaint if he didn't treat us exactly the same, despite her being an actual sergeant and my being a lowly specialist. He then informed me that I could appeal his decision. I would also be allowed to return to the school in February.

"Who does the appeal go to, sergeant major?" I asked.

"Me." He stated. "Are we good, then?" he followed.

"Hooah." I replied as the two infantry Staff Sergeants on either side of me cautiously turned their heads toward me in amazement.

"Dismissed" the sergeant major said.

I was then taken to my battalion headquarters where the acting sergeant major was 1st Sergeant Poe, my first company first sergeant and former Ranger instructor, who was about to be promoted to sergeant major himself. This was going to be a long day, I could tell.

"Slane....so your explanation is that you were just being a good soldier and helping another soldier out? Is that right? Her back hurt and you were just being a good buddy?" CSM Poe asked me.

"Roger than, Sergeant Major." I replied hesitantly.

"Oh, I see. Well, my back hurts, Slane. Can I have a back rub?" CSM Poe retored.

Fuck. I knew that next to myself and Earl, and maybe a handful of peers, Poe had the highest GT score in the entire battalion, meaning he was highly intelligent. And more so than I. After several minutes of uncomfortable silence, I decide that I would either be kicked out for being homosexual after agreeing to rub his back, or I could end my suffering and go back to my company for my next round of bashing.

"Point taken, Sergeant Major." I replied in acknowledgement of the futility of defending myself.

Once back in the company, I was first taken to my commander, CPT Geoff Hamill, who had led us in Somalia.

"Slane, the way I see it, you've done a lot of good and are probably under a lot of stress. I'm aware of your marriage situation as well. As far as I'm concerned, you've been punished enough and I see no point in doing anything more. Dismissed." Hamill said, to my relief.

Next stop, my platoon.

"Slane, you can forget sniper school. I know you're the most qualified person to go, but after this, I'm try like hell not to send you!" SFC Jones dictated.

"Do you have any idea how ridiculous that sounds, Sergeant Jones?" I replied.

"Hey, you fucked up. You gotta pay for it." He replied.

Sergeant Jones was a fair man and a great leader who had always stood up for all of us, myself included. Something he would do time and time again. I understood his position and gave no further argument. As a side note, I was promptly promoted to the rank of Corporal and given a new nickname. The masseuse. Sounded intriguing...." The Masseuse is coming for you mother fuckers! Better hide!" I don't know. It worked for a few months afterward.

By now, our Charlie company was in the shit with TF 2-14 in an ever increasingly dangerous situation. During a formation, our first sergeant asked for volunteers to return to Somalia. As I raised my hand, I received several rebukes from the NCO's as First Sergeant Rodriguez acted as though no one had raised their hand as he dismissed the company. I guess their feeling was that we had faced enough danger for now, and that the futility of Somalia wasn't worth anyone attending any funerals amongst us who had already survived it. Though I didn't appreciate it at the time, as a much older and wiser man, I wish I could find and thank them for ignoring my volunteering that day. And for those worried, I would eventually return to PLDC in February where I then received the Leadership Award, graduating top of my class. No backrubs. Immediately thereafter, I was promoted to the rank of sergeant, date of promotion 1 February, 1994, less than two years after graduating basic training.

As summer turned to fall in 1993, we weren't hearing much of anything about the situation in Somalia other than what the rest of the world knew. TF Ranger had been deployed to collect the bounty on Aidid's head and the fighting had steadily increased, as we had predicted. Several more troops were injured by yet another remote detonated mine, though all survived. People were questioning where the Somalis were getting weapons like remote detonated mines and personally, I already knew the answer. They were getting help from the same extremists we had faced in Merca, Ali Tahid, as well as Al Qaeda.

As far as the marriage woes, I wasn't alone. Several of us got married and divorced within a year of returning from Somalia. We had soldiers kicked out for alcohol abuse, and several careers that were nearly derailed. Spaceboy was trying counseling and finding no relief, while Hughes and Mangold were venting in other ways, having stolen a cab as it stopped for gas in Watertown, and even inadvertently taking a hostage during the following police chase. Luckily, the numerous felonies were reduced to a single misdemeanor and the Army chose to add nothing on top except maybe some alcohol abuse counseling.

Knowing the 3rd Ranger Battalion, Delta Force and our own 10th Mountain Division forces were in Somalia and closing in on Aidid, none of us could have predicted what September would bring.

Blood on the Altar

Setting: the early morning hours of September 25th, 1993 in Mogadishu Somalia. A chapter that could easily be called "The Original Black Hawk Down". Based on the firsthand accounts of 1-87 INF, 2-14 INF, 3-75 RGR, 101st Div Aviation and 5th Special Forces soldiers.

The incident we're about to re-live in this chapter is largely unknown by the American public as a whole, but not completely. It was briefly addressed in

"Black Hawk Down" and received a few paragraphs of mention in a handful of major newspapers. If I had to give the mission itself a title, it would be "The Original Black Hawk Down". The result of this mission was 3 American dead, and 3 American wounded with two of the wounded being what I would describe as brutally severe, and one of those two is a man I call a friend and a brother. My children know his name and his gift upon the altar. However, you do not; which is a major reason as to why I'm writing this book. Those of us who know Rolando "Poncho" Carrizales call him a hero, a title he would readily reject.

In July and August of 1993, at the end of the "Summer in Hell", the call was passed to C CO 1-87 Infantry as they were deployed to "The Mog" as attachments to TF 2-14, relieving 1-22 Infantry. By now, the US involvement in Somalia was dedicated as a Quick Reaction Force (QRF) in the city of Mogadishu. TF 2-87 had also been the main QRF for operations in Somalia, but unlike those of us in A CO 1-87 Infantry and the rest of TF 2-87, TF 2-14 was under UN control. Not only was their command structure vastly different while being under international control, their utilization was very different as well.

The 24th of September started out as just another day, a day they would refer to as another "Groundhog day". Wake up at 0530 hours, vehicles loaded by 0600 hours and by 0900 hours chow. The day would then continue with squad drills followed by cards and "bones" while the QRF say back, waiting to be called. SSG Rossman was the squad leader for 3rd platoon of C CO 1-87 Infantry. As a Ranger, SSG Rossman was viewed as one of the most competent leaders through his soldier's eyes as well as his superiors in the Mog. He spent the day listening to "Mad Man of the Mog" on the Armed Forces Network (AFN).

Called the Mobile Weapons Squad, their QRF mission was normally to pull rear security during missions for C CO 2-14 Infantry, while attached to the company's TOW platoon, which was similar to our own E-87 (Provisional). With their desert camouflaged fast back hummers which they had spray painted with "C CO 1-87", they had two .50 caliber M-2 machine guns, no fewer than TEN 7.62 M-60 machine guns and four MK-19 40 MM grenade launchers.

By mid to late afternoon, the squad began settling in for naps, which the chain of command encouraged. Being the QRF meant that at any moment you'd be called out without any idea of how long it would be before you'd get a chance to rest again. So, taking naps became a big part of "Groundhog Day" for the QRF in Mogadishu. However, today there was a birthday. Poncho was turning 23 today and the napping would have to wait a bit longer than usual while his squad mates took opportunity to celebrate a little; I imagine many of the same juvenile pranks we would pull on birthdays or holidays were much the same. Poncho still remembers the number they pulled on him that day, but I'm choosing to leave those details for him and his squad as a happy moment for them to hold on to.

At 1700 hours, the squad unloaded their vehicles for the day. As the evening turned to night and the squad lay fast asleep in their desert camouflaged uniforms and boots (DCU's).

At approximately 0145 hrs, Ranger Adam Bittner was on guard when he saw what he described as a "fireball" in the sky over the city.

By 0200 hours the squad was awoken by 1SG Tucker. It was "Go time". A black hawk helicopter was "missing" and the QRF was going to find them. SSG Rossman notified SPC Archibaul and SGT Boult ready the squad. This meant the QRF had to have the vehicles loaded and ready to go within 10 minutes, during which time Rossman received a five-minute briefing on the situation. During the briefing, Rossman learned that a black hawk had been shot down in the city; the pilots were alive and fleeing the crash site. SSG Rossman briefed his squad on the situation and presented their operations order. They would travel the K-4 circle to the airport, circumventing the 13 mile secure route, and they would follow aircraft to the site.

As the squad started out of the back gate, the atmosphere among the group was tense. How had Somalis managed to shoot down a black hawk, they wondered. The black hawk was said to have been traveling at over 100 knots as is flew over the city, an impossible shot with a mere Rocket Propelled Grenade (RPG). They had no idea what to expect. After a while Poncho began a conversation with SGT Boult, not sure why the route seemed to be taking so long. According to the briefing they had received, it wouldn't have taken this long to get to the crash site. As it turned out, the convoy had missed a turn to the crash site by about 100 meters.

At 0300 hours, Poncho's Humvee was the first to arrive at the crash site. Until SSG Rossman could get the rest of the vehicles turned around, they would have to secure the site alone. Immediately Poncho's group came under fire; an RPG exploded just behind them. They dismounted and began returning suppressive fire, with Archibald unleashing hell's furty with the M-60 machine gun. Archibald is the only M-60 gunner that I couldn't beat during M-60 qualification (though I was told I tied him eventually), having placed 3rd in the all Army competition, with Poncho as his AG. There couldn't have been a finer group of soldiers defending this crash site.

When Rossman arrived, he left part of the squad further down the road making an arc type perimeter around the crash site, with Poncho's Humvee at the 12 o'clock position, and everyone else placed at their 10 o'clock on down. Rather than being rear security, the squad was now on point. As they maneuvered into position, Poncho could see that while the left was secure, he was worried about a gap in the perimeter to his 1 o'clock.

As Rossman approached the scene on foot, having stopped two hundred meters shy, he encountered a head sized object in the road which turned out to be a smoking helmet, eventually learning it had been the helmet worn by the crew chief on the black hawk who was now dead and in the wreckage. As they approached the site, they looked for trip wires and booby traps, figuring at this point that they were walking into an ambush.

A call over the radio confirmed that the pilots had been safely recovered, so the rescue mission was now a recovery; they would be recovering the bodies of the 3 dead crew members. As Rossman moved over to Poncho's team, all hell was being unleashed as they unloaded on the Somali positions with everything they had. The other team was covering their six at an intersection just 50 meters away as Archibald suppressed the enemy positions, exercising good fire control. As abruptly as it started, the firing stopped. Having shot high, which was pretty typical, the Somalis hadn't managed to inflict any casualties on the group.

As SSG Rossman began to move toward the other fire team which had secured the intersection, their M-60 opened up when a Somali had come into the intersection firing an AK-47. He took cover until the firing subsided, which coincided with that team's M-60 jamming, making a sound "you hope you never hear in combat". After moving to Carr's position in the intersection, he used his Leatherman pliers to help Carr free up the machine gun. Once the machine gun was again operational, Carr again returned fire, this time quickly silencing a sniper.

By the time the sun began to come up, Rossman was able to make out the rotor of the downed black hawk, noticing that it looked as though it was "surgically removed". They were beginning to run low on ammo, having consumed about 50% of their basic M-60 load, and fearing the crash site was booby trapped, they initially stayed clear of the wreckage. In the center of their perimeter was a mosque; as their initial orders were to keep everyone away, they now had to adjust to civilians heading into the mosque for morning prayer. Rossman and his men redistributed ammo and Rossman secured another few hundred rounds of 7.62mm for the machine guns.

Then a call over the radio came for Rossman to bring a poncho to the crash site; the crew chief had been located. After getting a sitrep from his fire teams and learning that Carr's team reported only kids in front of their position, Rossman headed toward wreckage.

When he got to the wreckage, SFC Ed Ricord asked Rossman for his pliers before then reaching in and removing a dog tag from the deceased; SGT Ferdinand C. Richardson. As SFC Ricord instructed SSG Rossman on recovery procedures, the thing that stuck in Rossman's mind the most were SFC Ricord's instruction telling him "Above all, treat him with respect". During the recovery, those words echoed repeatedly through Rossman's mind. Treat him with respect. Even in death, maybe even especially in death, we respect and honor each other as soldiers. For the dead, the ultimate sacrifice has been laid upon the altar; their fight now over. As the recovery continued for the remaining crew members, the crash site again began taking more and more fire, rounds striking the wall just above the helicopter.

As Rossman moved to gather SITREP's (situation reports) from his fire teams, he could hear SGT Boult yell out as he returned fire.

"RPG! RPG!" Boult yelled as his team began suppressing a partially opened doorway in which stood an approximately 12-year-old boy with an RPG.

The boy fired, but fired short. Though Rossman reported that he was unaware of the boy's fate, Poncho confirms that he had been killed.

Now, as Poncho had feared, the group began taking heavy fire at their 10 and 1 o'clock positions, with the 1 o'clock being the most vulnerable. To their 1 o'clock, a 3 story building erupted with fire coming from each floor, causing the squad to return 40mm grenades in volume into the building, while the squad machine guns ripped each floor apart. Archibald yelled out that he was running low on ammo as the cobra gunships tore through the buildings around them in an attempt to cover the soldiers exposed on the ground. Rossman was able to secure another 200 rounds from 1SG Doody just as several more explosions ripped around Poncho's Humvee.

Poncho saw Archibald retrieving something from the Humvee. Believing his gunner needed his help, Poncho got up to assist him. As Rossman got to the site, several explosions rocked the group as they took a volley of several more

RPG's, followed by automatic gunfire. As Rossman got to the team, Poncho fell back into the street, seemingly unconscious. Rossman yelled for Poncho, believing that the explosions had knocked him unconscious, but to no avail.

As Rossman grabbed Poncho, he noticed a small one-inch hole in the left side of his neck. At first, there was no blood. Within a few seconds, the wound began pulsating, covering Rossman with Poncho's blood as Rossman immediately yelled for medic. The blood was shooting out waist high and Rossman tried his best to stop the bleeding. After several more minutes and no medic arriving to dress Poncho's wounds, Rossman continued to save Poncho as best he could, using Poncho's field dressing to apply pressure to the wound.

One of the FO's (Forward Observers) SPC Gregg Long exposed himself to heavy fire as he ran to retrieve a medic for Poncho.

As SFC Ed Ricord, a Special Forces Medic with 5th SFG, arrived at their position, Poncho was again conscious and able to speak.

"What do we have here? You picked a fine place to try and lay down." SFC Ricord calmly said to the pair.

"I think need to get the fuck out of here…" Poncho replied as he choked on his own blood from the wound in his neck.

"We're working on it buddy." SFC Ricord calmly replied as he took over treating Poncho's wound from SSG Rossman.

As Rossman started to re-assess the situation of the rest of his squad, Archibald yelled out that he had been hit. SGT Boult pulled Archibald out of the turret where he had been manning the machine gun which was now conspicuously silenced. Rossman noticed a bullet hole that had ripped through the windshield of the Humvee and had initially thought Archibald had been gut-shot, but it turned out to be his thigh.

"The only thing harder than self-pity is facing your own wounded soldiers."
– SFC (Ret) Olin Rossman

SFC Ricord worked frantically to save Poncho's life as the fight raged on. The skill of a Special Forces medic is second to none, and in the heat of the battle, they can perform surgery on a patient. Eventually Ricord was able to pinch of the artery in Poncho's neck enough to drastically slow the bleeding.

Rossman jumped into the turret to man the M-60, finding it difficult to operate with his hands slick with the blood of his soldiers. From the waist down he was soaked in blood, and his hands and wrists were as well. As the battle raged on, 1SG Doody and Rossman coordinated several more 40mm strikes at a sniper position, using HE and CS rounds. The gunships also took seveal passes ripping through the enemy positions in the surrounding buildings.

As the fight raged on, 2-14 was also completely engaged in the fight, as RPG after RPG ripped into the perimeter with nonstop machine gun fire. SGT Reid was struck with an RPG, blowing off one of his hands and a leg, blinding him in one eye, and leaving him covered with shrapnel wounds.

After pulling the mangled, charred Black Hawk apart by using a vehicle, and recovering the remains of the crew, the order would soon come to withdraw.

SSG Rossman, having taken 30% casualties in his squad, felt the weight of the events in a very personal way. His soldiers had been wounded, it must have been something he did wrong. As the group returned to the base, this time using the secure route, the look on everyone's face was the same. Complete horror and shock at what had just transpired over the last 5 hours; their brothers had been wounded, their brothers had been killed. The time to reflect on the events of the night and morning was taking its toll.

Back at the hospital in the Mog, Rossman saw Archibald as he lay getting treatment.

"I'd still follow you through the gates of hell" he told his squad leader.

Rossman then tried to see Poncho, who was heading off for surgery, but was told he'd have to wait at least an hour while they worked to save Poncho's life and stabilize him. Poncho, now awake, repeatedly asked the doctors and staff if he could call his wife in case he didn't make it. Though calm, he realized he may not survive this ordeal, and they still had some surgery to do. His request was denied or ignored, the priority being on saving his life.

After surgery in the Mog, Poncho was flown to Germany and then on to Walter Reed Army hospital, before being transferred to his home state of Texas. On his flight from Walter Reed to Texas, he was accompanied by our battalion Commander, LTC Sullivan. He gave Poncho the SITREP and proceeded to read him an article about the NY Yankees during the flight as the two talked, though the conversation was one way as Poncho had a breathing tube. Upon learning this detail, LTC Sullivan's stock went way up in my book. I would like to tell him "Thank you for being there with my brother when I couldn't". Poncho then spent 6 to 7 months recovering, learning to live life as a quadriplegic, coping with his demons, and ultimately becoming one of the strongest survivors of war I have ever known. War may have changed him physically and to some extent spiritually, he is the same strong soul I first met at Ft. Benning in 1991, even stronger.

Upon his return to Ft. Drum, LTC Sullivan gave the battalion a brief overview of our brother Poncho. I remember initially feeling dead inside, followed by a rage I cannot express. I had been quite close with Poncho during our time in basic training part of a cohort that had come to 1-87 Infantry. Harrison, Poncho, Smith and Ramirez among others. They were my brothers.

Back in Mogadishu, Gutierrez had been tasked with cleaning up the hummer that Poncho and Archibald were evacuated in after being shot. The back was full of blood and unspent ammunition. Out of morbid curiousity, he held an unspent 7.62 round and pressed it against his neck, trying to imagine what it must have felt like for Poncho. Ironically, he would soon find out.

The Broken Crown

The following is from the memoirs of Olin Rossman on the events of October 3rd and 4th, 1993.

I cannot remember how the day started. It probably started like any other day. Ground hog day of wake up; prep the vehicles for QRF mission or weapons maintenance, eat, nap, rinse, repeat. I do recall there was something special, almost like it was a day off but I cannot recall for sure. I know that there was a volleyball game and several members of the platoon participated. I know I wanted to sleep.

After, the events of September 25, I could not sleep well. On the evening of the Sept 25, the squad was ordered to replace the current squad on the MSR. And like good infantryman, we rucked up and went and we were on the MSR doing missions the next morning. Although the windshield had been replaced, the vehicles still had other bullet holes and pockmarks. The African heat supported the body odor, smell of cordite and blood throughout the vehicle and made me sick to my stomach. The MSR mission is a 3 or 4-day rotation and it involves securing points along the MSR that historically were either ambushed, had IEDs planted near or overlook weapon infiltration routes. Anyway, my squad was tired, defeated from the battle where Arch and Poncho was wounded and the MSR mission and truly needed a well-deserved day of rest.

October 3 and the platoon was at the volleyball courts at location I cant remember and I believe it was in the afternoon. I do remember someone rounding up the platoon and briefing us on Task Force Ranger being surrounded and asking for support. At that time, we went hauling ass back to the barracks and uploaded all equipment, weapons and water. This time, I ensured I had more ammo than the UBL and the vehicle was packed with ammo. I do not recall the exact moment or how it went down but we received word about the mission by Cco 2-14(?) as it tired to break through the K4 circle enroute to assist the Rangers to break out from encirclement. It mission was pushed back and several causalities were taken.

Here is what I do remember:

After dark, we moved from the old port to the new port to stage. Once again I do not remember the timeline. It is safe to assume that it was after 6pm since being so damn close the equator, it gets dark at 6pm and the sun it up at 6am. I want to say it was closer to 2100 or 2200 hrs when we started the rescue convoy. We received mixed briefings and updates throughout the night while staging but basically it was 'the Rangers and Delta are in the Bakara Market and have taken heavy casualties. Our mission is to assist in the breakout from encirclement. We will follow the APC and tanks and will be second in the order of movement". There was a 2-14 company that was assigned to the APCs and rode into battle with foreign drivers and TCs. We followed the APC and tanks.

While we were still staging and in the new port, LTC David rode up to the convoy on a semi truck full of ammo. I kid you not...it was a flatbed with every piece of ammo in country (hyperbole I know, but that is what is seemed like). He asked me what I needed. I need 40mm and M60 Ammo and he directed workers to give us cases of what we asked for. I also took M16 ammo for good measure. I may have taken flares and HC smoke since I never seemed to run out of those. The vehicle strained under the weight of the added ammo, water and personnel. I want to say my driver was Hannerhoff, Carr was manning the M60, Long was in the back left passenger seat and I was in the TC seat. Our orders were to smash/shoot/destroy everything in the area that is not identified as American. If the enemy could use it for cover or transportation we were to destroy it. Willie Boult used to say "if its brown, its down".

I do remember people cutting the parachutes off of a lot of flares. This was to give the flare more stability when used in a ground mode. The reasoning was simple, not everyone had NVGs and could not shoot flares in the air due to the possibility of either hitting or blinding a little bird. We would use the flares in alleys and we would shoot 200 meters down the alley in order to backlight the area. Movement would then be picked up and the targets would be engaged. The other unexpected use was to suck the oxygen out of shacks in the alley the enemy would use for cover. They were not afraid to be killed by bullets and used the tin shacks as cover/concealment. We would shoot at them and they would stay there and return fire. Shoot a flare in the window, it would pop and the magnesium flare would make it very hot, burn the throat, and suck all the oxygen out of the shack. They would leave the shack and we would shoot them when then did. Why not use 40mm HE you ask? I had a shit ton of flares and used the light so my shooters could engage. I did use 40mm HE if the flare in the window trick did not work but once again, it would limit my shooters ability to see the targets. Also, I learned very quickly that using 40mm HEDP with nods can be very tricky since it makes it very difficult to aim. I damn near blew myself up! We stopped at an alley and I got out the vehicle to cover an alley. I saw movement and received a few shots (way over my head) and my M16 was not having any effect. I decided to use 40mm HEDP. What I didn't know was that there was a thin piece of rebar (or similar metal) either sticking up from the ground or out from the wall but in my NVG, it was clear. I shot the 40mm and heard a "TANG" like a metal baseball bat hitting a rock, I had hit something. Luckily, the warhead's momentum carried it about 45m before it blew up. I am just glad the HEDP has a minimum rotational spin requirement to explode...and it was not point detonated. No one but me saw my mistake but damn it drove the point home.

The convoy into the fight

We started movement about 2200 hrs. The "fire fight" for us started kind of slow at first...A shot here, a shot there. The convoy was your typical stop and go mess of a slinky but when "under fire" and wanting to get to troops in trouble, it brings on a new meaning. Also what slowed us down was the pussies in the tanks would not drive over the roadblocks regardless of the size or makeup. The troops in the APCs had to dismount and break down the roadblocks. Most of the roadblocks were just burning tires or debris piled in the road and did not have any over watch (didn't know it at the time). Once the sammies learned that pussies were driving a 40ton war machine, the roadblock became less and less substantial. Their mission was to delay the convoy and did the sissified UN troops obliged.

We passed several places that I recognized such as war memorial and were heading towards National Street. Prior to getting on National Street proper, there is a large swooping curve. Once we made the curve, you could see damn near down the entire street. The scene was unexplainable: green and orange tracers being shot up from rooftops towards little birds and down from the rooftops towards our convoy. In retaliation, red tracers were being fired down and ricocheting from the little birds and being fired up towards "muzzle flashes" in the alleys, windows and rooftops that cover the street. There were many explosions from what I guess was RPGs. The air detonated RPG looked like fireworks on a 4th of July. The ones fired down to the street were all over the place. There was just so much to cover and we did the best we could. Hannerhoff and Long had the left side, Carr had where ever he thought he could do the most damage and I had the right side. The entire National Street has multi-level buildings, shit ton of alleys with makeshift shacks everywhere, vehicles/donkey carts parked and everything seemed to want us dead. Maps were damn near useless since the shacks would be built in roads and alleyways. You could not tell where the buildings began and the shacks ended, let alone the alleys.

We took RPG fire from the first alleyway we hit on National Street. The RPG came "screaming over the hood". It looked so close that I just knew our vehicle and everyone in it was FUCKED. In reality, the RPG was about 10 feet in front of vehicle but it did not calm the pucker factor. Getting a RPG broadside on a light skin HUMMER would have been devastating and would have killed us all. Of course, Carr was raking the area where it came from and I returned fire with my M16. We quickly started stopping short of the alleys and waiting for the vehicle in front of us to clear before forward movement...sort of IMT in vehicles. Something we should have not have to learn.

The entire rest of the movement to the end location was very similar. We went thru a metric shit ton of ammo. The entire convoy was a giant fucked slinky and information and communication was scarce outside the squad vehicles and platoon. We would fight to a stop, get out, return fire, load up, return fire, move 50 meters, stop, get out, return fire load up, return fire ad nauseam. There are very few details I remember outside the first RPG across the hood until reached National Street and Hawlwadig Road. I am not saying we had to fight for every inch of ground like Omaha Beach or Tet in Saigon, but it was a sustained fight in urban terrain and we were fighting as hard as the sammies.

National Street and Hawlwadig Road.

Once again, not sure of the time line since we have been moving and fighting for 2 or 3 hours (could be more, could be less) but we finally arrived were the convoy was to break off towards the crash site. The APCs and tanks were too big to travel down the alley to the crash site #1. So it was ordered that my section would secure the intersection of National Street and Hawlwadig Road, Gibb and his squad would travel to the crash site and assist in any way possible, Green and his squad would secure the egress route. The tanks and APCs were there but spread-out all over National Street and did not come anywhere near the intersections. To this day, I think those guys in the tanks had to have been the biggest fucking pussies that have ever worn a uniform (not knowing what their orders were from even a more pussified UN and host nations). God forbid those idiots ever get into a tank battle...

From the moment we "secured" the intersection, we would start receiving sniper fire. It was not very accurate at first due to the low light however as daylight came, the more effective the fire was becoming. The intersection described: On the main street there was very little cover outside our vehicles.

276

The up gunners were practically exposed the entire firefight. The buildings on the main street were 2 and 3 stories. There was a 3 or 4 story building across the "T" intersection at the 11 o'clock position. Crash site number 1 was around the corner to our right but unsure of how far. There was a small knee high wall in the area where my vehicle was parked. It did not offer a lot of protection but some is better than none. I had my vehicle combat parked and faced out towards the National Street. Carr's primary sector of fire an alley at the 9, the 3 story building at the 11 to where the street that led to the crash site. Long was Carr's back up and his primary sector overlapped Carr's. I was watching down towards the crash site to the right and to the multi-story building across the intersection.

Our mission was now to seal the area as best we could and not to let anyone in that is not American. During the night, we received sniper fire and could see shadows were running across the roads trying to get into the cordon. I could not tell you how many "laden" looking shadows I shot at running towards the crash site but it was a lot. I used the 40mm to shoot at groups of shadows a few times. I used gas, and smoke but it was ineffective for the most part.

Daybreak Oct 4th. I do not recall any "call for prayers" so that tells me it was still pretty early...hell I don't recall any call for prayers that day. Fire was still coming in hot and heavy but no RPGs for some reason (not complaining mind you). I would learn later that several of the upgunners were hit but not wounded. Laguna had a bullet pass horizontally thru his flak vest and one of the gunners showed me bullet holes in his pant leg. Neither was wounded. Anyway I digress...

I was worried about the building across from the intersection. It would be the perfect location to set up a barricaded heavy machine gun and it would have caused severe damage to the static soldiers conducting the cordon...it was a damn near perfect linear target. Every once in a while I would put a 40mm thru the window just to ensure that nobody would think about using it. I did think about asking to clear it and occupy it. It was perfect location for over watch however this building would have taken a platoon plus to clear and secure it correctly. We did not have the people to secure the building and the intersection.

Just after daybreak several things happened but I am not sure what happened first.

1)   Spaceboy Nanny was pulling security to the 3 o'clock position. He was shot in the back of the helmet. It knocked him forward a few steps. He turned around and started firing in the location where the bullet came from. Not sure if he hit the target but there was no further shots from that area.

2)   I heard don't shoot...don't shoot. I was confused by the command since it came from my 6 o'clock inside the perimeter. I just happened to turn to my left, weapon up ready for anything and there was a man, clearly a Somali, carrying someone in a bloody blanket. The fighting stopped and this man walked down the street oblivious to the firefight that was going on around him. I am not sure where he was going, not sure how he got to where I could reach out and touch him but I sure hope he got to where he was going safely.

3)   The big ass pussified tank driver must have been scared for his life or witnessed me putting 40mm in the building. The dumb motherfucker drove up to my near vehicle and fired his main gun into the building. This dumb ass did not check his surrounding and Long and myself were about 5 feet in front of the tank but off to the right of it. I thought my brain was coming out of my ears, the over pressure was damn near to much to bear. I am not sure how long my bell was rung but it couldn't have been more than a minute or two but in a firefight, that could cost you the mission.

Break from contact.

The word came down that it was time to leave. They have secured the fallen and the wounded have been loaded as much as possible. Once again, not sure what came first, the soldiers walking or the rest of our platoon coming off the crash site. I remember one of our vehicles came thru the intersection very fast and had to slam on the breaks to avoid crashing into a wall, the upgunner almost being thrown out of the turret. The next I know, I had dismounted soldiers from the crash site all over my location and across the street. There was a SSG (Delta or Ranger) with is squad that was next to me and I asked him if he needed water or ammo. We started passing out water bottles and ammo to these soldiers. We opened the 5.56 ammo crates and started handling out bandoliers of ammo. I do not remember handing out 7.62 but it could have happened.

I noticed another soldier across the street. Bullets were impacting a wall about 6 feet over his head. I guess if you have been thru what these guys have been thru, this was nothing. Anyway, I got his attention by waving my arms. Gave him the hand and arms signal for LOOK (finger to the eyes) and pointed UPWARD. He looked up, saw the bullets holes, pointed his weapon to where he thought the fire was coming from but I do not recall what happened after that.

Now it was time to leave but there was a call for the medic and the Gutierrez was hit and down hard. Hannerhoff grabs his medic stuff and head in that direction. I didn't know how bad he was hit, just that he was hit. Flashes of Arch and Poncho came back to mind.

It was time to leave. We were told to line the vehicles up in the road and standby to take on passengers. I am not sure who or how many I had in my vehicle but they were stacked like cord wood, covered in blood and sweat. We managed to get the passengers situated enough that the majority of them could point their weapons out of the vehicle. One of the passengers asked if I wanted "slap rounds" for the M60 and then he asked me if my gunner(Carr) knew what he was doing. I took the rounds, gave them to Carr and told him that my gunner was one of the best in the Army. It seemed to settle him down.

The convoy started to move and I had to pass by where Gutierrez was laying. I could see him laying down and Doc Foley was over him with an IV. I could not see Hannerhoff. I had to stop the vehicle and asked SFC Mooney where Hannerhoff was(since I brought him in the fight, I was responsible for making sure he got home). Mooney said that he had him and would make sure he got out. That was good an all, but by the time that was all sorted out, the convoy had left without me.

Not a fucking clue.

In the official AAR, it would say that the convoy headed to the soccer stadium and two vehicles headed to new port. Well can you guess what two vehicles made it to new port. That is right. I never received word that the convoy was headed to the soccer stadium. I had 20 people (estimated) and we were traveling thru the shit storm that over 30 vehicles and 200 men just fought thru ...but we were alone...in a hostile city. TO this day, I think my lucky stars, guardian angel, 4 leaf clover up my ass that nothing "bad" happened to us as it could have been the death of us.

I did not know the convoy was headed to the soccer stadium but I knew where we were and I knew where we had come from. It only made sense that the convoy would go back that way. After, I caused the break in contact with the convoy, conventional wisdom would tell you to travel faster to make up for it. Well that did not work. By the time, I realized the convoy did not come this way; it was better to just go back to the new port. We did. We did meet a little fire on the way out and there were several roadblock but we just drove over them. There were crowds ever where and on bot side of the street. They had guns in the crowds. We targeted the gun totters and shot at them. We must have been successful since we made it back to the new port.

New Port

There was very little conversation when we hit new port. There was little discussion with the gate guards and we were let in. We got in the secure gate and I felt a weight being lifted. The squad and passengers were safe however I still did not have a clue where the rest of the platoon was. Somehow, they figured out where we were and told to hang tight. About 30 minutes after arrival, we were told that there were soldiers still missing in the city and we were to go back out. Boult and I started ripping the vehicles apart, keeping only the good ammo, refilling mags, making sure we had a bite to eat...throwing everything else out into a heap of crates, brass and empty water bottles. Here comes the shit storm and I was not looking forward to it but we were prepared. The passengers had different orders; they were to return to the unit. The passengers gathered their equipment, thanked us and went back to their unit.

Sometime in the next 20-30 minutes we were told to stand down and hold in place. It was never clear if we(my squad plus passengers) were the soldiers that were missing in the city either way, I am glad we did not have to go back out.

The official AAR is that my squad made it back but somehow I came up one pair of nods less. I remember placing my nods under the passenger seat. My guess is that one of the passengers decided to take them. They were written off as a combat loss. The platoon was able to link back up and travel back to our barracks. Weapons and vehicle maintenance were priority followed by care for our bodies. It was claimed that out platoon went thru 22000 7.62 rounds.

We would learn the next day about the extent of the battle and the war crimes that happened to our fallen soldiers. It was a disgrace that Clinton pulled us out. Two weeks later, we had enough war power on hand to walk from one end of Somalia to the other and smash whatever fought us.

It is very interesting to note that on a inspection to fix or repair the vehicles after the firefight of Sept 25, I noticed a "lump" in the back left quarter panel of the vehicle. I looked inside and there was a pockmark from a bullet. I did my best CSI and determined the bullet came from the passenger side. I went to the passenger side window and sure enough, there was a small "gouge" from where it looks like the bullet hit the side of the window pane as it entered the vehicle and travelled to the rear where it landed. Upon further inspection, it looks like the AG gear absorbed the ricochet and fragments. I can't imagine what would happen if the bullet hit the passenger or if the fragments were not captured by the AG gear and spalled inside the vehicle. I was assigned as an OC at JRTC in late 1998. I happened to be traveling near an equipment holding area and a tan fast back hummer with "INFANTRY" painted on the side was inside. I went to the vehicle and ran my hand along the back left side and sure enough there was the bullet lump. The vehicle I used on Sept 25 …The vehicle that witnessed Poncho and Arch being wounded, the vehicle that witnessed the most severe fighting since Tet in 68… the vehicle that witnessed dark humor and arguments only grunts would understand...the vehicle that Hannerhoff tried to jump Duke style over a sand dune...the vehicle that had never ever let me down… the vehicle that I commanded for 6 months… had found me.

-SFC (RET) Olin Rossman

October 4th

As the sun came up at crash site 1, soldiers from C 1-87 worked frantically with the Rangers and Delta operators to free the body of Cliff Wolcott. Greg Long had been in the prone alongside one of the UN tanks when it suddenly fired without warning, rattling his brain and nearly knocking him unconscious. Today we know this as a Traumatic Brain Injury, or TBI. Back then it was just another suck it up moment.

Gutierrez turned and felt as though he had been hit in the face with a shovel. He had been shot through the face and neck, on the opposite side that Poncho had been shot. Doc Foley worked frantically to stabilize him while they continued to take fire.

The nose of the bird was impacted deep into the ground, trapping his remains in the cockpit. Loughhead's hummer was used in an attempt to pull the cockpit apart to retrieve the body, and they even attempted to pull the body directly out using the vehicle. With Loughhead were Zwetschek, Topmiller and Smith. When they finally recovered his remains, Topmiller helped carry them to the hummer. He cradled them as though he was carrying a small child.

As word got to the family of Gutierrez, his brother who was a US Airmen, got on a flight to Mogadishu to see his brother. When he arrived, he was told his brother had gone to Germany, so he took the next flight there. By the time he got to Germany, his brother had been flown back to the US, where he would eventually be in the same hospital room as Poncho.

As October 3rd and 4th had been underway, 1SG Poe had been staged to head to Mogadishu with HHC and B CO 1-87. B CO was in the air before they got word of what was transpiring on the ground, and HHC was told to stand down. Our involvement in Somalia would be short lived and we would have no troops there after the New Year.

After the Storm

As the sun came up in Haiti and the waters began to recede, I believe I was still in shock from the night's events. I felt angry and betrayed, but I was also glad that we were alive.

The 1SG came a full day after the storm had passed, and he came with news....I would be heading home. I was to PCS from Ft. Drum to Ft. Lewis, something that wouldn't actually happen until January. But it gave me a small sense of relief to know I was leaving this place. Ironically, so would the 1SG as he was relieved of his command.

Before leaving I was given my first NCOER (performance evaluation), which is required after 1 year, or when a noncommissioned officer changes raters (like by going elsewhere). They also tried to send me to the E-6 promotion board. But my time in grade (10 months) and my time in service (2 years and 10 months) were not enough to even allow that to be possible, and it would be over a year before that opportunity came again.

As I waited to board a plane out of Haiti, I asked a SSG sitting near me to look at my NCOER to see if he thought it was done right. Ironically, it was Olin Rossman that was looking over my NCOER. I would not see him again until 2018.

After returning to the states and leaving 1-87 IN, I would go on to serve in C CO 2/9 IN 7th Infantry Div. and C CO 5/20 IN of the 25th Infantry Div. before receiving a lump sum early retirement for medical disability. I took that money and moved my family to Ellensburg, WA where I received my Bachelor's Degree in Biology with emphasis in Microbiology, but began working in Information Technology the day I graduated. I met my 3rd wife in Ellensburg, as I divorced the 2nd. My military obligation was complete in September 1999.

I am still there; Behind the Gun.

- Bravo Charles

Bibliography

Alderete, Greg. 1995. Land of Unknown, memoirs from the basement of hell. https://www.scribd.com/document/146622583/BASEMENT-OF-HELL

Linderer, Gary. 1991. Eyes of the Eagle: F Company LRPs in Vietnam, 1968. Ballantine Books; 1st edition (March 2, 1991).

Stanton, Martin. 2001. Somalia on Five Dollars a Day. Presidio Press (July 2001).

Acknowledgments

Roland Carrizales, John Wasik, Greg Alderete and Rick Beem were instrumental in motivating me to write this book early on in the process. Brian Szulwach, T. Walker Peterson, Christopher Cooke, Christopher Grish, Adam Jovino, Thomas Corey, Gerrard Gutierrez, Robert Loughhead, Darron Evans, Greg Long, Roderick Forde, Luke Carr and many other former members of the 87th Infantry regiment were instrumental in this endeavor.

For more pictures and soldier biographies, visit:

https://behindthegun.wordpress.com

About the Author

Bravo Charles (Steve Slane) was born in Orange, CA in 1970. He grew up mostly in the Pacific Northwest and in North Carolina. He attended Meadowdale High School in Lynnwood, WA and Wilkes Central High School in Wilkesboro, NC, graduating in 1988. In the Army, he served in the 10th Mountain Division, the 7th Infantry Division, and the 25th Infantry Division. His Military awards include the coveted Combat Infantryman Badge. He currently works as a software engineer and spends his time raising chickens with his wife Kimberly, and their 7 children: Emily, Paige, Bishop, James, Sarah, Jacob and Logan.

Rick "Earl" Beem was born in 1970 and raised in Shell Rock, IA. He had a younger sister, older brother, and two older step brothers. He attended Waverly-Shell Rock High School graduating in 1989 then Hawkeye Community College machinist program graduating in 1991. Rick worked as a mold maker apprentice while attending school during the first Gulf War. With his 3 older brothers already serving their country it was an easy sell for the Army recruiter. He briefly entertained technical job fields, ultimately he sought the challenge of being an Infantryman with the famed 10th Mountain Division

Rick returned to his apprenticeship after his Army enlistment and worked through various positions and many job losses until eventually settling with the US Forest Service as a Research Laboratory Mechanic. Rick lives in Wisconsin with his wife Jess and two children Abbey and Logan. Abbey is currently serving with the Wisconsin Army National Guard as a combat medic.

In 1996 Ricks older brother Bradley Charles Beem was killed when the Army CH-47E helicopter crashed during a training flight. He served with the 160th SOAR "Night Stalkers" and was a larger than life personality. Brad was a huge influence on his younger brothers' decision to serve with the Army, he is dearly missed.